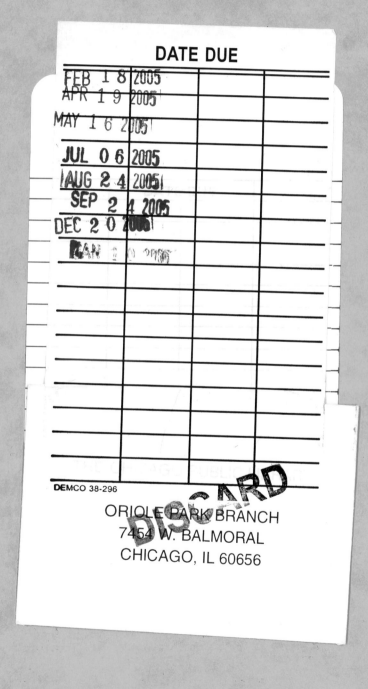

DATE DUE

FEB 1 8 2005		
APR 1 9 2005		
MAY 1 6 2005		
JUL 0 6 2005		
AUG 2 4 2005		
SEP 2 4 2005		
DEC 2 0 2005		
JAN 2 0 2006		

new decorating book

Better Homes and Gardens® Books
Des Moines, Iowa

Better Homes and Gardens® Books
An imprint of Meredith® Books

new decorating book
Editor: Denise L. Caringer
Project Editor/Writer: Sharon Novotne O'Keefe
Art Director: The Design Office of Jerry J. Rank
Copy Chief: Terri Fredrickson
Copy and Production Editor: Victoria Forlini
Editorial Operations Manager: Karen Schirm
Managers, Book Production: Pam Kvitne, Marjorie J. Schenkelberg
Contributing Copy Editor: Jane Woychick
Contributing Proofreaders: Julie Cahalan, Sarah Henderson, Gretchen Kauffman, Vivian Mason, Erin McKay
Indexer: Kathleen Poole
Electronic Production Coordinator: Paula Forest
Editorial and Design Assistants: Kaye Chabot, Karen McFadden, Mary Lee Gavin

Meredith® Books
Editor in Chief: Linda Raglan Cunningham
Design Director: Matt Strelecki
Executive Editor, Home Decorating and Design: Denise L. Caringer

Publisher: James D. Blume
Executive Director, Marketing: Jeffrey Myers
Executive Director, New Business Development: Todd M. Davis
Executive Director, Sales: Ken Zagor
Director, Operations: George A. Susral
Director, Production: Douglas M. Johnston
Business Director: Jim Leonard

Vice President and General Manager: Douglas J. Guendel

***Better Homes and Gardens®* Magazine**
Editor in Chief: Karol DeWulf Nickell

Meredith Publishing Group
President, Publishing Group: Stephen M. Lacy
Vice President-Publishing Director: Bob Mate

Meredith Corporation
Chairman and Chief Executive Officer: William T. Kerr

Chairman of the Executive Committee: E. T. Meredith III

Cover photograph: Bill Stites

All of us at Better Homes and Gardens® Books are dedicated to providing you with information and ideas to enhance your home. We welcome your comments and suggestions. Write to us at: Better Homes and Gardens Books, Home Decorating and Design Editorial Department, 1716 Locust St., Des Moines, IA 50309-3023.

If you would like to purchase any of our home decorating and design, cooking, crafts, gardening, or home improvement books, check wherever quality books are sold. Or visit us at: bhgbooks.com

If you had to list one or two absolutely essential ingredients for your home, what would they be? Answer with your heart, not your head. For me, no place would be home without a piano. As a child, I spent some of my happiest times in what we called "the piano room." French doors opened to reveal comfortable seating and the venerable old piano that my mother received as a child. Home was St. Louis, and Mother's spirited renditions of "St. *Louie* Blues" could rattle the walls. I myself began to play when I could barely reach the keys.

It's no wonder that when my husband and I moved into our first home, I bought a piano even before every room had furniture. It simply wouldn't have been home without it. Today, a grand piano is the centerpiece of the loft of our barn-inspired home. Because the loft is actually the master suite, some people might find it an odd place to put a piano. Who cares? It's the only place in the house where it would fit. If you have a passion for it, find a place for it—and don't let anyone else tell you what's "supposed" to go where. Let's say you have a little-used formal living room but long for a studio for crafting or painting. Great! Tailor the room to fit your *real* need. Similarly, if your dining room often sits idle but your soul absolutely craves a book-lined library for reading and relaxing, line the walls with shelves and move the table to one side to make space for a reading chair and ottoman. It's your house; do it *your* way.

What are your passions? What are the must-haves that encourage you to be who you really are—and

Decorating
for the *real you*

perhaps remind you of where you've come from too? Walls of books? A great sound system? Grandma's desk? A collection of '50s furnishings, 19th-century landscapes, or the kids' art from school? A chaise placed under a skylight for celestial meditation? A fountain whose sound reminds you of a favorite creekside camping spot? An easel set in front of a stack of sleek cubes piled with art supplies?

On these pages, we can't tell you what to put into your home—and you wouldn't want us to. Instead, we offer hundreds of great photos, solid decorating information, and options, options, options so you can do your own thing. Just be sure to let your heart lead the way. Although playing music definitely is a here-and-now source of joy for me, I've no doubt that a part of me happily wanders back to the beloved "piano room" of my childhood every time I touch the keys.

Denise L. Caringer

Editor, *New Decorating Book*

Contents

Room Decorating

FRESH IDEAS FOR EVERY ROOM OF YOUR HOME

Design Topics

HELP WITH SPECIFIC DECORATING ELEMENTS

Special Features

INSPIRATION, HOW-TO, SMART SOLUTIONS

Your Style

Does your home truly reflect who you are, what you love, and the way you really live?

What are the elements of *your* style? Know yourself, and you're on

the way to creating your own design vision. For inspiration, join this

coast-to-coast decorating tour and meet creative people who prove

that getting personal is the best path to beautiful rooms. To learn

more about yourself, take our fun Decorating Taste Test.

Tulsa, Meet Provence

Tulsa, Meet Provence

MICKEY AND TOM HARRIS OF TULSA, OKLAHOMA

PREVIOUS PAGES: Mickey Harris pulled in powerful pieces—a 17th-century limestone mantel and a towering armoire—to match the scale of the 20×30-foot great-room. A trumeau mirror, stone garden statue, and painted dogcart accent the mantel. Provençal spirit greets guests at the antique front doors, Paris flea market finds Mickey weathered with a painted finish and framed in limestone slabs. BELOW: After giving their Tulsa home a French twist and filling it with treasures, Mickey and Tom Harris and their Cavalier King Charles Spaniel, Sadie, feel at home at last. OPPOSITE: Layers of soft color, pattern, and texture cozy up the living area, at ease with club chairs and squashy pillows on the sofa. "Railroading" inexpensive striped fabric across drapery valances and adding elegant fringe give the windows professional polish.

All slick tile and white walls, the modern Tulsa home seemed a century or two too new for Mickey and Tom Harris. Their enchanting style story is an old French tale with a cast of rustic and refined characters they've come to cherish—and collect—over 30 years.

Trekking from Paris flea markets to provincial country fairs, they've taken time to define their passions and focus their design vision. That's why Mickey was able to spot "good French bones" in the spare shell of their house. Instead of a contemporary great-room, she saw a cottage in Provence with one gracious space for living and dining.

RICH IN HISTORY

"Country French will always be my first love," Mickey says. "It's sophisticated, yet it's casual. It's the mix, not the match, so whatever you love, you can make it fit." Tulsa interior designer Charles Faudree, who guided the redesign, attributes the timeless appeal of country French rooms to their "approachable elegance."

Timeworn and painted woods mingle amiably with polished and pedigreed pieces such as the living room's Louis XVI walnut armoire. Countrified checks and plaid "dress down" the 1850 fruitwood sofa and a carved wing chair, giving pieces once clad in velvet a fresh, relaxed attitude. In the scenic spirit of 18th-century French toile de Jouy, the new log cabin print on dining chairs inspired the palette.

"Serious rooms are hard to live in, but all of this has been fun," says Mickey, who has edited down to her "first loves." French icons—tole chandeliers, creamware, and salvaged trumeau mirrors—artfully mix with country cousins, such as English figurines of farm folk and cows and primitive toy wheelbarrows that Mickey fills with flowers.

For "past-perfect" context, walls were stuccoed and ceilings were vaulted with old beams and grape-stake fencing. Floors were stripped to the original concrete slab, then stained and scored to mimic stone.

If you're shopping for vintage pieces, Charles Faudree offers this advice: Use old pieces in new ways. Cheese makers and wine tasters once toiled over the couple's tables; the vanity was an iron stove; and the kitchen island was a cashier's stand in a French shop. Lamps had past lives as a tole samovar, an olive jar, and candlesticks. "You can make anything into a lamp as long as it stands still," says Charles.

"Serious rooms are hard to live in, but all of this has been fun. Mixing is the fun of decorating," Mickey says.

ABOVE: In the dining area, Staffordshire figurines and 18th-century pewterware line the shelves of a French *estagnier*, which is backed in original fabric and "married" to a French dresser below. A marble-top patisserie table holds antique decanters and a tole planter and doubles as a serving piece. **OPPOSITE:** Mickey loves vintage stitchery and collects examples that capture the innocence of childhood and the joys of rural life. She showcases favorite English and French works from her extensive collection above an old oak commode she painted a sun-faded Provençal blue.

ABOVE: Terra-cotta-hued concrete countertops and a ceiling clad in grape-stake fencing give the kitchen its rustic roots. The island is an old French cashier's stand made of pearwood, the chandelier is fashioned from bronze mistletoe boughs, and the cow head is a recycled sign from a French butcher. **OPPOSITE:** In the new breakfast bay, dressy chairs upholstered in the palette-setting print pull up to a French farm table with a slatted drawer for draining cheeses. The whitewashed 18th-century clock and the porcelain room stove, now used as a plant pedestal, may share Swedish roots, Mickey says.

If you're shopping for vintage pieces for your home, consider these words of wisdom: Think reincarnation.

OPPOSITE: In the master bedroom, Mickey indulges her passion for toile with golden pattern on walls and windows and aubergine on the upholstered headboard. The tole chandelier is English Directoire, circa 1850. The limestone mantel is a flea market find. **1** Framed stitchery and botanical prints lend a country air

to the guest room. A lighthearted mix of toiles, checks, and plaid fabrics dresses the antique bed. **2** Mickey favors furniture over built-ins, so a tall French *bonnetiere* stores towels in the guest bath. **3** A marble top, sink, and reproduction fixtures turned an old iron *poele*, or room stove, into a vanity just the right size for the tiny powder bath. **4** An early-19th-century English Regency piece, this faux-bamboo buffet with a marble top and storage potential makes a perfect master-bath vanity. The couple used salvaged architectural elements such as the arched window to add authenticity.

Big Apple, Little Bite

Big Apple, Little Bite

CAROL MARYAN AND JOEL BERSTEIN OF NEW YORK, NEW YORK

Architect Carol Maryan is no Chicken Little. When her home's living room ceiling really was falling, she didn't panic. She designed an oasis. Far above the madding crowds, her family's 1,250-square-foot co-op is an airy whitescape awash in soul-soothing neutrals. Over that major hole in her "sky" caused by a leaky roof Carol built the most soothing space of all—a skylit bedroom loft with postcard vistas by day and city lights by night.

NURTURING NATURE

"When I'm in the city, it's very frantic, but up here, I'm in this pure space looking out at the city. It feels very cocoonish, very safe, like being in a womb almost," Carol says.

Carol bought two dinky, dingy apartments—"my trailer park in the sky"—with merger and renovation in mind. She removed the water-damaged ceiling and covered the 8×16-foot void by building a skylight-topped loft bedroom over it. White scaffolding doubles as the loft floor and living room ceiling. "I wanted big light in here," she says, and sunshine pours down the spiral staircase.

The serenity of cool white walls and earthy hues is contagious the second you walk inside. Carol keeps her color options open with a wardrobe of slipcovers in browns, grays, and whites for a quick seasonal shift or mood change. "All white is when I've had too much of everything," she says. "Some people clean their closets. I just slipcover."

With relaxed neutrals, it's easy for this adept mixer of textures and treasures to add and subtract when new loves—worn leather chairs or a 1960s acrylic lamp—follow her home. Clean modern pieces settle in beautifully with retro, rustic, and functional finds, such as weathered wood panels from an old mansion that she hinged into a screen behind a sofa. The old-new mix is "like a family," she says. "You have grandparents, and you have children, and I think it's great when you watch them interact. That's life."

Carol made use of every inch and then some to create her live-big spaces. Floor-to-ceiling mirrors bounce light around to expand space. Floating bookshelves define "rooms." The supersize, glass coffee table keeps the eye flowing, and the kitchen sink and dining banquette scoot out mere inches into greenhouse windows.

You can take the girl out of the country—in Carol's case, Indiana—but she'll still crave that nature connection. To keep the river in view over a parapet, a platform elevates living spaces; glass doors with window-box gardens replace windows.

PREVIOUS PAGES: Carol Maryan layered on warm pattern, texture, and more sink-in comfort by substituting big, squashy pillows for back cushions on the petit point sofa. Satiny slipcovers on the chairs remind her of "old-fashioned quilted robes." For parties, the paneled screen folds back to open up the space even more. On casters for easy moving, a floating "wall" has a splash of bright yellow color that stops the eye but hints at space behind it. The leather chairs are from the 1930s or 1940s; the triangular nesting tables between them are space-savers that go anywhere.
RIGHT: From the rooftop terrace of their New York co-op, Carol Maryan, husband Joel Berstein, and sons Nathan (seated) and Lyle enjoy views of the Empire State Building and the Hudson River.
OPPOSITE: Behind the stretch-out sofa, built-ins with adjustable shelves add functional focus to the family room, which steps down to the original floor level. An ottoman scoots under the coffee table, angled to make the simple shape—and the room—more interesting.

ABOVE: Carol jokingly calls this space-saver counter "a Popeil pocketknife" because it's multifunctional. It handles food prep, casual meals, and party buffets, and the undercounter refrigerator opens on two sides so kids can get juice without squeezing into the kitchen. **OPPOSITE:** Contemporary wire chairs and an antique table pull up to the window box banquette for dining. When plumbing pipes spoiled the see-through view, Carol sandwiched them between a glass-door mahogany cupboard and matching shelves on the kitchen side. Checkerboard ceramic floor tiles set on the diagonal visually expand the space.

The serenity of cool white walls and an earthy palette is contagious.

Postcard vistas by day;
by night, a planetarium view

As the sun sets and city lights blink on, the skyline view from the glass-loft bedroom is as magical as the stars. "It's like being in a tree house," Carol says. "It's a lot of fun, and at night, it's so pretty."

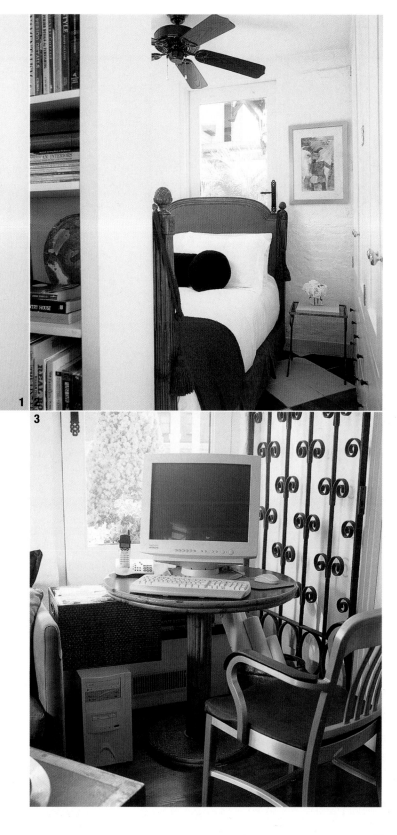

1

3

OPPOSITE: Yards and yards of white sheeting for sun control and privacy make the skylight bedroom a dreamy space at any time of day. Carol linked the tops of the sheets together by sewing on lengths of grosgrain ribbon; then she draped the fabric panels over cables so they slide back easily. The panels are rarely closed, because Carol loves her "postcard view." **1** After fitting in necessities, this tiny bath had nary an inch to spare for decoration, but Carol gave it a dramatic color shot with periwinkle blue wall tile. She then mixed textures, pairing a brushed-metal mirror with a $3.50 outdoor light fixture and a rustic towel bench. **2** By tucking an antique canvas-upholstered bed behind the living room's floating wall of bookshelves, Carol created a cozy guest room with all the requisite comforts, privacy, and even a view of terrace greenery. Guests can stow their stuff in the adjacent wall of built-ins. **3** For parents' and kids' homework, Carol set up a corner office in the family room. Instead of a utilitarian desk, she installed a round table to hold the computer. An old wrought-iron gate climbs the wall as a decorative yet space-efficient accent.

Pacific Sun and Soul

Pacific Sun and Soul

LINDA APPLEWHITE AND MARSHALL MILLER OF SAN RAFAEL, CALIFORNIA

It could be the saucy sundresses on serious chairs. It could be the cheery grin of an ancient bronze horse. But sooner or later, some treasure or unexpected twist in this captivating cottage will coax a smile. That's the point, interior designer Linda Applewhite insists: "I love whimsy. It's a big motivator. Why not have things in your rooms that make you smile?"

She does, and the relaxed, sun-washed spaces in the home she shares with husband Marshall are rich in the art and the handcrafted objects that Linda believes bring uncommon joy and spirit to any home. What's her style? Call it "rustic elegance," because it welcomes any humble or precious object that happens to win her heart.

CREATIVE BLISS

Warm Mediterranean yellows, corals, oranges, and greens flow through every room. Linda layered on custom-mixed pigments by hand, so walls glow as if drenched in liquid sunshine. Iron remnants and judiciously placed art with touches of black make the otherwise lighthearted hues more sophisticated. "Everybody deserves to live in beauty. You can do a lot with a bucket of paint," she says. But, she adds, "If you didn't have black to ground it, these colors would fly away." Fresh fabrics blend orphaned chairs she rescued and rebuilt. In the dining room, the chairs' leopard-print sundresses, with dressmaker plackets and button-up backs, play beautifully against the dark wood table.

Linda's collections range from quirky metalworks and pottery to edgy contemporary art and Chinese tomb figures. Whether it's color, shape, or texture, Linda finds artful links to unify vignettes and she headlines doors and windows with architectural fragments to draw the eye up to newly vaulted ceilings.

"It's fun to put a funky old shutter next to a piece of art. It's art by Mother Nature," she says. "Things made by somebody's hands and things that are old nurture the human spirit and give a home soul."

Linda erases boundaries between indoors and out, explaining that "when those worlds cross, it's a great way to live." She invites garden objects inside, welcoming lichen-crusted finials, terra-cotta pots and statues, and weathered columns. Then she decorates in reverse, pulling indoor colors, furnishings, and signature collections outside to the terraces. "I like to live in a place where you can put your feet up, and you don't have to just tiptoe around in it," Linda says.

PREVIOUS PAGES: A dramatic juxtaposition of modern art, a meat-and-poultry-hook chandelier, and an old table with layers of peeling paint reveals Linda's respect for all things handmade. Once a closet, the entry introduces samples from her collections: a rare Chinese horse and rider atop an old tripod table, a hand-painted vase, and a remnant of "found" ironwork. BELOW LEFT: On the terrace of her remodeled cottage, interior designer and artist Linda Applewhite soaks up some California sun and inspiration from Mother Nature, one of her favorite decorating resources. OPPOSITE: Walls faux-finished for an old plaster look set the stage for collections of artwork, Chinese and Asian figures, salvaged objects, and just-plain-fun finds that add personality to each room. The living room's 1920s mahogany sofa is updated with fabric in an intriguing Indian tree-of-life pattern. The fireplace wall is a study in textures, with abundant treasures filling new built-ins and a modern Russian painting above the weathered mantel.

Linda erases boundaries between indoors and out:
"When those worlds cross, it's a great way to live."

OPPOSITE: Spinning off Linda's disciplined palette, fresh fabrics and lighthearted patterns energize mixed seating, from the two-toned easy chair in the living room to "dressed for dinner" French chairs around a century-old painted table. ABOVE: On this dining-out terrace, wicker assumes a more elegant air when it's paired with an Italian wall fountain and a rusty table with an ornate base and a concrete top. Colorful cans holding votive candles form an impromptu chandelier.

OPPOSITE: To age the new family room, Linda added salvaged windows with old, wavy glass. Open to the kitchen, the sun-dappled space mixes comfy slipcovered seating, distressed woods, and quirky finds such as the rusty blade above the window. **RIGHT:** Triumphal arches that link the home's spaces repeat in the kitchen's display niche above the cooktop and in the cabinetry above the French-paver countertop. Lower cabinets stop short, leaving a slot to slide in the Mexican dining table. Open shelves display "functional art," French confits, and handmade pottery in a rainbow of glazes.

ABOVE: Instead of a predictable wall-to-wall mirror in the new master bath, a little window was inserted between the two framed vanity mirrors. Repetition comforts the eye, says Linda, so a diamond pattern links the Mexican tile on the backsplash, the French chair's upholstery fabric, and the rickrack trim on the sconce shades. **OPPOSITE:** As airy as a summer garden pavilion, the master bedroom includes a new iron bed with a vintage quilt and a mix of new and old linens. Linda accented the vaulted ceiling with architectural elements from a Victorian porch and marked the pinnacle with a handcrafted wreath of fragrant eucalyptus, moss, and dried flowers.

Relaxed Gulf Classic

Relaxed Gulf Classic

SUNNY AND JAMES ENDICOTT OF PASS-A-GRILLE, FLORIDA

PREVIOUS PAGES: A telescope in the "den" end of the living room brings the ocean view even closer. Rollaway chairs gather at the games table but can glide away easily for reading, relaxing, and entertaining. As construction began, James Endicott scaled scaffolding to check out the view, which proved so spectacular they perched the main living spaces and an expansive terrace on the third level. Everyday meals are alfresco, served up with vistas of dunes, breeze-ruffled sea oats, and boats plying Gulf waters. BELOW: Emptynesters Sunny and James Endicott take tea on the terrace of the beach home that they designed to be easy-going and elegant. OPPOSITE: The unexpected addition of a pair of roll-arm wicker chairs by the fireplace boosts living room comfort. On the mantel, Sunny displays an oversize poster that adds a bolt of dramatic color and graphic pattern and fits the room in scale.

When Sunny Endicott packed her beach bag, in went the gold-leaf demilune, the ormolu planter, and Chinese exportware from the 1700s. They're not exactly the typical take-alongs for fun in the sun, but Sunny and James were off to the beach—for good—and couldn't leave behind the classic furnishings, art, and antiques they love. Barefoot elegance was their goal.

"Everybody's so laid back at the beach. It's much slower paced," Sunny says. "We didn't want things too formal. We wanted to take that edge off." Relaxing the palette was easy enough: Open the doors and let snappy sail-whites, cool ocean-blues, and sunshine-yellows flow in.

TIME AND TIDES

"You've got to be comfortable in your home," Sunny says. "You go into it, and it picks you up. It should be constantly renewing." The icy white cottons on the mix of upholstered seating feel cool and refined, yet they're easy to clean. Friendly wicker chairs tone down the gilt and mirrors with warm natural texture. Comfort includes pleasing the eye, and white backdrops showcase works of American artists and the rich woods of heirloom furniture.

Hard decorating choices come with the territory when you down-scale, Sunny says. Beyond favorites, what made the cut? Double-duty pieces with inherent flexibility. Antique chests add character, storage, and visual weight in the high-ceiling spaces. The dining table is two pedestal tables that also can go solo. Chairs on casters and a French bench tucked under the sofa table provide extra seating.

"We do a lot of gathering up and entertaining, so this home is all about family and friends," says Sunny, who likes intimate dinner parties—no matter how long the guest list—with small tables spilling from inside onto the terrace. Tampa interior designer David van Ling tamed the rambling living room so it's as cozy for two as it is for a crowd. Towering built-in shelves make up for the library in their previous home, and the conversation area moves center stage to focus on the fireplace, leaving end zones for a mini observatory and the piano.

Sunny nurtures roses, perennials, and orchids to match the home's interior colors because the blooms end up inside. "I'm not a kitchen person. I'm a gardener. I'll spend all day in my garden," she says.

Filled with cherished heirlooms and grandchildren's laughter, "our home is all about family," Sunny says.

ABOVE: Wing and slipper chairs, in dress whites, gather around the twin dining tables that serve in tandem or separately. Chinese export pieces on the burled walnut sideboard echo the refreshing blue and white palette. **OPPOSITE:** A mirrored wall reflects the seascape outside and adds visual width and depth to the living room. Blue ceilings temper bright sunlight. Centering the sofa freed up space for a music "room," built-in bar, and more high-rise bookshelves.

ABOVE: Even if guests in the adjacent dining room are seated facing the kitchen, they enjoy a peek at the sea, thanks to a mirrored backsplash that reflects the view behind them. White cabinetry and a black granite countertop create a crisp backdrop for art. OPPOSITE: For high drama in the third-floor foyer off the living room, an 1800s gold-leaf demilune holds a marquetry planter with Sunny's homegrown orchids. Framed etchings of shells and shellfish accent striped walls.

Sun and sea colors flow through
the home, emphasizing a sense
of place and a feeling
of grace and ease.

Cool, calming comfort reflects the ocean's presence, and the palette is as romantic as a sunset.

ABOVE: An antique dressing screen fitted with sheers and mirrors reflects the master suite's soft peach hues, chosen because they're flattering to complexions and always soothing. The down-filled chaise is a relaxing spot for reading, writing, and watching the sunset beyond the French doors. **OPPOSITE:** Although Sunny loves antiques, she's not a purist, especially if comfort is at stake. Instead of reworking an old bed to fit a new mattress, she chose a new, reproduction bed with an ornate headboard to set a classic mood; then she layered on vintage, hand-embroidered linens and lacy shams collected from French fairs and street markets.

HomeSweetSeattle

Home Sweet Seattle
JANET AND SHELLY JONES OF SEATTLE, WASHINGTON

PREVIOUS PAGES: Overlooking the backyard and garden, a covered patio has old-fashioned porch appeal for relaxing and entertaining, rain or shine. The blue-gray shingle siding and architectural details capture classic Cape Cod spirit. The galley kitchen may be small, but it's bright and efficient with glass cabinets that match panes in the new bay window. The built-in dining nook is dressed in crisp navy blue fabric, from the cushions to the chandelier shades. BELOW LEFT: Tradition lightens up and comfort rules in Janet Jones's home, where Emmett, the family's golden retriever, happily volunteers as the sofa-tester. OPPOSITE: Warm red on the walls of the family room is the perfect antidote to Seattle's frequent rainy days. Translucent lamp shades also impart a soft glow. Fabrics with color in common link the reupholstered sofa with the new wing chair and club chairs. In this dog-lover's retreat, the couple's four-legged favorites pop up in mantel art, coffee-table books, and accent pillows that Janet mixes with her own needlepoint creations.

"Down, boy!" isn't in Emmett's vocabulary. Neither is the word "metaphor." But the golden boy—retriever, that is— who shares this cozy Cape Cod-style home with Janet Jones and her husband, Shelly, is a tail-wagging symbol of its fetching personality. "We didn't want an all-white home that looks like people visit from time to time," Janet says. "Emmett's the kind of dog you saddle, so it's definitely his house."

TRADITION ON THE FUN SIDE

Keeping up with the Joneses means showing the world what you love, in a casual yet elegant context. They define "home" with lots of family photos, books, nature art, Janet's needlepoint, and the French and English antiques and accessories they've accumulated. It's the details, from hand-pleated lampshades to red animal-print upholstery, that takes the starch out of a proper wing chair. It's dreaming of butterflies in the bedroom, then searching high and low for that perfectly fanciful fabric. And it's color, always warm and bright in Seattle's rainy climate.

Dogs, however, rule the day. "I collect anything that's got a dog motif—dog books, dog art, dog dishes," Janet says. Etchings and prized Wedgwood plates on the sideboard display canine portraits by British artist Marguerite Kirmse, who illustrated

1940s *Lassie* books. Guests have favorite antique, dog-theme napkin rings they expect to see by their plates.

Janet would rather reupholster furniture than buy all-new pieces. "There's no such thing as a furniture graveyard," she says. Because the family room sofa is a favorite lounging spot for Emmett and Phoebe, the couple's elderly collie, it's reupholstered in $10-a-yard cotton duck. Two sets of cushions, one set for daily use and one for company, make it dog- and guest-friendly.

On evening strolls with Emmett, Janet found that she was drawn to one special Georgian colonial home. "There were beautiful lamps, beautiful oil paintings of the children and of dogs," she says. "It was the most inviting thing." It was also the home of British designer Bambi Goodhew, living temporarily in Seattle. Her warm, personalized style clicked with the couple's vision, and she guided the redesign of their home.

Originally a "mongrel, Cape Cod, ranch," the home underwent seven years of remodeling and decorating and has emerged with a fresh, easygoing take on classic style. "It's a lovely house," Janet says. "It's casual and cozy. I think we just made it what it wanted to become all along."

Let it rain. Inside, the mood is always cozy with a warm palette of reds and yellows.

To create the golden hue on living room walls, paint was mixed on-site and applied in test spots to view in changing light. Botanical-print pillows punch up the sofa, and Janet dipped into her collection of antique tea caddies and Battersea boxes for coffee-table accents.

ABOVE: Deep "military blue" walls create an intimate mood for entertaining in the dining room, where Janet mixes pieces new and old that share a noble profile, such as the reproduction table and shield-back chairs. **OPPOSITE:** A distinctive collection of transferware plates featuring drawings of dogs by British artist Marguerite Kirmse turns the sideboard into an art gallery that also displays antique figural napkin rings, most with a canine motif, from the late 1800s.

ABOVE: Designed for pampering visiting family and friends, the guest room is "a chameleon," Janet says, because light changes the stipple-look wallcovering from robin's-egg blue to soft green through the day. Fabrics link the suite, and the English rose pattern on the triple-fringed draperies repeats in the bath's shade.

Playful patterns and luxurious fabrics are the dream-weavers in everyday getaways.

ABOVE: Wallpapered from the ceiling to the baseboards in a soft yellow miniprint, the charming master bedroom layers English chintz onto the duvet-topped bed. Eton checks act as a crisp foil. Treating the cushioned window seat to an ottoman gives it extra comfort for reading or lounging.

Decorating Taste Test: What's Your Style?

Decorating at its best is a self-portrait. Your rooms reflect your individuality through the colors, furnishings, and accessories you choose. Created in the spirit of fun, the Decorating Taste Test is designed to help you explore your personal style. Choose your answers honestly. If none of the answers is exactly you, select the one closest to your taste. When you've finished, transfer your answers to the scoring columns on the next page; then analyze the results to find what your answers reveal about your decorating personality. (For more fun, have your partner take the test too and then compare answers.)

1. **In your dream-house dreams, you picture yourself settled happily into:**
a. A Victorian "painted lady" with a carriage house and garden, all lovingly restored
b. An architect-designed log home wrapped in window walls and woods and lake views
c. A gallery-style loft with skylights and skyline views in a renovated warehouse

2. **Browsing through the neighborhood bookstore, you spot one title you can't resist adding to your decorating library:**
a. Romantic Style
b. Second Home: Finding Your Place in the Fun
c. Bauhaus for Today

3. **You've inherited an antique pine farm table for the dining room. For seating, you:**
a. Search for chairs of the same vintage
b. Paint mismatched chairs cottage-style white
c. Pull up post-modern metal chairs

4. **You never miss your favorite TV "home" show:**
a. This Old House
b. Trading Spaces
c. Extreme Homes

5. **Out of three invitations, you choose to attend:**
a. An estate sale at an 1896 mansion
b. A street fair featuring local artisans
c. A lecture on Japanese pottery

6. **The colors you love to live with come from:**
a. The jewel box
b. The flower garden
c. The beach

7. **For you, the perfect reading chair would be:**
a. An antique Chippendale wing chair, upholstered in toile de Jouy
b. A down-filled chair-and-a-half and ottoman, upholstered in chenille
c. A steel-and-leather Le Corbusier chaise with a pashmina throw

8. **On a "do as you please" weekend, you:**
a. Work on genealogy on the Internet
b. Dive into that long list of do-it-yourself projects around the house
c. Grab your camera and shoot some arty black and white images for framing

9. **Your sofa needs fluffing up, so you choose:**
a. Matching accent pillows for each end
b. A large pillow at one end and two or three smaller ones in mixed fabrics at the other
c. One or two exquisite handcrafted pillows

10. **For a special dinner party, you dress the table to the nines with:**
a. Grandmother's Limoges china, antique crystal, and a big bouquet of cabbage roses
b. Mismatched handcrafted pottery, stainless flatware, and wildflowers in a basket
c. Square white plates, colorful chopsticks, and gerbera daisies in a metal pitcher

11. **Your living room seating has been begging for slipcovers, so you choose:**
a. Damask for the sofa, velvet for chairs
b. Cotton duck for the sofa, denim for chairs
c. Natural linen over all

12. **If you could find a special piece of art for that needy spot over the mantel, it would be:**
a. A gilt-framed, period English landscape
b. A folk-art painting of children
c. An African kuba cloth framed in black

13. **You're off on that long-awaited vacation to:**
a. Tour the homes of Colonial Williamsburg
b. Cruise the Mississippi River on a houseboat
c. Visit the Napa Valley for a wine-tasting tour

14. **When the Antiques Roadshow rolls into town, the treasure you bring for appraisal is:**
a. Your Grandmother's Imari plate
b. The crazy quilt you found at a garage sale
c. Your childhood cache of Star Wars figures

15. **For your living room windows, you choose:**
a. An English floral swag-and-jabot treatment
b. Roman shades in natural linen
c. The view, so you leave windows undressed

16. **The person, past or present, you'd love to invite to your next dinner party is:**
a. English gardener Gertrude Jekyll
b. Actor Tom Hanks
c. Architect Frank Lloyd Wright

17. **If you bought a new bed, it would be:**
a. A carved mahogany four-poster
b. A pine frame and garden-gate headboard
c. An upholstered platform bed

18. **On weekends, you're likely to wear:**
a. Khakis and a cashmere sweater
b. Jeans and a buffalo-check shirt
c. Jeans and a white silk shirt

19. **The best gift your home ever received is:**
a. Antique candlesticks you wired into lamps
b. A wicker trunk you use as a coffee table
c. Iron finials you display as sculpture

20. **To reflect your personality and interests, what mood do you want your home to convey?**
a. Gracious ease with timeless furnishings—nothing stuffy, but tradition is important
b. Comfort first with relaxed furnishings and natural textures in an un-self-conscious mix
c. A sophisticated love of design with restrained schemes and varied-vintage classics—editing is your forte because you dislike clutter.

Scoring

After you've circled "a," "b," or "c" for each question, transfer your answers to the appropriate columns below. Then total each column at the bottom. The column with the highest score indicates the decorating mood that suits you best.

COLUMN 1	COLUMN 2	COLUMN 3
1. a	1. b	1. c
2. a	2. b	2. c
3. a	3. b	3. c
4. a	4. b	4. c
5. a	5. b	5. c
6. a	6. b	6. c
7. a	7. b	7. c
8. a	8. b	8. c
9. a	9. b	9. c
10. a	10. b	10. c
11. a	11. b	11. c
12. a	12. b	12. c
13. a	13. b	13. c
14. a	14. b	14. c
15. a	15. b	15. c
16. a	16. b	16. c
17. a	17. b	17. c
18. a	18. b	18. c
19. a	19. b	19. c
20. a	20. b	20. c
TOTAL	TOTAL	TOTAL

Analyzing the Results

Now have fun using your answers to decide which of three main decorating moods best suits your tastes—classic, casual, clean and simple, or a mix. No matter what decorating style you prefer—romantic, cottage, 18th century, Art Deco, modern—it can fit into any of these basic categories. For instance, graceful Chippendale chairs can go formal or minimalist, depending on your room's mood.

CLEARLY CLASSIC If most of your answers were in Column 1, you like formality, and your home may be a gracious melding of timeless, classic furnishings in symmetrical groupings. In this broad category, you may choose from period French, 18th-century Chippendale, or Queen Anne furnishings, as well as Oriental and formal modern pieces. You mix antiques, quality reproductions, and lovingly collected accessories. Colors are often rich and mellow.

CASUAL COMFORT If the majority of your answers were in Column 2, you like a casual decorating style. You choose furnishings with relaxed comfort in mind, and you prefer unfussy seating with carefree fabrics in earthy or neutral colors. Seating is arranged in informal groupings for easy conversation. Your favorite things include lighthearted and whimsical accessories. Your home's only demand: Put your feet up and enjoy.

CLEAN AND SIMPLE If most of your answers were in Column 3, you like a sophisticated, elegantly simple look inspired by your interests in art and design. You carefully edit furnishings and accessories, choosing each element, whether modern or traditional, for its distinctive lines and integrity of form. Even color is often kept to a minimum, with hues drawn from the neutrals—especially black, white, and gray—often punched up with a brilliant accent color, such as red.

PERSONALITY MIX If your answers are spread over all three categories, you're confident about your personal style and want to combine the best from several design periods and styles. Chances are that your answers lean, at least slightly, toward one of the main categories. The key is to understand and heed your main attitude toward furnishing your home so you can combine disparate elements into a harmonious whole. For instance, if you lean toward simplicity but also love the classics, you might team Chippendale dining chairs with a sleek glass-top dining table for the best of both styles.

Your fun challenge is to create beautiful, comfortable rooms that draw on the best resource of all—your personality.

TO FIND OUT MORE ONLINE, VISIT US @ www.bhg.com/bkhousehome

CHAPTER 2

Living rooms

Your living room can be one of the most versatile rooms in your home. Whatever your style, the space can be as cozy for conversation, as gracious for entertaining, and as comfortable for relaxing as this New England-style classic. What else would you like it to be? Could you add a home office or library? Could it become a music room too? Whether your space is big or small, the right furnishings can help you put more life, style, and function into your living room.

Express Yourself

A well-designed living room lives and entertains the way you do. What's in the script for yours?

Is it a guests-only space? Is it the family's everyday gathering spot? You'll put yourself and your guests at ease by tailoring furnishings to the way you use your living room. Analyze your space and decide if the furnishings and the arrangement work. If you're a put-your-feet-up, casual type, a room with white upholstery and no ottoman in sight may be a bit too formal for you. However, if your living room is more for entertaining than for watching television, the formality of classic furnishings and traditional arrangements could be the best choice.

ABOVE LEFT: Classic forms and details in the upholstery, window treatments, Louis XVI chairs and console, and the symmetrical arrangements exude formality in this room. **ABOVE RIGHT:** Neutral walls set a serene backdrop for a simple room where shapely, comfy seating is a priority. Accents are edited to a dramatic few.

ELEMENTS OF YOUR STYLE

Whether your design style is formal, casual, spare, or a funky mix, take a thoughtful look at the design elements and furniture arrangement in your living room. Is your room in sync with your style? If not, use these tips to do a little redecorating. *(For more ideas, see chapters on "Elements," pages 286–309, and "Arranging," pages 260–285.)*

■ **USE FABRICS CREATIVELY.** Fabric weaves, finishes, and patterns express different degrees of formality. Linen, for example, is a good choice for an eclectic room that's sleek yet casual; use it in natural hues in understated window treatments. To express a casual attitude—whether your style is contemporary or country—dress sofas and chairs in the same textural denims, plaids, and cottons you wear on weekends. Mix patterns for eclectic and casual styles. Matched fabrics convey a formal look, as do elegant silk, damask, and glazed chintz. *(For more tips on choosing fabrics, turn to the "Fabrics" chapter, pages 336–357.)*

■ **FRAME A NEW VIEW.** Window treatments play a major role in building your style. Loosely draped curtains express a casual, clean, or eclectic look. For a minimal look, stick to unadorned shades, blinds, or shutters. For a formal, traditional feel, consider traditional draperies with flowing floor-to-ceiling panels, valances, and elegant trims.

■ **LET FURNITURE TELL YOUR STORY.** Create a formal look with antiques and reproductions featuring classic details: camelbacks on sofas, cabriole legs, ball-and-claw feet, or shield- or lyre-shape chair backs. Make a formal yet modern statement with 20th-century classics such as Barcelona and Wassily chairs. Oversize roll-arm sofas with squashy cushions can set a casual mood.

■ **FACTOR IN TEXTURE.** Rough textures such as berber carpet, natural-fiber rugs, and twig furniture work in casual and eclectic rooms. Smooth textures—lacquer, glass, mirrors, and polished woods—can combine to convey a sleek yet formal attitude.

ABOVE LEFT: Classic, sink-in seating and a bright mix of colors and patterns give this room its outgoing look. The upbeat mood is enhanced by yellow paint on the end wall and on the back wall of the open shelves. **ABOVE RIGHT:** A Victorian sofa, a sleek ottoman, and graphic pillows add personality to a romantic room.

Formal or Casual?

To put your best "style foot" forward in your living room, would you wear a silk pump or a cross-trainer?

Most living rooms fall somewhere between formal and casual. Whatever their degree of formality, they all share a goal—gracious comfort and ease—but take different paths to get there. What's your lifestyle, and what are your entertaining needs?

ABOVE: Free-spirited color beckons from this easygoing room. A playful mix of fabrics on the slipcovered sofa and pillows contrasts with the textures of distressed wood and wicker. No window treatment is needed; a folding screen easily moves in front of the windows to add privacy or fend off harsh rays. OPPOSITE: Classic furnishings, antiques, and gilt-framed art give this room a formal air; seating reupholstered in highly textured chenille relaxes the mood. The modern cocktail table makes a delightful and unexpected contrast to the oversize French mirror behind the sofa.

FORMAL FLAVOR

A living room used for formal entertaining demands a few special considerations.

■ **HOW DO YOU ENTERTAIN?** If serving cocktails to a few friends or business associates is your thing, you don't need as much seating or as many pull-around tables as you do if your "party style" is buffets for 50 guests. Do you need smaller-scale furniture pieces to free up space for a piano?

■ **DESIGN FOR FLEXIBILITY.** Create flexible furniture groupings that include lightweight, open-arm chairs that rearrange easily as guests gather during a party. Upholstered ottomans work as tables and extra seating.

■ **MAKE IT EASY FOR GUESTS.** Put tables within reach of sitting areas. A sofa table can be a mini oasis for plates and drinks.

CASUAL DAYS

Live and entertain casually? Remember that any style, including traditional, can be casual if you decorate with these ideas in mind.

■ **ARRANGE CASUALLY.** Instead of placing sofas in a formal face-off at the fireplace, let seating mill around informally. Add a sturdy ottoman or coffee table for a footrest. Arrange collections and art asymmetrically.

■ **MIX IT UP.** Toss a wicker chair, a wood rocker, even an unexpected log chair into an upholstered grouping to loosen things up. Mixing knotty woods and painted or distressed finishes relaxes the mood, as do gathered skirts on traditional sofas.

■ **ADD FAMILY ROOM TOUCHES.** Add a dining or game table to a corner of a traditional room. Pull a table up to a bookcase for a snug reading, homework, or dining spot.

Design for Flexibility

Pull together the versatile basics in furnishings and other design elements, and your living room can sail gracefully from casual daytime living to dressier evening entertaining with only a subtle change of accessories. Whether your style leans toward traditional or modern, your living room can be inviting around the clock if you make comfort a priority and keep backdrops simple.

■ **GO LIGHT.** Neutral, or at least subtle, backdrops entertain well, day or night, making it easy to add more color and pattern in accessories. White walls, ceilings, mantels, and window treatments are crisp and appealing with any decorating style.

■ **STOW IN STYLE.** Storage ottomans and window seats, armoires, and bookcases with enclosed compartments hide daytime clutter when company arrives.

■ **PUT COMFORT FIRST.** Use overstuffed versions of traditional seating pieces, such as roll-arm sofas and club chairs. For long wear and beauty, make your biggest decorating investment the sofa and cover it in a durable fabric, such as tapestry or cotton.

■ **DRESS UP ACCESSORIES.** Substituting silk accent pillows for daytime cotton ones or arranging candles and collections on the coffee table sets a special occasion mood. Build a fire or fill the fireplace with a cluster of candles.

■ **PLAN FOR LIGHT, DAY AND NIGHT.** Minimal window treatments, from classic swags and jabots to chic window-framing drapery panels, invite the most light by day, yet they still look dressy for parties. Turn on accent lights at night; a picture light over your favorite painting adds drama to a dark wall.

ABOVE: When the owners of this home chose the room's main focal point, the fireplace lost out to the view, but it's the center of attention in an alcove that includes a desk and striped seating. The fireplace wall glows in sun or candlelight thanks to pearly paint used in the cloud-effect finish. RIGHT: Striped, floral, and plaid fabrics make a friendly mix against the sail-white backdrop, wicker and wood tables, and yellow berber rug. An unexpected and witty touch, a frilly yellow lampshade tops a floor lamp. OPPOSITE: Golden sunshine and ocean blue inspired the palette and breezy attitude of this living room. The slipcovered sofas are angled to focus on the spectacular Pacific view. The arrangement also keeps this main conversation area open to the action at the other end of the long space.

Choose Your Focus

Every sitting spot needs a focal point. Think of it as the sun in your furnishings universe—an anchor around which all your furnishings revolve. If your living room has a natural architectural focus, such as a rustic fireplace, built-ins, or a great view, group seating around it. If not, accept the challenge and create your own focal point. Arrange seating to focus on a bold painting, a grouping of colorful prints, a large decorative mirror hung above a console table, a bookcase, or an armoire. A focal point gives the eye a starting point from which your eye can take in the whole space with ease.

FEATURE ATTRACTIONS

■ **DO IT YOURSELF.** If your home's builder left out architectural character, add some yourself. An antique fireplace mantel, a large-scale furniture piece, or a grand painting underlined with a cabinet or a bench can anchor a seating group. Or, center seating with a hunt board or sideboard teamed with an oversize mirror.

■ **GRAB THE EYE WITH COLOR AND PATTERN.** Use bright or bold hues to create a focal point. A boldly colored and artfully shaped sofa or a brightly painted armoire can grab the eye in an otherwise bland living room. Or, use a beautifully patterned area rug to draw the eye and anchor seating pieces.

■ **TURN TO THE VIEW.** If you have a great window or view, arrange seating to take advantage of it. Paint the window trim an accent color or add curtain panels that capture the eye without competing with the view.

OPPOSITE: Embellishing this plain window with rustic shutters transforms a plain wall into a focal point for living room seating. The expanded window is more in scale with the sideboard beneath it. Colorful wall art draws the eye to the new focus. RIGHT: Why choose when you have two views that are worth savoring? By arranging upholstered seating at a right angle and tucking a chaise under the window, the family and their guests can enjoy the rocky hearth in this seaside living room and still watch for passing boats. A large area rug and a slim sofa table help set the seating group apart from the adjacent dining area.

More Grace Than Space

Your living room can be small or midsize and still offer big style and comfort.

How you design a small, featureless space is more important than its square footage. With the right furnishings and creative arrangements, small spaces can be as gracious as larger ones—and offer even more coziness and intimacy too.

LESS CAN BE MORE

■ **RESHAPE THE BOX.** Put the sofa on a casual, room-widening angle and enhance the effect with a diagonal area rug. Hang a window valance on a rod mounted on the wall above the window so the fabric clears the glass completely. Add tall items, such as a lofty secretary or a ceiling-high ficus tree, to make an 8-foot ceiling seem higher.

■ **MAKE COLOR A PLAYER.** White walls and sparkling mirrors make a room look bigger, but if you love color, use bolder hues for a cozier feel. Forge a space-expanding link with the outdoors by bringing in the colors seen outside your windows—desert neutrals, forest greens, or garden-flower brights, for instance.

■ **PUT WALLS TO WORK.** Give a small space grand architectural character with built-in shelves or bookcases. Such storage creates a focal point and corrals clutter. A bookcase built to stretch from wall to wall and floor to ceiling expands space by pushing the walls out and the ceiling up. Balance furniture groupings with wall displays of art or collections.

■ **PARE FURNISHINGS.** Use fewer, bigger furniture pieces and include some light-scale and dual-purpose items. A drop-leaf sofa table expands for dining and entertaining. An over-size ottoman offers extra seating.

■ **LIGHTEN UP.** Light fabrics and wall finishes and simple window treatments, such as trim, light-hued draperies, curtains, or shades, give rooms an expansive and open feeling by keeping things bright and airy.

■ **STRETCH YOUR SPACE.** To create long sight lines, link adjacent spaces with the same colors and flooring.

ABOVE: Ample seating plumped with floral cushions snugs up to one wall, allowing space to move through the room to the terrace beyond. Simple drapery panels frame the atrium door without blocking precious light. Artwork turns a blank wall into a secondary focal point. **OPPOSITE:** A sofa and armchair are angled to break up boxiness in this living room. Flanking the window with shelves turns the entire wall into a focal point. New canvas slipcovers, light pattern-free walls, and a light rug bordered in flowers also give the room a gracious, expansive look.

Make a Large Space Inviting

Variety is the decorating solution for large living rooms. By dividing your rambling space into several intimate seating and activity areas, you can create islands for relaxing, reading, enjoying a garden view from a window seat, or letter writing at a corner desk. Instead of arranging a single, overly large conversation area, divide up the seating. Two smaller sitting areas for guests to gather around are friendlier for entertaining too.

■ **DEFINE WITH FURNITURE.** To subtly separate two sitting areas, arrange a pair of seating pieces with their backs to each other. Include some lightweight chairs that can be moved from one group to another as needed. Use the room's narrow ends for tall case goods or a desk. Tuck functional tea or console tables for serving and display into alcoves and corners.

■ **UNIFY YOUR SPACE.** Even when you've subdivided its functions, treat the room as a whole, weaving it together with the same window treatments, the same wall color or wallcovering pattern, and the same sweep of carpet or hardwood flooring. Define separate conversation spots by using area rugs.

■ **FIND FOCAL POINTS BEYOND THE FIREPLACE.** Pull up a chaise lounge, a desk, or a couple of chairs to a window with a great view. Adding a window seat creates seating, storage, and architectural interest.

LEFT: The original, early-1900s hearth in this art-filled home is a natural focal point for one seating group. A chair by the tall window takes advantage of the view. A movable ottoman provides extra seating. OPPOSITE: Back-to-back leather sofas define two conversation areas in this oversize living room. In a large space like this, one focal point isn't enough. The fireplace, a tall grouping of artwork between the windows, and an alcove accented with a console table and decorative mirror attract the eye and balance each other.

Changing Seasons

When falling temperatures and snowflakes
make cocooning indoors so appealing, warm body and soul by redecorating with slip-covers in rich colors and a seasonal change of accessories. In the living room of this 1920s Arts and Crafts-style home, the French settee and windows dress in cut velvet, and fireside seating dons chenille cover-ups and textured pillows in winter. Even lampshades change to dark-hued silk. Iron masks of the North Wind and clay pots of winterberries accent the fireplace and mantel. Turn the page to see how this cozy room cools off when summer arrives.

Changing Seasons

It's summertime, and the livin' really is easy—and easy care. The living room sheds the warm winter wear shown on the previous pages and slips into something cooler and more comfortable. White is the unifier, making the space feel and look airy and expansive. Tapestry slipper chairs pop on white canvas slipcovers, windows dress in crisp linen, and the settee and fireside seating shrug off their extra layer. Pillows are brighter, lampshades are lighter, and the mantel is "seascaped" with beachcomber shells and sea glass. Displaying art on an easel makes it easy to change the scene to fit the season.

CHAPTER 3

Family rooms

Your home is your haven, and for many families, the family room is the heart of it.

No wonder you have great expectations for that great All-American space where you log lots of family time, relaxing together, dining, entertaining, and being entertained. Whatever the size of your gathering spot, it can be as great-looking as this easygoing space. Good design will make your space work and play as stylishly as the family rooms in this chapter.

Success in the Family Business

Once the family's retreat to avoid messing up the "good" furniture in the formal living room,

family rooms and great-rooms are today's casual but stylish hub for everybody, including guests. To design for comfort, flexibility, convenience, and, of course, your personal style, consider the four Ws: Who's using the family room? What's going on? Where are the activity areas? When is it used most?

■ **PICK YOUR FOCAL POINT(S).** Yes, there may be more than one. In family rooms, seating often must focus on a fireplace and a media center—a problem often solved with a diagonal furniture arrangement that can focus on two walls at once. Let your focal point anchor your furniture arrangement.

■ **USE FURNITURE WISELY.** Break a large great-room into two or more seating areas to increase versatility and provide solo spots for reading, watching television, or playing video games. A table can double as a desk and a crafts or games spot. Let furniture direct traffic around, not through, activity areas.

■ **DESIGN FOR COMFORT.** Durable, easy-clean upholstery, natural-fiber rugs, and cotton, denim, and other no-fuss fabrics relax the mood.

■ **INCREASE STORAGE.** Built-ins and free-standing storage organize an active room filled with books, magazines, electronics, toys, and more.

OPPOSITE: Sharing neutral hues, natural materials, and a fireplace view, the great-room's living and dining areas flow seamlessly into the kitchen. The limestone island incorporates shaded lamps—an especially warm touch for any kitchen that is part of a larger great-room. A cloud painting draws the eye to the sky. The bright yet mellow scheme of warm woods, warm whites, and dashes of black is punctuated by tangy lemon and lime accents. The kitchen's focal point wall presents an uncluttered face on the family room side, but turn the page and you'll see the storage bonus it holds.

BELOW: Grab the remote, a good book, or the kids for cuddling and sink back among the citrus and white pillows on this spacious daybed that serves as the great-room sofa. Its shapely legs end in wheels, giving it the flexibility to move anywhere in the room. The seating piece is pulled away from the wall, so traffic glides behind it and not through the seating area.

GREAT-ROOM, GREAT IDEAS

Cares of the day melt away when family and friends gather in this simply dramatic great-room where sail-white backdrops, snuggle-in seating, and a mix of warm, natural textures create its getaway mood. Every detail in this talented three-in-one space was thoughtfully designed to enhance family living.

1 Refreshments, anyone? Convenience inspired the features at this handy intersection, where you can grab a log for the fire, make a snack on the stone-slab island or a cappuccino in the beverage center, and plop down on one of the dining table's leather chairs. To keep the mood airy and expansive, cabinetry is a pale maple, and glass doors are lined with rice paper for a frosty, textured look. **2** Remember the kitchen's focal point wall on page 80? It turns a clean-and-pretty face toward the living space, but it works hard behind the scenes too. Step behind it into the "butler's pantry" with built-in freezer, refrigerator, bar sink, food prep counter, and storage for table linens, serving pieces, and great-room "stuff." (Clutter doesn't play in this contemporary scheme.) At the end, the built-in desk keeps the household organized. **3** Not in the mood to cook on a sultry summer night? Try take-out—without leaving home to fetch the food. With a circle of cheery chairs under backyard oaks, impromptu picnicking on the shore is just steps away. Creating access to the outdoors, be it a big yard or a sliver of garden, makes any family room live bigger and adds the fun option of fresh-air dining.

ABOVE: This room offers fun for all ages. Ask the kids what activities would turn your family room into a great-room. Here, it's a child-size table and chairs for art projects, a soft wool rug for floor games, and nearby, a TV on a bench that lies low so it doesn't obscure the view. Remote-controlled blinds temper the sun, clerestory windows all around invite natural light, and uplight sconces, such as the one on the wall high above the TV, handle general lighting.

New Look
Smarter Storage

BEFORE

Well-loved family rooms have a way of becoming well-worn family rooms, overstuffed with accumulated treasures—and, yes, clutter. Still, updating your family room doesn't mean out with everything old and in with all new. It means dressing up that broken-in sofa, arranging for more function, and putting lazy walls to work. Here's how this family room kept its best and changed the rest:

■ **TWO UNFINISHED PINE CORNER HUTCHES,** simply stained, make a powerful addition to the fireplace wall. They expand storage and display space, introduce needed vertical interest, and widen the room by carrying the eye from wall to wall—and around the corner. Remember: With the right cabinetry, 12 to 24 inches of floor space along a wall yields a lot of storage between the floor and ceiling.

■ **THE DECADE-OLD YET STILL-COMFY SOFA** was spiffed up with a washable slipcover in multicolor paisley that disguises spills. Accent pillows in coordinating fabrics link the "new" sofa and "old" woven chair.

■ **TWO SMALL TRUNKS** replace the ho-hum coffee table. They add character, are handy for stashing toys before company arrives, and they're easily moved aside when the kids play floor games.

■ **A NEW WOOD-LOOK LAMINATE FLOOR** accented with an inexpensive sisal rug replaces the old beige carpet, underscoring the room's traditional character in fuss-free style.

■ **CHECKED FABRIC** on the window's pleated valance and side panels complements the paisley sofa. Full-length shades control sun more effectively than the half-shutters did.

RIGHT: With extra storage and easy-clean fabrics and flooring, this family room is now more kid-friendly and more carefree for parents too. Rearranged seating and a versatile two-trunk "coffee table" open up the space, making it more inviting. Corner hutches add storage and architectural impact.

Link with Color and Style

Today's most popular floor plan, the great-room with kitchen, dining, and living space

flowing together, poses some tricky decorating challenges. Forge links with design elements and you can blend those rambling spaces into an inviting, unified whole.

MARRYING SPACES

■ **CREATE FLOW WITH FLOORS.** Use the same flooring throughout, especially in smaller spaces. If you do change flooring materials between adjacent areas, it's wise to stay in the same color family to avoid jarring contrast. Use area rugs to define and anchor groupings.

■ **LET WALLS AND WINDOWS CARRY YOUR EYE.** In this French Country-inspired room, the walls are drenched in yellow paint, and topiary-print fabric carries the hue to Roman shades and draperies. Window treatments don't have to match, but, like floors, should be color-related.

■ **REPEAT FABRICS,** accent colors, and surface materials, varying intensities and patterns. Here, stripes, prints, and miniflorals spin off the sofa's dominant blue-and-yellow fabric. The same tile tops the dining area built-ins and the kitchen counters—a shade of blue echoed in the sofa.

■ **USE EASY GO-BETWEENS.** Work in mixable naturals, such as wicker and mellow woods. Punch up your scheme with painted pieces. Here the dining chairs and antique table base were painted blue to pull the hue through to the dining area.

■ **SHARE COLLECTIONS AND ACCENTS.** Blue and white ware, displayed on kitchen soffits, walls, and tabletops, inspired this palette.

■ **KEY COLORS** to the natural light. Add "sun" to a north-facing room or a room used mainly at night by including touches of yellow or red; cool a sunny room with green or blue. *(For more color tips, check the "Color" chapter, pages 310–335.)*

ABOVE: A parade of blue and white plates sets off in the kitchen and then marches around the great-room. Tile on the peninsula and fabric on the stool cushions repeat in the dining area. **OPPOSITE:** Terra-cotta flooring, birch cabinetry built in as a buffet, and fabrics in golden yellow and blue carry the flavor of the kitchen to the living and dining areas where this family likes to entertain.

Add to the Fun

What would it take to make your family room more family-friendly?

Is seating a tight squeeze when you enter-tain? Would you stay more organized or homework get done faster if the computer were handy? Small changes may be a better solution than extra square footage.

FAMILY-FRIENDLY ZONE

■ **CATER TO YOUR CROWD.** Add an oversize coffee table or a drop-leaf sofa table for play-ing board games. (Have little ones? Pull some child-size chairs around it.) Tuck a desk or computer center into a wall of built-ins. Add a comfy chair for the book lover and build in a window seat for extra seating with bonus storage below.

■ **PROVIDE FLEXIBLE LIGHTING** and spread it around. Include general lighting for kids' play, task lights for reading, and over-the-table lighting—a pendant, recessed fixtures, or a strip of track—on a dimmer so it can be turned up for reading and down for dining.

■ **MAKE IT PERSONAL.** This is where you display and enjoy belongings that reflect your family at its happiest. Create a portrait of your loved ones by displaying family trea-sures and just-for-fun finds. Items such as vacation souvenirs, handcrafted textiles, and children's artwork make great conversation starters when guests arrive.

■ **ACCENT ARTFULLY.** Consider larger artwork or groupings that can hold their own in typ-ically large or vaulted great-room spaces. Artwork should be hung at eye level; in plop-down family rooms, hang artwork lower so you can better view the art while seated.

ABOVE: Too small for even a sofa, this den wasn't very entertaining until this sofa-sized window seat was built in. Now there's room for a few guests and a place to store games and other gear below the cushioned seat. **RIGHT:** Togetherness in this family room starts with a wall of built-ins where Mom or Dad can read or pay bills and the kids can do their homework on the computer. Wrapping built-ins like these around two walls creates work space on one wall and home entertainment space on the other. **OPPOSITE:** With a dining table, an oversize coffee table for board games and casual meals, and gather-around seating, this family room is ready for action. Distressed woods and easy-care fabrics relax the mood.

TO FIND OUT MORE ONLINE, VISIT US @ www.bhg.com/bkdecoratingcenter

Living in the Library

With a little ingenuity, you can transform

an infrequently used space into a book-lined retreat that welcomes family activities and entertaining. Do you walk past a standoffish formal dining room every day? Could you turn that often-idle guest room into an evening retreat for the family? A little-used room and a lot of shelves can perform this decorating trick.

CREATE DO-IT-ALL SPACES

Wrapped in floor-to-ceiling shelves that hold a collection of books, this ambitious library added a few more tasks to its job description. With the addition of a desk and round game table at one end, a set-for-eight dining table, and leather chairs and sofa, the library also serves as an office, game room, dining space, and den. Even in smaller spaces, you can pull off this kind of practical room transformation. Start with shelves to set the mood, then follow these tips:

■ **MAKE MULTIFUNCTIONAL ARRANGEMENTS.** Move the dining table to one side to make way for a deep love seat and an armchair. Dining chairs can pull around for dining or conversation as needed.

■ **LIGHTEN UP.** Make lighting less formal by swapping the typical dining chandelier for dimmable recessed lights or track lights that can illuminate the table, spotlight artwork, and bounce light off walls for an indirect, general glow. Add lamps for reading, hobbies, and homework and accent lights for art.

■ **EXPAND STORAGE.** For almost every activity that goes on in a family room, there's a corresponding set of items and equipment to be neatly housed nearby. Use shelves and storage furniture, from armoires to chests and trunk tables, to neatly corral electronics, games, dishes, and table linens.

ABOVE: Lightweight faux-bamboo stools upholstered in fluttery "eyelash" fabric serve the desk at the library's sunny office end and provide extra seating at the round game table nearby. Behind the desk, an English fishing box on a new base holds the phone. **OPPOSITE:** Family-friendly activity areas defined by vintage Oriental rugs break up the long, narrow shape of this Arts and Crafts library. Bentwood chairs wearing dressmaker-style slipcovers edge the crackle-finish table that hosts everything from casual everyday meals to elegant dinners for guests, who love dining in the library.

At Your Service

Your rooms don't have to be small to benefit from the talents of flexible and double-duty furnishings.

In spaces large and small, these clever, well-designed pieces always add a dimension of comfort and function. Family rooms are inherently spontaneous spaces, and they're more fun if lightweight seating scoots where it's needed, if tables expand for dining and impromptu games, and if practical storage adds character to the space.

ADDING FLEXIBILITY

■ **LET OTTOMANS RULE.** Because these talented pieces can be used for dining, storage, seating, and resting tired feet, they've taken over for coffee tables,

which once stood in front of every sofa. Group seating around an over-size ottoman, or for flexibility, pair two smaller ottomans that can serve or seat. Add a tray to protect the fabric and hold drinks and snacks.

■ **TURN THE TABLES.** Versatile drop-leaf, gateleg, extendable, or flip-top tables are ideal for any family room. Drop-leaf tables can serve as everyday sofa tables, then quickly flip up into company dining spots.

■ **SHOP FOR FURNITURE THAT CAN DO TWO JOBS.** Chests or trunks work well as coffee tables and end tables—and hold games, work files, and guest linens if your sofa hides a bed inside. Dressed-up daybeds make invit-ing settees when piled with enough pillows for back support.

■ **RECAST COLLECTIBLE FURNITURE.** Antique armoires, painted cupboards, dry sinks, and pie safes can stow entertainment gear. An old bench or a flea market chest makes a perfect surface for a TV—and an instant focal point when you hang eyecatching artwork above it.

■ **CUSTOMIZE WITH MODULARS.** From upholstered seating to stackable chests and wall storage units, flexible modular furniture lets you tailor—and re-tailor—the configuration to suit changing needs. Modulars come in styles from clean-lined contemporary to tradi-tional; some are scaled down to fit compact spaces.

OPPOSITE LEFT: Casters make this artful trio of diamond-shaped ottomans a functional gem. Clad in synthetic suede fabric, these soft seats roll around individually, but when they are lined up in front of the sofa, they become a colorful server for snacks. CENTER: Classically detailed with shapely wood legs, this oversize ottoman makes a modern design statement. An inviting feet-up spot, the ottoman also serves as a handy table when a large tray is placed on top of it. BELOW: A small living room yields grand comfort when a table-size ottoman pulls up to the sofa. In addition to its regular footrest duties, the ottoman offers a spot for hors d'oeuvres and casual dinners.

TelevisionSpots

Whether your family room boasts a home theater
or an old-but-reliable 20-inch portable, living in this media age means the TV is never far from view. Of course, there are times when you wish it weren't so visually demanding, especially when friends are gathered for lively conversation or the family converges to catch up on each other's news. Creative storage and customized furniture pieces can solve the "big black eye" problem by corralling and camouflaging the television and other electronics. Before building or buying storage, measure your TV and electronics components; not all storage units are deep enough to hold big TVs. If you're considering a home theater, ask an electronics expert's advice on selecting and placing speakers in your family room and install window treatments that block sunlight and glare.

CHAPTER 4

Dining rooms

At your home, are mealtimes a leisurely taste of gourmet fare, served family style for a crowd, or something quick and simple before everyone scatters? No matter who's at the table or what's on the menu, you deserve a dining area that's as inviting as this New England classic—one that reflects your decorating taste and your lifestyle. In this chapter, you'll find ideas for creating attractive dining spaces—even in unlikely places.

Formal or Casual?

You know how awkward it feels to dress formally if you're a jeans-and-T-shirt person,

but proper dining to you may mean the works—fine china, crystal, and silver. To relax yourself and your guests, define your dining style and design for it.

A CIVILIZED TWIST

Formal dining can be a getaway activity in itself—a civilized, unhurried sharing of your best, from manners to food and wines. The design principles for creating a formal look work equally well in contemporary and traditional spaces.

■ **USE SYMMETRY** (mirror images on either side of an imaginary centerline) for wall and furniture arrangements.

■ **DRESS UP** with gleaming mirrors, gilt frames on artwork, lacquered finishes, polished veneers, and crystal stemware and candlesticks.

■ **FORGO FUSSINESS.** Nothing makes a stronger formal statement than furniture with pure, classic lines, be it 18th-century antiques or contemporary classics, and lustrous fabrics—from silks and taffetas to brocades.

RELAX IN STYLE

Whether your style is cottage-casual or urban-sleek, your own unique mix of fabrics and furnishings will give guests a warm and welcoming taste of your personality.

■ **RELAX WITH TEXTURES.** As a general rule, choose rough textures instead of smooth; wicker, rattan, pine, and iron are less formal than polished woods and glass.

■ **MIX THINGS UP.** Consider a collection of unmatched vintage chairs around the table. Even one unmatched chair at the end breaks up formal uniformity. Or pair matching chairs with a table of a different material. Team wood chairs with an iron-base table or wicker chairs with distressed wood or stone. Mixing stained and painted wood finishes also adds an informal air.

■ **BRING FABRIC TO THE TABLE.** Choose casual, coarse weaves over shiny silk or damask. Easy-care cottons and wrinkle-resistant fabrics make a casual dining room more approachable. Dress down formal chairs with slipcovers and a formal table with a floor-length cotton skirt.

ABOVE: Is this dining room in a European villa or in the suburbs? It's the latter, but with an aged paint treatment on the walls and ceiling, elegant fabrics, and a graceful mix of furnishings, home entertaining here has "new" old-world flavor. OPPOSITE: Relaxed yet sophisticated in its juxtaposition of natural textures, this dining room has an oversize soapstone-top table to match its hospitality. Antique fabric on the woven chairs' cushions, charming folk art on the wall, and a painted chest as sideboard reflect the homeowners' travels and collections.

Plan to Dine

Dining rooms are among the easiest spaces to plan. Their dimensions dictate what's needed. Use common sense, a tape measure, and these tips to pull your dining room together. *(For more help with space planning, turn to the room-arranging kit on pages 280–285.)*

DESIGN FOR DINING

■ **CHOOSE A DINING TABLE** to suit the area's shape. Long tables—formal banquet or casual farm tables—fit long, narrow spaces. A square or oblong table teamed with a bench that can tuck under the table to save space when not in use—can suit small spaces. A round table softens the angles of a square room.

■ **KEEP ROOM SCALE AND BALANCE IN MIND.** You can squeeze a large table into a tiny room or place a table for two in a cavernous space, but proportionally neither will look right. If you must use a large table in a smallish room, consider a glass top to consume less visual space. Evaluate vertical space too; a room with a soaring ceiling may require high-back chairs and perhaps a weighty patterned area rug to anchor dining pieces. Plan for a mix of high and low pieces, adding a tall hutch or sideboard topped with a wall-hung painting.

■ **POSITION THE TABLE SO TRAFFIC FLOWS** smoothly around it—usually near the room's center. To turn a dining room into a multiuse space, push the table to one side to make room for lounge chairs or a sofa. Plan at least 8 square feet for a table for four, plus about 36 inches so chairs can be pulled out. To make the dining table a focal point, set it atop a colorful area rug.

■ **ALLOW ELBOW ROOM.** To determine how many can dine at a table, allow a space of 20 to 24 inches wide and 15 inches deep for each place setting. Ideally, reserve a 12-inch-wide strip down the table's center for centerpieces and serving dishes.

RIGHT: Raspberry walls set a cheery and gracious stage for formal or family dining. Relaxed and casual, the well-worn farm table gets an unexpected sophisticated touch from faux-bamboo chairs and a wrought-iron console. The console, a pine hutch, and slim built-ins on one wall handle storage, display, and serving.

TO FIND OUT MORE ONLINE, VISIT US
☞ @ www.bhg.com/bkarrangearoom

Dining-In Personality

Beyond the scrumptious menu at your favorite restaurant, what is it about the decor and ambience that keeps you coming back for more? Do aged walls and old-world furnishings transport you to a Mediterranean villa—if only for an evening? Does colorful art make you feel as if you're dining in a gallery? Or do you love to look at the collections? Borrow some decorating ideas and turn your own space into the hot spot to dine.

■ **FRESHEN UP WITH PAINT.** Consider the time of day the dining room is most frequently used. Depending on your lighting, wall color in a bold apple

green may be dramatic for dinner but overbearing at brunch. Pretty by day, soft pastels may wash out by night. Create special effects—aged plaster, stone, or fabric—with painted wall finishes.

■ **SLIPCOVER IN STYLE.** It's an easy way to change the look of your chairs and the entire room. Bold colors and busy patterns are best when window treatments and walls are pattern-free. For a quick change, make or buy simple seat cushions to add color and texture without concealing the chair design. Or pop fabric "cozies" over chair backs and miniskirts over seats. Floor-length slipcovers give wood chairs an upholstered look and provide visual relief in a room full of exposed-leg pieces.

■ **SHARE YOUR PASSIONS.** Set the style stage with your era-evoking antiques, quirky collections, art, and artful lighting. Pick personality-packed furnishings and accessories to add a bit of unexpected visual spice and color. Instead of the predictable hutch, a French baker's rack can serve as a sideboard while also showcasing collections.

OPPOSITE LEFT: This gracious dining room, with its faux-aged walls, arched windows, and antique French table, is like a Tuscan getaway for guests. Dining chairs are slipcovered in burlap with monograms on the chair backs. The wall finish was achieved with bronze and gold-tone glazes. CENTER: Enclosing a terrace created this lively dining space, which celebrates a collector's love of art, whimsical art glass, and contemporary style. The sculptural bent-maple table and chairs host casual meals; diners enjoy the view and, on the brick wall, a painting done by the homeowner. BELOW RIGHT: A tulle-dressed mannequin is a glamorous and unexpected guest at this fete. Slipcovered wing chairs and an oak server anchor the setting, illuminated by a tulle-draped chandelier. Color punch comes from art that's actually gift wrap from Germany, hanging from a curtain tieback.

Dining Out at Home
Today many of us dine all around the house.

Tonight it might be dinner for eight in the dining room. Tomorrow morning? Coffee and a bagel in the kitchen. And on Sunday—if you're lucky—it might be a leisurely brunch in the master suite. All that variety demands creative space planning. Start with a good understanding of your special lifestyle needs.

DOUBLE-DUTY DINING

■ **ARRANGE A DINNER DATE.** As home building costs soar and square footage shrinks, a formal dining room may not be your priority. If you require an everyday den and rarely a formal dining room, plan one room to do both. Let the table double as a desk. A hutch can hold books and dishes. Or push the table to one side and add a small love seat or easy chairs that can double as dining seating. (Just be sure the seats of such pieces are close to the 18-inch seat height needed for dining.)

■ **SQUEEZE A TABLE** into unexpected places. A half-round (demilune) or drop-leaf table in a wide hallway can be a lunch-for-two spot. Or set a modest rectangular dining table behind a sofa or against a wall in the family room or living room. Even a slim sofa table can serve dinner when you pull up a couple of chairs. To give B&B-style romance to a master bedroom, snug a slim dining table or sofa table against the foot of the bed or in front of a window, or replace a nightstand with a larger table that can serve for cozy, late-night snacks.

LEFT: Designed to look like an English garden folly on the outside but serving up Swedish cottage charm inside, this poolside pavilion gives elegant new meaning to backyard dining. This steps-away getaway is also a garden room and library. OPPOSITE: No reservations are needed for this romantic table for two. The library fireside makes an inviting spot for tea and casual dinners. An armchair in sunny yellow toile and a scoot-anywhere ottoman for extra seating at the bistro table add comfort and convenience.

Dining in the Kitchen

A staple of older homes and a selling point for new ones,

the big, eat-in kitchen beckons family and friends with its casual, back-door air, bringing back heartwarming memories of gathering around that icon of the American home—the kitchen table. Give your kitchen's informal eating area special decorating attention and make some memories of your own.

KEEP IT CASUAL

■ **USE EASY-CARE FABRICS** and finishes for fuss-free kitchen dining. Use hard-wearing stain- and water-resistant fabrics, add chair pads with zippered covers for easy removal for washing, or have your kitchen's signature fabric laminated and fashioned

into wipe-clean chair pads. Tabletops finished with paint or polyurethane are easier to clean than those that have an oil-base finish.

■ **CONSIDER EFFICIENT BUILT-INS.** Pull a table up to a window seat for dining. Built-in banquettes make efficient use of floor space and corners and give the kitchen a cozy look. New freestanding booths that tuck into corners offer similar space efficiency.

■ **KEEP TRAFFIC IN MIND.** Position the dining table and chairs so they're out of the everyday flow of traffic.

■ **LIGHT THE SCENE.** Replace the ceiling light switch with a mood-setting dimmer. If the kitchen lacks an over-the-table light, use a plug-in swag light or wire in a hanging fixture, recessed lights, or a strip of track lighting so diners aren't kept in the dark.

LEFT: A walk-through space between the den and kitchen now stops traffic. Reupholstered garage-sale chairs and a discount-store wicker table funnel traffic around this new breakfast spot. The chandelier both lights and defines the space. ABOVE: Beaded-board paneling and a built-in banquette make for cozy corner dining. Shelves above the seating create space for the owner's cookbook library and collectibles. OPPOSITE: An all-in-one cabinetry-and-table unit transforms a blank wall into a dining spot and focal point. Wrapped around an early-1900s French poster, the shelves hold books, pottery, and collectibles.

ServeUpStyle

Dining rooms don't require as much storage

as kitchens, but mealtimes are easier when linens, dishes, and serving pieces are close at hand. Dining rooms also benefit style-wise from open storage that allows you to show off your favorite collectibles. Use these tips to expand storage.

■ **PULL IN A HUTCH,** buffet, or cupboard. A low sideboard is ideal if you have a large painting, a mirror, or a plate rack to hang above it. If not, maximize vertical storage

space with an armoire, a hutch, or a Welsh dresser.

■ **HANG IT ON THE WALL.** A small wall rack, wall-mounted shelves above a table, or a unifying shelf encircling the room can add style and stow your dishes too.

■ **BUILD IT IN.** Built-in china cabinets or shelf-lined niches turn blank walls into storage assets. Put dead corner space to work with corner cupboards. For formal symmetry, treat corners identically.

OPPOSITE: A pretty mix of fancy and Irish country, this garden-style room relaxes a classic pedestal table and ornate chandelier by mating them with cottage-white chairs, a primitive cupboard, and a shelf above the wainscot. **1** Found at a flea market, this focal-point buffet was primed and painted before toile wallpaper was applied with adhesive, then aged with a tea-hued glaze. **2** Built-ins that served this space when it was a library adapt beautifully to the room's

new dining role. Although the table is an antique Biedermeier, seating is a casual mix of nothing-fancy, Italian-style chairs and a wicker settee. **3** Two dining room classics—a hand-me-down sideboard and new Swedish-style plate rack—add up to one dramatic focal point with linen storage below and display for china and pewter servers above. Fresh paint blends old chairs with the new table. **4** An old storage piece gains new life when treated to a fresh coat of paint. Blue accents inspired the choice of blue rod-back dining chairs. Table linens and patterned chandelier shades pull the new color scheme together.

Plain-to-Pretty Focal Points

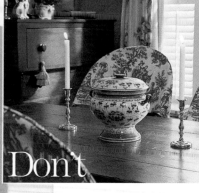

Don't

Do

DON'T bare it all. With the spare and predictable trio of candlesticks and tureen, **ABOVE,** the big table looks as if it's waiting for dinner. Although the minimal accents work during mealtime because they allow room for serving dishes and plates, in the room's off-hours, it's not a tempting time-out spot.

DO delight the senses. Between meals, make the dining room more inviting with tablescapes that make a style statement or convey a seasonal theme, such as this nature-inspired vignette, **LEFT.** A woven runner underscores the texture-rich centerpiece, scented with candles and flowers. Windsor chairs are softened with fabric "cozies," inviting family to settle back and munch the grapes.

When there are no guests on the horizon, does your dining room sit idly by, undressed and unused? Does your hutch look more like shelves of random clutter than a striking focal point? Making your dining room more inviting every day could help you reclaim that underused space and turn it into a pleasant spot for a cup of tea or an afternoon of reading or conversation. Here's a designer's secret: Successful decorating appeals to all five senses. Think beyond visual delights: In centerpieces and shelf displays, incorporate.touch by mixing items of varying textures, add fragrance with fresh flowers and scented candles, and tempt taste buds with a plate of fruit or bowl of candy. Add sound with soft music, wind chimes, or by opening windows to nature.

Don't

DON'T miss the point. A few pieces of the homeowner's collection of blue and white dishes are displayed in the hutch, ABOVE, but they are lost in a sea of unrelated objects. Symmetrical in some spots and asymmetrical in others, this hutch grouping can't decide whether it wants to be formal or casual.

DO make a statement. To give the hutch stronger focus and the collections more impact, additional pieces of blue and white porcelain are brought in, RIGHT. The pieces are arranged to create consistent formal symmetry. A flower-filled vase and a candlestick lamp add vertical interest and function. To bring more interest to your own displays, tour your home and borrow accents from other rooms.

Do

CHAPTER 5

Bedrooms

Busy lives have turned bedrooms into round-the-clock retreats. New-home master suites are packed with amenities from entertainment centers to mini refrigerators—details you can add to any bedroom if you employ some decorating ingenuity. Even a small bedroom needs a spot to tuck in a TV and maybe a computer. What little luxury does your bedroom need? A sitting spot? A fresh mood? Filmy curtains on pegged rods sparked a new romance for this four-poster. Whatever you add, put your comfort first.

Sleep Styles

For sweet dreams, do a little decorating matchmaking. Although it applies to every room, decorating with what you love is most important in the bedroom. What colors and materials relax you most at bedtime? What sights—and even scents—would you love waking up to each day? Play matchmaker— put colors, furnishings, and accessories together in a way that reflects your tastes and comfort needs—to create a bedroom that serves as your ultimate time-out spot. For starters, are you formal or casual? Do you lean toward cozy clutter or artful displays of a few select objects?

ANALYZE YOUR DREAM SPACE

Forget style labels and instead use these tips as a guide for gathering

accessories and choosing and arranging major bedroom furnishings to serve your practical needs and make you feel utterly at ease.

■ **IF YOU PREFER FORMALITY**, you won't feel quite right unless you center the bed along a wall or between two windows and then flank it with matched lamps and nightstands. Balance accessories such as wall art and collections on the mantel in a similar orderly way.

■ **IF YOU EQUATE RELAXING** with casual ambience, you may lean toward looser, asymmetrical room arrangements. Move the bed to one side of the room or angle it headfirst into a corner. Placing furniture on the diagonal can make rooms look larger and free up floor space for a desk or love seat. Balance an off-center bed with a weighty armoire or other storage piece, a reading chair and lamp, or bold artwork.

■ **IF YOU LEAN TOWARD CLEAN-AND-SIMPLE** minimalism, comfort may mean paring down to the beautiful, clutter-free basics. Start with an eye-grabbing bed, then add a few well-designed accents. Provide plenty of closed storage to keep your retreat free of visual clutter.

■ **IF YOUR TASTES ARE ECLECTIC** and don't fit neatly into one style category or degree of formality but you aren't sure how to create your own mix, clip magazine photos of rooms you love. Before you decorate, study the clippings for hints of your true style and mood preferences. Then use the photos as a guide to creating your own perfect blend of design styles and approaches.

OPPOSITE LEFT: An antique Victorian settee and handsome secretary team with a classic canopy bed to hint at formality, but checked fabric, the angled placement of the settee, and the gathered canopy and chair skirt lend a touch of casual ambience. OPPOSITE RIGHT: Simplicity reigns in this clean-lined retreat. Textures and rich woods turn up the heat while a sleek bed dressed for comfort softens hard edges. BELOW LEFT: Bold colors echoed in the velvety duvet, accent fabrics, and dramatic rug unify this personal mix of the modern and the unexpected. BELOW RIGHT: Symmetrically placed lamps and nightstands please formal sensibilities, but soft textures and feel-good fabrics, including a quilted headboard, create a comfortably casual air.

Bedroom Essentials

Only you can define what's "essential" in your personal retreat.

To do so, first determine the role your space plays. Is it for sleeping only? Does it work part-time as a den or office? How you use your room determines your essential furnishings.

■ **LIST THE BASICS**—sleeping, storage, seating, work space. What size bed fits your room and the way you live? Do you need a king-size bed, or a queen-size with space left over for a lounge chair and ottoman? What are your storage needs? If you have a large walk-in closet with built-in shelves and drawers, can you forgo a dresser and free up space for the writing table or chaise you long for? If you take newspapers and stacks of books to bed, use a larger bedside table. Dimmers and lamps with three-way switches let you control light levels for reading and relaxing. Sculpt space with accent lights and art lights; use strip lights to illuminate collectibles or books. *(For more help, see "Arranging," pages 260–285 and "Lighting," pages 390–405.)*

■ **DRESS THE BED FOR COMFORT.** Cotton sheets soften with washing and let the body breathe; cotton-polyester blends wrinkle less but aren't as soft. Pima and Egyptian cottons are silky to the touch. Thread count, the number of threads per square inch, indicates sheet quality—180 to 200 is standard; 350 means luxury. Do you want a spread or a plump duvet? (A duvet is a comforter, usually down-filled, with a removable cover; it serves as top sheet, blanket, and bedcover all in one.) Duvet covers can be pricey, but you can make one by sewing two flat sheets together on three sides and adding buttons or snaps to close the end. (Update an old comforter the same way.) A feather bed atop the mattress adds luxury.

LEFT: Stargazing over the ocean and waking up to the waves were "essentials" in this seaside cottage bedroom, so the owners used double box springs to raise the duvet-covered bed for a better view. A freestanding armoire handles storage, and a roomy built-in seat for lounging stretches across the bay window.

> **TO FIND OUT MORE ONLINE, VISIT US**
> **@ www.bhg.com/bkarrangearoom**

Customize Your Retreat

Whether your sleep space is large or small, careful floor planning can help you make the most of it. Measure your room and major furnishings, then sketch it all out on paper using our room-arranging kit on pages 280–285, or pop floor-planning software into your computer. Use these design tips as you plan.

A PERFECT FIT

■ **CONSIDER THE SIZE OF THE BED.** Treat yourself to a larger bed if you have a large closet or built-ins and can forgo freestanding storage. Also remember that the bed's visual size is determined by more than its mere dimensions. A tall scrolled-metal headboard consumes less visual space than a carved-wood headboard of similar size and shape; visually, dark woods and finishes consume more space than light ones. Size bedside tables to mattress height.

■ **CREATE EASY ACCESS.** Avoid placing the bed so close to a door that the bed becomes a speed bump. For easy bed making, allow at least 2 feet on both sides. In front of the closet allow about 3 feet for dressing (or more if door swing demands it). Allow at least 36 to 40 inches in front of chests and dressers for using drawers.

■ **TUCK IN STORAGE.** Add a highboy or armoire or a dresser-mirror combination to a wall of built-ins. If you have space for freestanding storage, consider turning the closet into a home office with a built-in desk and shelves.

■ **THINK BIG IN SMALL ROOMS.** Scale up furnishings. Fewer but larger high-function pieces can handle practical needs and help you avoid the visual clutter created by a scattering of small furniture pieces. Stick with an arrangement of major pieces parallel or perpendicular to walls; a diagonal bed may steal too much floor space in a small room.

LEFT: An upholstered bed with an ocean view serves as an island of comfort in this whitewashed master suite addition. A long desk, a comfy chair, and a computer turn a windowed alcove into a convenient home office spot. **OPPOSITE:** Across from the bed, upholstered armchairs with high backs that invite settling in pull up to a cast-concrete fireplace. A built-in conceals a pop-up television. Wall-to-wall sea-grass carpet and neutral hues are naturally relaxing touches.

ABOVE: Walls in this luxurious master suite look as if they're draped in elegant fabric, but it's actually wallcovering that flows into the bath. Fabric in a neoclassic floral print—used for the coverlet, the graceful window treatments, and the roll-arm bench at the foot of the bed—inspired the soft rose-and-green palette. **OPPOSITE:** In the tranquil bath, the wallcovering teams with crisp white trim and pale marble floors. The green-checked fabric on the chair cushions reinforces the green stripes on the wall. Plantation shutters afford the focal-point tub a river view. An Oriental rug pulls in the traditional mood set in the bedroom.

SuiteInspiration
Decorating a master suite presents special creative challenges.

Let your bedroom and bath share style and mood so they flow together into a retreat where you can relax and rejuvenate. Why settle for a chrome-and-mirrors bath if your sleep space is swathed in country French fabrics? Why live with a bathroom's aging floral wallpaper or busy tiles if you've gone clean and modern in your bedroom? Forge links between the two spaces with color, pattern, finishes, and decorative accessories.

SUITE REWARDS

■ **COUNT ON COLOR** to make this marriage of spaces work. Start with the same palette for bed and bath, perhaps changing the color emphasis in each room for design interest.

■ **UNIFY WITH FABRICS, PATTERNS, AND MOTIFS.** In the bath, you won't use as much fabric as you do in your comfy bedroom, but carry fabrics and pattern through in bath window treatments, chair cushions, and wall coverings.

■ **PICK FINISHES THAT FIT YOUR STYLE.** If your bedroom sets a classic mood with a marble fireplace, use marble or a stone-look material on the vanity top or the bathroom floor. If rich natural wood is your bedroom look, add an antique cupboard to the bath—you'll appreciate the extra storage.

■ **SHARE THE ACCESSORIES.** An Oriental rug or Japanese bench at the side of the tub, well-edited collections, and framed wall art can bring the bedroom mood to the bath. If your vanity is long enough, top it with a mood-enhancing lamp for soft light.

Redo
With A New View

BEFORE

A big helping
of illusion
brings the mood
and the magic

to many beautifully decorated rooms. Plain closet doors may be the last place you'd look for help in coaxing your bed room out of its sleepy style rut, but the wall of clutter-shutters is exactly where this space started to capture French country flavor. On the new "French door" closets, the mirrored panes are subtle—not glitzy—and hardworking, reflecting space and light. These elegant doors are custom-made and open beneath a top row of fixed panes. Running mirrors to the soffit visually raises the roof and coaxes the eye to gable windows. Here are less expensive ways to get the look:

■ **GLUE LIGHTWEIGHT MIRRORS** to closet doors; then top them with glued-on batten strips or country lattice. Paint or stain the strips or lattice before applying to the doors.

■ **HAVE MIRRORS CUT TO FIT DOORS,** leaving a border all around about one-sixth of each door's width and length. Attach them to the doors with mirror clips. Top mirrors with pop-in window muntins secured to the mirrors with pieces of cushioned, double-stick tape.

In the lighten-up spirit of this redo, fresh fabrics and a floral carpet moved in. A graceful pencil-post bed more in scale with the space replaced an old brass one. But the roomy antique linen press, stowing the television, stayed put.

RIGHT: Inspired by the garden air of new "French door" closets, this bedroom—once a garage—gets both its palette and its alfresco look from the floral patterns of the needlepoint carpet and the bed skirt. The blue quilt not only echoes the blue in the carpet, it also provides welcome, cool contrast to the room's golden woods and warm accent colors.

Make It Personal

If you yearn to let your design fantasies take flight, the best place to launch them is your bedroom. By surrounding yourself with favorite things, you'll create a truly personal refuge that soothes the body and delights the eye—and the soul. Treasures such as antique quilts, pretty plates, and heirloom furniture may be too fragile for a high-traffic family room, but they're perfect in the bedroom where you can display them to enjoy every day.

ACCENT YOUR SIGNATURE STYLE

■ **SHOW YOUR STUFF.** No matter how quirky your collections, if you love them, let them show. Grouping objects adds impact; arrange flea market teacups on a wall-hung shelf or enameled boxes on a tabletop; you'll recall the fun of the hunt every time you pass by. Is art your passion? Turn a wall into a gallery. To display family photos, frame them to match; have some enlarged to make displays more interesting.

■ **PLAY WITH FABRICS.** Give the bed an unexpected twist: Instead of the typical spread, use a tablecloth, a vintage throw, a lightweight kilim rug, or your grandmother's quilt that you've had packed away. Dress your bed in a mix of prints, breaking up florals with snappy stripes, gingham checks, and colorful solids. Mix up the pillows too, blending new ones with those covered in vintage fabrics.

■ **SET YOUR PRIORITIES.** What makes you feel pampered? Eyelet-edged sheets? A sound system for the music lover? A library full of favorite books? Plants from your garden? Even a sleeping spot for a pet may top the priority list in your domain.

LEFT: The English plant-drying rack and the 19th-century transferware that inspired the bedroom's fabrics are clues that the room belongs to a gardener and collector. A French silk-taffeta remnant accents the creamy silk draperies, the garden bench wears original paint, and the lamp is an electrified pitcher. OPPOSITE: Giving this country bedroom colorful personality was child's play: The homeowner pulled out 1940s and 1950s sandbox toys and tin dishes from her own childhood to display on a hand-painted shelf above the bed. Fabrics with farmhouse spirit mix it up on the iron bed, a family heirloom.

HeadboardClass
Making your bed the focal point of your sleep space often means giving that expanse of empty

wall above the headboard some creative attention. For an easy solution, hang one great piece of artwork or perhaps a trio of favorite prints in frames faux-finished in your bedroom colors. Here are more finishing touches to make your bed a standout:

■ **SOFTEN THE SCENE WITH FABRIC.** Canopies and flowing bed curtains guarantee a feeling of luxury and privacy. Or treat the wall like a window: Wall-mount two rods at ceiling height behind the headboard; shirr a curtain on one, a valance on the other, and add tiebacks on both sides of the bed. Kits for wall-mounted coronas are available at home centers—all you add are the fabric and trims. Even

a big quilting hoop, suspended from the ceiling and draped in mosquito netting or a gauzy sari, can conjure an exotic mood. Replace a ho-hum headboard with a screen made of louvered panels hinged together or plain panels upholstered in fabric.

■ **ADD ARCHITECTURAL CHARACTER.** Salvaged gingerbread trim from old porches, aged ironwork brackets, or lacy garden lattice add interest and texture to the headboard wall.

■ **STORE AND DISPLAY.** Wall-mount a carved antique shelf or a new antique-style one above the bed to highlight the headboard, display accessories, and keep bedtime books close at hand.

RIGHT: This collector's retreat accents the heirloom bed with an arc of blue and white plates echoing the headboard's curve. The window treatments and accessories, including the lampshades, pull the crisp colors around the entire room. OPPOSITE: Floral fabric drapes from a gilded, wrought-iron crown, marking the French fruitwood bed as the place of honor in this elegant bedroom. Two sets of portieres in the same fabric define a vestibule and a sitting spot in the bay window.

A Place for Everything

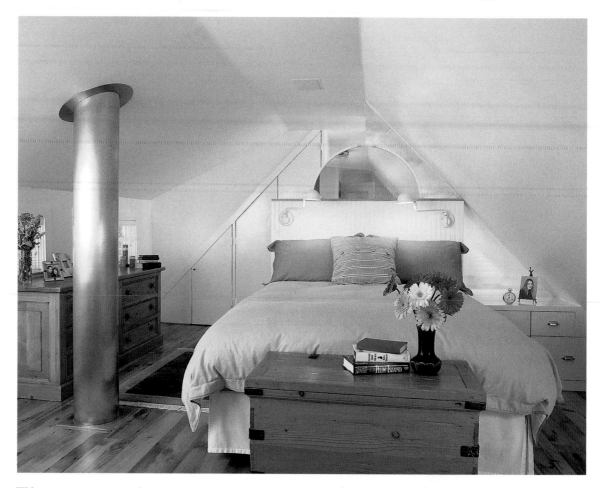

First comes the television, then the home office, and before you know it, the bedroom is getting a bit crowded. A threat in so many other living spaces, clutter can be downright disastrous in a bedroom where serenity is the goal. Cast a creative eye around your bedroom. Could you outfit that sliver of wall with shelves to hold tidy wicker baskets for "stuff"? Could you scoot fabric-covered storage boxes and baskets under the bed? With such pretty storage, you might want to shed the bed skirt. Whether it stores a little or a lot, any freestanding piece is welcome if you have room.

■ **OUTFIT THE FOOT OF THE BED.** Bed linens and sweaters can hide inside a chest; on top, display collectibles and books. Slide an antique bench or an oblong cocktail table against the foot of the bed to hold books and magazines.

■ **LOOK FOR STORAGE FURNITURE.** Consider beds with headboard caches or drawers built in below the mattress and nightstands with drawers or shelves. A vertical stack or a horizontal lineup of slick storage cubes can hold TV and video gear on top and corral folded clothes below. Always practical, an armoire also can house a TV and clothing.

■ **EXPLORE FOR CLOSET-DEPTH SPACE.** By bumping out a wall between windows or on both sides of the bed, you can add architectural interest to a square space and gain a new spot to hang your hat.

OPPOSITE: Built-ins outwit angled attic walls, providing this redone bedroom with storage in the end wall and dividing the bed and bath with a headboard "wall." **1** Instead of letting this bedroom's spacious bay window sit idle, built-in, sill-high shelving organizes bedtime reading, displays accessories, and adds warmth and texture. **2** This compact master suite makes all the right moves to live big. Neutral colors open it up, glass-panel walls invite light, and the bed has built-

in drawers and pullout nightstands. **3** Just a few feet of space at the end of the bed works wonders when it's this well planned. A chest hugs a side wall, freeing up under-window space for a small but efficient desk and storage pieces. Note how the leggy desk and the airy, cantilevered chair consume little visual space and allow the eye to follow the floor all the way to the wall—a fool-the-eye space expander. **4** Working vintage doors into a newly crafted armoire brings unrivaled character, plus great storage, to a serene bedroom, romanced with a mix of fabrics and flea market finds.

CHAPTER 6

Guest rooms

To create a welcoming retreat for your overnight guests, think about what made your last getaway memorable. Maybe a quaint bed-and-breakfast pampered you with the same luxurious linens, fresh flowers, and thoughtful amenities that beckon from this serene guest room. Even though your guest space may do double duty and work every day as a family room or home office, you can make it inviting and comfortable with a few well-planned decorative touches.

Welcoming Amenities

Decorating a room especially for overnight visitors is the ultimate in hospitality. It's great if you have

a spare room to redo, but you may find guest space in unexpected places. For starters, consider last year's overnight-guest list and plan accordingly.

DEFINE GUEST NEEDS

Choose a bed that fits the space and the needs of your most frequent guests. One or two twin beds or a queen-size bed are good choices. For extra company or visiting children, supplement sleep space by renting a crib or a rollaway bed. Offer guests a choice of synthetic or natural fillings in fluffy pillows. Dress the bed in charming linens, a sink-in feather bed, and a down-filled duvet, and provide bedside reading lamps that hold 75- to 100-watt bulbs.

SHOP FOR SPACE

Take a tour of your home, and assess each room, alcove, walk-in closet, and hallway as possible guest quarters. Tuck a daybed or sleep sofa into an alcove, put up an antique screen for privacy, and you have an instant guest spot. Or turn that spacious closet into a snug sleeper with built-in bunk beds. Add a futon sofa to a finished attic or reserve a top-of-the-stairs loft for guests. If you don't have a full-time guest room with a closet, find ways to help your visitors stay organized.

■ CLEAN OUT A HALL CLOSET near the guest space and add plenty of hangers, including custom hangers for suits and skirts.

■ STOW GUESTS' clothes on an over-the-door hanger, a decorative Shaker-style peg rack mounted on the wall, or a corner coat tree.

■ WICKER BASKETS and colorful bins and boxes can corral bath and personal items. Size them to fit on bookshelves or under a lamp table, coffee table, or bed. Use a trunk or hamper as an end table.

■ A LUGGAGE RACK makes a thoughtful addition that eases unpacking chores, and it can double as a tea-tray table.

OPPOSITE: A Midas touch with pattern and color pulls this classically furnished space together, imbuing it with a sense of luxury that guests are sure to appreciate. Striped walls blend with a mini-check fabric that dresses the bed and lines silk-taffeta curtains. BELOW: Whether guests use it for a laptop, writing postcards, or morning coffee, a desk is always a thoughtful amenity to tuck into any guest room, and in this small space, it expands storage. A sunburst mirror adds graphic energy.

Double Up on Comfort

In many homes, the guest "room" is a sofa bed, but the chunky heavyweights of yesterday have slimmed down and prettied up. Today, however, sofa beds aren't your only option for creating dual-purpose guest quarters.

■ **THINK DOUBLE DUTY.** Let a sofa bed turn a family room or den into guest quarters. Position a sofa bed so guests can walk around the open bed safely and easily. Choose chairs and tables that move easily when the bed is opened. Dual purpose applies to accessories too, so decorate with day and night uses in mind. A cozy quilt doubles as a daytime throw and a footstool as a bedside table. A three-way lamp provides mood or reading light.

■ **SHOP FOR OPTIONS.** Consider daybeds (piled with pillows, they double for lounging when guests leave), futon sofas, flip-open chairs, and wall beds that tuck away into cabinets and wall units. New wall beds bolt to the wall studs and have a safety mechanism for raising and lowering slowly. *(For an example of a wall bed, see pages 164–165.)*

■ **GIVE GUESTS PRIVACY.** If windows are covered only in sheers or cafe curtains, add opaque shades or blinds to give guests privacy. Portieres—curtains hung across doorways—can turn even a living room into a guest spot. (Hint: Hang portieres on tension rods; remove them when guests leave.)

ABOVE: Curtains flow from ceiling-hung rods, and a twin bed dresses up in mixed-pattern linens in this home office. The bed serves as seating by day; at night, it becomes a private sleeping spot for guests. Projects in progress stow beneath the draped table. RIGHT: With the beach steps away, this cottage welcomes its fair share of guests, but the den is ready to accommodate them with a foldout sofa and a diminutive coffee table that scoots easily out of the bed's way.

TO FIND OUT MORE ONLINE, VISIT US
@ www.bhg.com/bkarrangearoom

ABOVE: Usually it's a comfy chair in the family room, but when a guest arrives it folds out into a twin-size bed. Chinese chests serve as nightstands, and Asian wedding baskets double as tables that offer hidden storage.

Create B&B Ambience
What was it about that charming inn that won your heart in a weekend?

A rustic pine bed piled with quilts? The romantic mood set by linens and lace? Collections of antiques inviting you to step back in time? Make the space you provide for guests a true getaway by taking cues from your favorite bed-and-breakfast.

■ **SCOUR YOUR HOME, FLEA MARKETS,** and antiques shops for accessories and furniture you can refinish or paint. Beware of antique beds; measure carefully to be sure the one you're considering can handle a modern-day mattress. Sort through collections and linens you've had tucked away; they could inspire a guest room palette and add character.

■ **MAKE GUESTS FEEL AT HOME** by designing comfort and convenience into your guest space. Is there a reading lamp, a cozy chair and ottoman for relaxing, a writing desk, mirror, alarm clock, radio, television, closet space, an empty drawer or two, a phone, and an outlet to plug in a laptop? Thoughtful touches such as scented, padded hangers; a unisex terry robe; a hair dryer; thick towels; and a basket of shampoos, soaps, and lotions are always appreciated.

■ **BE YOUR OWN GUEST.** Before your official guests arrive, invite yourself to spend the night in the guest space. You'll quickly find out if the mattress is comfortable, if the room temperature is OK, if the lighting is practical and inviting, and if the furniture placement is safe and easy to navigate at night.

LEFT: Old wood paneling painted sage green gets this guest room off to a fresh start. Between the handcrafted four-poster beds dressed in floral and striped linens, a circa-1800 tiger maple chest holds an antique shaving mirror, and bird prints nest above each bed. **OPPOSITE:** The world's fast pace slows instantly when guests enter this simply romantic guest room in an 1800s home. Twin beds have a new-old mix of linens—fuzzy white blankets, floral coverlets, and lace-edged pillows—and the rusty nightstand has a new glass top.

Bring the Baby

To provide safe, comfy sleeping space for your littlest guests, do you end up renting a crib?

Although that's a practical solution, the owners of this airy guest room came up with a different plan, turning a seating nook into optional crib space. Slide on the crib rail and the nook turns into a nursery, with sleep space roomy enough for even a toddler. The custom mattress/cushion fits snugly, and other than adding baby linens, the only accessory change is removing the painting. What makes this nook a quick-change artist is a pair of wooden brackets on each side of the opening. The wooden crib rail, with 1¾ inches between the slats, slides securely into upper and lower brackets. Pullout drawers below

keep baby linens and toys handy. When they want to switch the nook back to a sitting spot, the owners slide out the crib rail and pile on pillows so guests can snuggle into the lighted nook with a good book.

With antique French-style beds dressed in new striped quilts and crisp linens, this space is a treat for other guests too. (Twin beds offer the ultimate in flexibility for guest rooms.) Swing-arm lamps for reading serve each of the antique beds, and the nightstand is a circa-1880 faux-bamboo bed cupboard. Access to a porch also makes this room a guest favorite.

Guest-Ready In a Weekend

BEFORE

Feathering a luxurious guest nest doesn't demand a big budget
or a lot of time. With ready-made linens and curtains, simple projects, and savvy shopping, this "leftovers" bedroom now welcomes weary travelers in charming style. Adapt these strategies to rediscover the art of pampering.

■ **GET INSPIRATION.** Remember the children's story about the princess and the pea and the princess's high-rise bed? The homeowner who decorated this room did. The existing iron bed gained elevated focus and comfort with a second set of box springs. Each box spring wears its own matelassé bed skirt.

■ **WARM IT UP.** Walls painted corn-silk yellow take the chill off the north-facing room. Crisp green accents add cool contrast.

■ **TREAT THE WINDOWS.** Provide window treatments that create privacy and block unwanted early-morning sun. If using sheers, add a blind or shade behind them.

■ **DO SOME "HOME SHOPPING."** This owner scavenged other rooms for the vintage armoire and the silver, wrought-iron, and ceramic accents. The armoire packs entertainment gear and baskets of books, magazines, candles, stationery, CDs, bottled water, bath scents, and even raffia slippers and a jar of peppermint candies.

OPPOSITE PAGE: An apple green checked duvet, pristine linens, and an architectural headboard accent make both the bed and pure comfort the focus of this room scheme. **1** This low iron table stands ready to hold a suitcase for unpacking or a tray for afternoon tea. **2** Bow closures—daisy trim glued onto sheer wired

ribbon—add custom detailing to plain, ready-made curtains. **3** An old garden chair—its cushion re-covered in a fabric remnant—joins the inexpensive iron table at the foot of the bed for casual dining and relaxing. **4** Borrowed from another room, the painted armoire delivers the storage, display space, and character that every guest room needs. Here, it holds blankets, robes, bottled water, toiletries, and even a TV.

CHAPTER 7

Kids' rooms

Delightful children's rooms are the stuff of dreams. That's why they're fun to decorate.

This little boy's blue room is fit for a prince, and his pillow proclaims "The Prince Sleeps Here." A storybook canopy and antique daybed could make the space regal enough for a little princess. Creating spaces where little ones learn, explore, and dream takes imagination, but unlike forever-young Peter Pan, this chapter's charmers grow with your child.

Rooms Grow Too

With bold colors and playful touches, kids' rooms are among the most fun spaces to decorate. Plan on reworking your child's room three times during the growing years: baby-to-toddler transition, the early school years, and adolescence. Careful planning and wise furniture choices can reduce the extent (and cost) of that inevitable redecorating.

DESIGN TOGETHER

Fortunately, you have an in-house expert—your child—for decorating inspiration. It's important to get a child involved in choosing colors, themes, and accents. Starting at age 3 or 4, kids can help choose wall coverings, paints, and fabrics; however, resist the temptation to overembellish. In addition, always retain veto power; if a child wants a color you truly abhor, compromise by using it for easy-to-change accents.

FURNITURE WITH A FUTURE

Opt for sturdiness and easy care over style. Laminates, plastics, and painted surfaces are ideal. Look for on-the-grow cribs that convert to youth beds, changing-table chests that can store items beyond the diaper stage, and modular storage with adjustable shelves. For a child's first big bed, consider a full size; it will allow growing room and space for parent–child talks and stories. In major furniture pieces, avoid themes. Winnie the Pooh may suit a child today, not tomorrow.

KID-FRIENDLY SCHEMES

Children naturally head for the brightest hues in the crayon box. Bold, primary colors and defined shapes stimulate learning. Cast those bright hues in accents; for backdrops, pick enduring neutrals and classic wall coverings in stripes, checks, or florals. Use a neutral-plus-one scheme—for example, white walls and red curtains, bed linens, cushions, and area rug. If a child's favorite color changes from red to, say, blue, you can switch accessories without repainting. Other quick-change accents include drawer knobs and pulls, lampshades, wall and bulletin board art, reversible rugs, colorful storage bins, and, of course, bed linens.

> **TO FIND OUT MORE ONLINE, VISIT US** @ www.bhg.com/bkarrangearoom

OPPOSITE: Nary a cartoon character can be found in this nursery. It's wisely designed for the baby-to-toddler transition, with a neutral backdrop, bright primary accents, and a convertible crib. The gingham and vintage-print fabrics are sweet but not too babyish. **BELOW:** When it's toddler time, the wall color and nautical theme still work. The crib converts to a daybed with the removal of a side rail, and colorful toy bins and a child-size armchair slipcovered in chenille move in.

Planning a Nursery

A baby is coming! It's cause for celebrating—and decorating. The list of nursery necessities is long. When you consider the hours you'll spend in your baby's nursery, you'll understand why nursery schemes must please you as well as your baby.

NURSERY STARTERS

■ **A CRIB THAT MEETS TODAY'S SAFETY STANDARDS.** Only use pre-1992 cribs if they are in good repair and have slats no more than 2⅜ inches apart and a drop-side that, when lowered, is at least 9 inches above the mattress. Two-stage, drop-side catches are best. Avoid vintage cribs; check secondhand cribs for lead paint, shaky construction, missing slats, or removable knobs and decorations. If in doubt, buy a new crib. Place the crib away from the window to

prevent falls against the glass or tampering with the window blinds, curtains, and cords.

- **A STANDARD CRIB MATTRESS,** $27\frac{1}{2} \times 51\frac{7}{8}$ inches. For baby's safety, no more than two of your fingers should fit between the mattress and crib.
- **ROCK-A-BYE SEATING.** A rocking chair or glider with flat arms and an ottoman make feedings comfy. How about a daybed, a futon sofa, or a twin-size bed for your own naps too?
- **A DOUBLE-DUTY CHANGING TABLE** with a high top rail and open shelves for diapers now and toys and books later. Some styles double as dressers to adapt to changing storage needs.
- **ADJUSTABLE LIGHTING.** Dimmers allow brighter light for changing baby and softer illumination for feedings. Add a night-light too.

COLOR AND PATTERN

- **TRY A SOFT-TOUCH PALETTE.** Infants respond to contrast, bright colors, and patterns, but avoid going overboard. White or pastel backdrops may be more soothing; add brighter colors and patterns with accessories.
- **DRESS UP WALLS** with scrubbable wallcoverings in simple prints that aren't too babyish. On painted walls, use decorations you can remove and change when your child outgrows them. If walls have pattern, keep rugs neutral or a solid color.
- **ADD A MOTIF** to painted walls at crib height for your baby to see. A graphic wallpaper border, even if only on one wall, provides definition and charm—and is easy to change in the future.

OPPOSITE: A sophisticated scheme of bright pastels and a ragged paint finish on the walls will welcome changing accessories later. CENTER: Playful and bilingual, this nursery underlines the walls' hand-painted stripes with a border of words and kid-pleasing images that were traced onto the wall, then painted. BELOW: Stripes and mini prints add depth and interest to the Peter Rabbit print hopping around this room. The cornice's freehand flowers and checkerboard trim match the changing-table chest.

Looks to Last
Think of kids' rooms as whimsical canvases for their ever-changing dreams and creations.

The trick is choosing versatile design elements and timeless themes that make your child's room inviting now and for years to come.

PAINT ON MAGIC

Painting is a quick and low-cost way to splash on a child's favorite colors. Shop for low-VOC (volatile organic compound) latex paints; they're less toxic and nearly odor-free. Paint a thrift store chest color-block style, or let the kids help with simple paint techniques such as sponging, stamping, or stenciling on walls and unfinished furniture. Frame a wall section with molding and brush on blackboard paint so kids can do all the doodling they want.

SPACE AND STORAGE

With double-duty furnishings—beds with drawers and wall units with pull-down desks—even a small space can play, study, sleep, and grow. For crafts and homework, fit a triangular desk into a tight corner; skirt an old table for today's little-girl vanity and tomorrow's computer station. Check that all drawers have stoppers for safety. Bolt tall chests or bookcases to studs so kids can't accidentally pull them over. For shelves, use ¾-inch plywood spanning no longer than 30 to 36 inches between supports. Need sleepover space? Don't forget trundle beds or air beds plopped on the floor.

DETAILS COUNT

Low-pile carpet and wood floors offer good floor play space. Tailored Roman shades, valances, cafe curtains, and shutters stay out of a groping toddler's way. For safety, cut all cord pulls short so toddlers can't grab them. New blinds have split cords so kids can't get caught in them; on older blinds, cut loop-style cords to create split cords.

OPPOSITE LEFT: In this little pet-lover's retreat, stuffed toy dogs scamper over the plaid duvet. Attached with hook-and-loop tape, they're easily removed for washing. Dog art is hand-painted on linens and the toy chest, and the dog bed doubles as floor seating. OPPOSITE RIGHT: Fun fish accent the coverlet, pillows, and wall border in this boy's room. The coverlet's fitted corners convey nautical style with cording laced through brass grommets. Peg racks turn walls into efficient storage for nautical accents, keepsakes, clothes, and play gear. ABOVE: Thanks to Mom's passion for collecting vintage fabrics and on-sale remnants, this room includes fun colors and lively prints designed to last well into high school. The daybed for sleeping and lounging is draped in a chenille spread that inspired the palette.

ABOVE: Two-toned, painted walls and rope create a pinstriped wainscoting effect in this teenage equestrian's bedroom. Spaced 15 inches apart, the rope pieces were glued on, secured with finish nails, and coated with polyurethane. Heavy fringe on the pillows and plaid fabric on the bedskirt echo the room's English riding theme. **OPPOSITE:** Brothers share this bedroom; its crisp red, black, and white scheme is lively without seeming juvenile. Featuring an upholstered headboard with piping detail, the bed is one of a pair, each featuring a pullout trundle for overnight guests.

Teen Pleasers

Eager to establish their own identities, teens want to personalize their rooms, so give them space. Letting them express their creativity—with reasonable guidance from you—is a great opportunity to help them develop good design and budget sense.

PLAN TOGETHER

How does your teen want the room to function? Do you need more storage for collections, electronics, books, or sports gear? Does your teen need a bigger desk for a computer or spots for grooming or exercising? For visiting friends, use oversize floor pillows, a daybed, or an upholstered chair. Does the closet need a do-it-yourself organizing system? Now is the time to strike compromises. Instead of taping posters to newly painted walls, consider a corkboard wall or an oversize bulletin board for changing displays.

FIX UP FURNITURE

Whether it's from your attic, a yard sale, or the secondhand shop, hand-me-down furniture can become fun, funky, and functional with a fresh coat of paint and new hardware. Also consider modular, unfinished furniture for lining a wall with bookshelves and a computer desk. Slipcovers are easy-care coverups for seating.

FIT IN HOMEWORK

Writing desks have a standard height of 30 inches; computer desks are about 26 inches high. Are file cabinets and drawers adequate and within easy reach? Create a quick-and-easy study spot by placing a door atop two file cabinets. Your teen can personalize the desk top with decoupage or paint.

LIGHT WITH CARE

Choose desk lamps that place the bulb about 15 inches above the desk top. Bedside reading lamps need to be 28 to 32 inches tall, or use wall-mounted swing-arm lamps. Choose lamps with stable, weighted bases. Because they produce extreme heat and can be a fire hazard, avoid halogen lamps in younger kids' rooms. For daytime computer use, control glare but preserve light with miniblinds or sheer curtains.

Suite Sharing

When siblings bunk together, make their room a cozy sleep space and a fun place to play and study. Sharing works best if children are the same sex and close in age. Don't put a toddler with a 9-year-old whose tiny toys could pose a choking hazard for the little one. When well planned, a shared room can nurture each child's individuality with spaces for hobbies and separate lockable storage for treasures.

DOUBLE-UP STYLE

■ **EXPLORE FOR SPACE.** Underused rooms and attics, such as this top-of-the-stairs redo, offer plenty of privacy for siblings. Built-in shelves, back-to-back chests or bookcases, or a ceiling-hung blind can define territories. Avoid top-heavy floor screens unless they are safely anchored at the ceiling.

■ **MIX, DON'T MATCH.** Let children pick accessories and bed linens in their favorite colors. Then separate beds by hanging two back-to-back curtains, each of a different color or pattern.

■ **SLEEP SAFE.** Choose twin, trundle, or bunk beds that meet American Society of Testing Materials standards. Children younger than 6 years are too young to sleep on top bunks. Beds should be made of strong, durable materials with smooth, rounded edges. Look for securely attached posts; bolted-on side rails; guardrails with a fastening device; and sturdy, securely attached ladders with steps 10 inches wide and 12-inch vertical spaces between steps. Mattresses must lie at least 5 inches below the guardrail top, and there should be no more than 1 inch between the mattress and frame.

ABOVE: Removing interior walls and adding new drywall, dormers, and windows opened up this once-dark attic into a sunny sleep-and-play suite with easy-care fabrics and a minimalist Scandinavian spirit. Now the family cuddles up on the canvas-covered sofa for bedtime stories. OPPOSITE LEFT: Creating the children's suite was a family affair. Dad crafted the beds and the toy and sports gear chests out of cypress. Mom upholstered the headboards and stitched bed linens, and "Grandmom" created the quilts beneath the duvets. OPPOSITE RIGHT: Recycled one more time, this flea market chest was once the children's changing table, but with a new sink, it's now the vanity in their shared bath. The muted red, white, and blue tile is from a tile salvage company.

Just for Kids

Imagine a room decorated with sailing ships, twirling ballerinas,

soccer gear, or friendly dinosaurs. Kids do. They love rooms that reflect their interests, but those interests change quickly, often long before the cartoon-character sheets wear out. So let the kids redecorate by making their own unique bed linens, art gallery, and blackboard furniture—with parents as assistants.

PICK A PATTERN

A salute to red, white, and blue is always fun and never looks dated. The linens and pillows on this kid-pleasing bed are straight from the department store white sale, but they earn their stars and stripes with nontoxic fabric paints, stamps, stencils, and sponge cutouts. Magazines, coloring books, and storybooks can inspire other motifs. Crafts stores offer dry stamp motifs, including children's names.

PATRIOTIC LINENS

Start with laundered ready-made bed linens: Duvet cover, bed skirt, and shams in white and sheets and pillowcases in red.

■ **FOR THE DUVET:** Slide a tarp inside the duvet; smooth it out. Use a 3-inch roller and non-toxic fabric paint to make horizontal stripes. Work paint into the fabric, but don't worry about uniformity; the

stripes are meant to have a slightly uneven, hand-painted look.

■ **FOR THE BED SKIRT:** Lay the ready-made skirt over waxed paper. Cut stars from a sheet of sponge. Dip large stars in fabric paint; press firmly around the skirt. Repeat with small stars. When dry, use a fabric marking pen to outline each star.

■ **FOR THE PILLOW SHAMS:** Line the sham with waxed paper. With a 1½-inch brush dipped in fabric paint, make stripes around the sham border. Cut a large star stencil for the sham center and a small star stencil for the corners; fill in the stencils with a sponge dipped in fabric paint. When dry, use a dry stamp to top the center star with a small star in a contrasting color. Using a fabric marking pen, link the corner stars with a wavy border.

■ **FOR THE SHEETS AND PILLOWCASES:** Cut stars in three sizes from a large sheet of sponge, dip the stars in fabric paint, and press firmly along the borders.

JUST-FOR-FUN PILLOWS

■ **FOR THE WHIZ KID STAR PILLOW:** Computer scan a favorite photo and print it out on fabric transfer paper; iron the image onto fabric. Tack the fabric photo at the corners.

■ **FOR THE FLAG PILLOW:** Glue a small fabric flag onto a ready-made pillow; add USA with fabric marking pens.

1 With two coats of blackboard paint and tied-on chalk, this thrift store nightstand is parent-approved for graffiti. It's dressed up with new red knobs to match painted legs. Oversized paper clips turn the lampshade into a family photo gallery. **2** Clipboards painted in lively colors display the works of a young artist, and it's easy for a youngster to change the day's featured masterpieces. Three sturdy screws attached to the painted wooden shelf hold the clipboards. **3** A computer-transfer photo of the kid in residence gives this red, white, and blue pillow its star power. This image is stitched onto a store-bought pillow, but yours could be ironed onto a homemade one. **ABOVE:** Little artists, old enough to handle paints, stencils, and stamps, hand-painted these linens as an affordable alternative to kid-theme designer bedding. The bonus? You and the kids get to pick the colors you want.

Build a Picnic Table Bed

Decorating gives teens a chance to show off—and experiment with—their budding personal styles. Like most of her teen peers, the clever teenager who collaborated on this fresh and fun space had definite ideas about everything that went into her room, including her own hand-painted picture frames. An outdoors enthusiast with an artistic streak and an interest in design, she combined those interests to create her room's clever and sturdy star—a bed frame inspired by campsite picnic tables. Then she painted it hot pink. Constructed with 2×4 legs and braces and a mattress deck of ¾-inch plywood, this platform bed will turn kids of all ages into happy campers. This queen-size bed is 14 inches tall from the floor to the top of the deck, but the simple design can be raised or sized to fit twin- and full-size mattresses. Use these mattress measurements as your guide: A twin mattress is 75×39 inches, a full is 75×54 inches, and a queen is 80×60 inches. Top it with a standard mattress or futon; for smaller children, add a nonskid pad beneath the mattress to prevent sliding during rambunctious play.

PUTTING IT TOGETHER

The amount of wood you'll need depends on the size of the bed you're making. Use one or two sheets of ¾-inch plywood for the deck. In addition, you'll need wood screws, wood putty, a miter box, saw, sandpaper or sander, primer, and paint.

Make four legs, cut from 2×4s with mitered ends. Each leg forms a capital letter A with a flat top to hold the deck level. Use wood screws to attach the two leg side pieces together at the top and to secure the leg's horizontal brace. Connect a 2×4, cut to appropriate bed width, to the inside top of two of the A-shaped legs with wood screws; repeat the process to connect the other two legs. Now you have two sets of connected A's. Connect your A sets together with a 2×4 brace, cut to the appropriate bed length, and attach to the middle of each cross-brace with wood screws. Now your bed frame should resemble a capital letter H. Countersink screws and fill with putty for a smoother finish, then sand and paint. To form the bed deck, cut plywood to bed size, sand to round off corners for comfort; screw the deck to the frame, prime, and paint.

ABOVE: The bed frame's four, A-shape legs are connected lengthwise and crosswise with 2×4 braces, and the mattress deck is made of plywood. After sanding, the bed was primed and painted in flat latex paint. OPPOSITE: Playful pillows and a patchwork duvet of spring greens and rosy pinks top this custom-designed picnic table bed that reminds the room's teenage resident of camping in the great outdoors. A wispy canopy and colorful, high-rise photo gallery create "headboard" interest for the platform bed.

CHAPTER 8

Home offices

Whether you're the CEO of a home-based business, in charge of keeping a busy family organized, or both, going to work can be a pleasure when you put the "home" into your home office. With efficient furnishings, thoughtful space planning, and bonus personality, your home office can be much more than a landing pad for your laptop. This bright and breezy writer's retreat headed upstairs for peace and quiet and tree-house views.

WorkStyle MakeItCozy

Every day can be casual day when you work at home. There's no morning rush, no freeway commute, and no dress code, so take that conference call in your jeans and fuzzy slippers. And why not make your work space as personal as the rest of your home? After all, it doesn't have to look like a conventional office; it only has to work like one. To select the right space for a home office, consider how you plan to use it.

■ **IS IT STRICTLY FOR BUSINESS?** Is it a research library, a hobby room, or a multipurpose hobby and home management center? Is it strictly for desk work or will it double as a guest room?

■ **HOW IMPORTANT IS PRIVACY?** The family room may be a perfect spot for a bill-paying desk, but if you're writing the great American novel, the area may be too distracting. Will other family members use the office? If you hold client meetings, you'll need privacy and maybe a separate entrance.

■ **WHAT WILL YOU STORE?** Do you need space for research materials, sample books, blueprints, a computer and office equipment, a drafting table, or crafts items?

PERSONALITY PLUS FUNCTION

If you want to wallpaper your "corporate suite" in raspberry red toile and add a comfy chaise for stretching out to ponder a project, go ahead. An author did exactly that in turning a spare bedroom into this creative haven. From the closet's quick-and-easy desk—two filing cabinets and a three-board top—to handsome cabinetry, every inch works beautifully. Open shelves keep photos, reference books, collections, baskets, and fabric-covered boxes in view; doored storage hides messy projects. Fabric-covered foam-core panels turn closet doors into a message board/photo gallery crisscrossed with ribbon.

LEFT: This clever closet office gets to work with soft touches, such as the chenille-clad slipper chair and lots of family photos on display, even under desktop glass. The laptop may be high tech, but the accents—an old-fashioned phone and fresh flowers—are pure home.

> **TO FIND OUT MORE ONLINE, VISIT US**
> ☞ @ www.bhg.com/bkarrangearoom

ABOVE: Upholstered in a luscious plaid that spins off the room's cheery palette, the sink-in chaise works double duty as a spot to relax and read and as "guest" seating when the family drops in to check on Mom's projects.

WorkStyle Make It Sleek

Designing a home office that truly helps you succeed
requires careful planning. How do you work? Do you like cozy clutter and leaving projects and paperwork spread out? Or does neatness count? Know your needs; then use these tips for setting up shop:

■ **CONSIDER BUILT-IN** or modular shelves, desks, and storage to optimize space. Custom built-ins are pricey, so check out stock kitchen cabinetry for its custom look and storage options.

■ **UTILIZE TALL STORAGE UNITS** that add vertical interest without gobbling up floor space. For an expansive look, combine open shelves and doored storage.

■ **WHAT'S YOUR REACH RADIUS?** You'll need everything within a comfortable arm's reach, so arrange your work area in an efficient L- or U-shape.

■ **LIGHT YOUR WAY.** To cut glare on computer monitors, use adjustable desk lamps, general lighting on dimmers, and lamps or sconces that bounce light off the ceiling.

PARTNERS BY DESIGN

Wrapped in rich woods from beams to built-ins, this home office doubles up on workstations for the couple who works here. Colorful pottery, collectibles, and family photos add the personality these home workers and their clients enjoy. The items also contribute to the textural mix that makes this space warm and welcoming. For client comfort, oversize chairs were reupholstered in plush mohair fabric,

OPPOSITE: Designed to flow seamlessly from the home's light-filled living spaces, this workplace-for-two opted for warmth and personality and left the heavy metals and austerity of conventional offices behind. Each workstation is designed in an efficient U-shape, and both share back-wall storage. **ABOVE:** Although this desk turns its back on the inner office, it still has a view of a colorful accent wall and art in the hallway. The hall functions as an annex, including custom storage to help the main space maintain its sleek good looks.

and breezes and natural light flood in from a lineup of transom windows. With room for supplies and files below decks in clean-lined cabinetry, workday clutter disappears after business hours, so the couple can pluck a good book from their office library, settle back, and relax.

A Do-It-All Office

Many homes—including this one—have precious little space to cast separately as a home office, a guest room, and a hobby spot. To ease its space crunch, this home called on clever cabinetry, flexible comfort, and warm, round-the-clock color to triple the function of a spare bedroom. Granite countertop wraps the office area, which has sitting and legroom for adults to use laptops on the side while the kids work at the computer angled into the corner. When guests are due, projects stow away behind doors and in ample drawers and wicker baskets and the countertop is swept clean so guests have room to spread out. Then out of the cabinetry comes the queen-size wall bed,

OPPOSITE LEFT: With a warm palette and three walls wrapped in action-packed cabinetry, this ambitious home office has turned into a family hub where everybody can do homework or pursue their hobbies. The vintage rocker invites settling in for a chat or a good read. BELOW CENTER: The everyday space makes quick work of changing into a guest room that has all the comforts of home. When the bed is in the open position, it reveals niches for nightstands on either side with rear outlets for reading lights and a clock. BELOW RIGHT: For safety, the fold-down sewing table has a lock inside the upper cabinet so it can't fall or be pulled down accidentally. The cabinet is outfitted with an adjustable light and has plenty of specialized storage for sewing supplies.

lightweight and well balanced so it raises and lowers easily and safely. With dressed-up touches such as crown molding that gives cabinetry a furniture look, faux-finished aubergine walls, and a cheery floral-fabric window treatment, the space is always ready for a quick and smooth transition from work to relaxation. The cabinetry holds one more surprise—a fold-down table for sewing projects and gift wrapping. The sewing machine slides out and plugs in inside the cabinet, and there's plenty of adjacent storage for fabrics, wrapping papers, ribbons, and the stitcher's library.

Make Room for Homework

When it comes to squeezing in a home office,

your bedroom can handle desk work with a slim sofa table at the foot of the bed or with a farm table in place of a nightstand. But if you like to burn late-night oil while your partner tries to sleep, it may not work as a full-service office.

WHERE TO WORK?

■ **FOR QUIET,** forget busy kitchens. Spare rooms away from household hubbub are obvious winners. Can you tuck a vintage secretary into a corner of a little-used living room?

■ **FOR FAMILIES WHO SURF** the Internet, the family room or dining room may be the answer.

■ **CONVERTED GARAGES OR WALK-OUT** basements with streetside access are ideal if you need privacy and receive clients.

■ **WALK-IN CLOSETS,** under the-stairs nooks, and corners make cozy work spaces.

■ **KNOW YOUR MEASUREMENTS.** Desks are 30 inches high; computer tables about 26 inches high—important to know if you are converting an antique table to office use.

■ **KNOW YOUR FILE NEEDS.** File cabinets offer letter-size or legal-size drawers. Hanging-file and specialized drawer inserts can convert ordinary chests into officeware.

■ **SQUEEZE IN THE FUNCTION.** Laptops fit the smallest office, and flat-screen monitors free up desktop space.

■ **CUSTOMIZE VERTICALLY** with prebuilt shelves; open-bookcase sizes begin at about 18×30 inches, with shelf depths starting at 12 or 13 inches.

■ **CONSIDER CLOSET ORGANIZER SYSTEMS.** Freestanding units offer good looks and storage.

■ **MODULAR STORAGE** comes in varying dimensions, from stackable cubes to shelf units with optional drop lids, shelves, doors, and drawers.

ABOVE LEFT: Scooting the sofa out from the wall frees up a living room corner for an antique secretary that's convenient for writing, reading, and paying bills. With doors open to showcase collectibles, it adds charm and focus plus function. **ABOVE RIGHT:** Crisp white cabinetry and a split-level counter put this tiny top-of-the-stairs room to work as a home office. An antique weaver's chair serves the high counter—handy for gift wrapping and projects—and baskets keep supplies organized on open shelves. **OPPOSITE:** This airy home office features beaded-board paneling—a remnant from its past life as a porch. A cushioned window seat nestles into new built-in shelves. An antique desk handles correspondence. Sentimental collections abound in this book-lover's retreat.

ABOVE: With antique woods, natural textures, and a tranquil neutral backdrop, this busy office stays user-friendly around the clock. The soft leather chair swivels easily from the English pine desk to the computer, which takes a backseat on a metal stand. **LEFT:** To emphasize the "home" in this home office and make it an inviting space for after-hours entertaining, cold metal file cabinets are camouflaged with pull-back slipcovers in a linen-cotton fabric.

Working the Swing Shift
Home offices don't have to be all work and no play.

Linked in color and style with other living spaces, they can move gracefully from day job to nighttime relaxing and entertaining when you choose anything-but-corporate furnishings and plenty of clever storage.

AFTER-HOURS ELEMENTS

■ **A SPACE THAT'S AN OFFICE BY DAY** and a den by night needs decidedly homey furnishings, such as graceful round tables instead of massive, hard-edged desks. Add comfortable seating—even a dining table—and the space can host after-work cocktails or dinners for two.

■ **USE COLOR TO FORGE** visual links between your home and office if the work spot is open for entertaining. Choose hues for office walls and other design elements from your home's palette. As guests flow in and out, a drastic color change won't jar the senses.

■ **MAKE CLUTTER DISAPPEAR.** Files, books, and projects in progress need to stay organized but out of sight. If romance is your style, pop slipcovers over your metal file cabinets. Rolling metal shelves can hide in closets.

■ **TO PUT THE OFFICE** in an after-hours mood, supplement desk lamps with reading lamps, accent lights, candles, and recessed lights. Put general lighting on dimmers.

■ **FLEXIBLE WINDOW TREATMENTS** can bridge the gap between day and night. Shutters and blinds, perhaps softened with fabric curtains, modulate natural light to control glare on work surfaces; then they add privacy when the sun goes down.

BELOW LEFT: Travel souvenirs and books gather on this "table," which is actually hardworking storage made of metal file cabinets covered in fabric. The louvered office door is always open and accented with art. **BELOW RIGHT:** Open shelves that served this former bedroom now hold books and collections. The homeowner annexed the adjacent closet for storage by rolling in a freestanding wire unit to keep magazines organized behind doors.

CHAPTER 9

Special spaces

Your home's quirky spaces—entries, hallways, attics, landings, odd nooks and crannies—often get second-class decorating treatment or none at all.

Instead of letting them sit idle, make every square inch contribute personality and function to your home's overall design. A slim bench and painted walls turned this entry into a welcoming woodland bower. Here's how to put the bloom on your own "leftover" spaces.

First Impressions

When guests cross your threshold, what's their instant opinion of your home? Is the entry inviting? Does it reflect your personality? If it's just a pass through, coax it into living up to its design potential with a few warming touches.

INTRODUCE PERSONALITY

■ **CHANGE THE SCENE WITH PAINT** and wallcovering. In a tiny entry, stencil on a checkerboard for impact. In small entries, use a wallpaper border instead of a busy all-over pattern.

■ **CONSIDER THE FRONT DOOR** as a potential design element, whether you faux-finish it, paint it one bright hue, or leave it natural.

■ **SELECT FAVORITES.** If art, collections, or plants are part of your home's charm, introduce them in the entry. Greetings will be leisurely because guests will linger for a look.

■ **ADD COMFORT.** Choose functional furniture pieces such as a bench, small chairs, or a console table to hold keys and packages and to display collections.

■ **REFLECT THE GLORY.** Mirrors visually enlarge small entries and create a spot for last-minute primping before leaving the house.

■ **MAKE AN ENTRANCE.** If your front door opens right into your living room, create an entryway with a floor screen, a fabric panel, or a tall bookcase placed perpendicular to the door.

■ **LIGHT CREATIVELY.** Focus accent lights on art or collections. Stack sconces to dramatize a corner. Direct uplights on plants to cast dappled shadows on a wall.

■ **ADD A KILIM OR COLORFUL RAG RUG** to casual or contemporary entries. Consider an Oriental rug or needlepoint rug in more traditional spaces. Secure rugs with no-slip liners.

ABOVE: Size doesn't stop this small cottage entry from showing off the homeowner's creativity and love of antiques, such as the Victorian Eastlake table paired with a Victorian chair. Stair risers were wallpapered in scenic toile, then sealed with polyurethane for cleanability. RIGHT: Porch-style wicker pieces and an old love-seat-size settee piled with pillows transform this tiny kitchen laundry area into a pleasant and functional entry, handy for slipping on shoes, reading cookbooks, setting down grocery bags, or chatting with the neighbors.

ABOVE: Guests can't wait to see the next act once they step into the drama of this romantic entry. A 19th-century mirror provides a space-expanding backdrop for the painted table, accented with the home's hallmark—intriguing collections.

Passing Pleasures

Anyone who thinks hallways should function as elevator music, in the background and hardly noticed, is missing a major decorating opportunity. Even the smallest home has some kind of hallway connection, so why not turn those ho-hum passageways into places worth enjoying?

MAKE IT WORTH THE TRIP

■ **DISPLAY FAVORITES.** Walls decorated in gallery fashion convey style without taking up square footage. If you don't have a collection of art or prints, gather framed family photos; frame posters, hobby or sports mementos, textiles, or other collectibles for wall art. For uniformity, keep framing treatments similar in style—no sleek metal frames mixed with ornate carved and gilded ones.

■ **ADD FUNCTION.** When the hallway offers ample space, consider subtracting a foot or more from its width for an antique chest or floor-to-ceiling shelves, either built-in or freestanding. Add shelves at the short end where a hallway terminates. Because hallways are transition spaces between living areas, group two chairs and a small table for a conversation and afternoon tea spot.

■ **GET DOWN TO BUSINESS.** Dead-end hallways are prime spots for home offices. If there isn't a window, you can build in desk and storage space from floor to ceiling. If you want to preserve light from a window, consider a variety of modular pieces that will allow you to customize and organize even the smallest spaces.

OPPOSITE: A long, 5-foot-wide hallway turns into a library with the addition of sleek built-in bookcases. Mixed in with the floor-to-ceiling volumes, framed photos tell the family's story. FAR LEFT: Linking a new family-room addition with the kitchen, this breezeway invites passersby to linger for a look at collections. Blue Willow dishes fill a handcrafted child's cupboard, and wall-hung platters and a striped wall covering create vertical interest in this narrow space. LEFT: Once a screened-in dumping ground for boots, shoes, and outdoor gear, this breezeway gained year-round solarium appeal with the addition of new windows and French doors, whitewashed board-and-batten cedar panel-ing, and casual seating for reading and enjoying the view.

ABOVE: Attics can be dark and boxy, but this suite lightens up with neutral hues and a recessed wall of new windows. Slim blinds allow privacy and sun control. Built-ins combine drawers for clothes and shelves for books and the television. **OPPOSITE:** The low-flying beams in this attic bedroom were imposing until a space-expanding brush of white over all turned them into architectural assets. Skylights on the angled wall above the bed brighten the space by day and frame the stars at night.

Retreat to the Attic

If you've considered adding a new room to your home, think vertical, not horizontal. Transforming an old-house attic or a new-house bonus room above a garage into living space makes economic sense. The storybook charm of a treetop hideout or quirky sloped ceiling is romantic reason enough to put such underused spaces to work. With these ideas, attics and bonus rooms can become idyllic playrooms, children's bedrooms, adult sitting rooms, home offices, or master suites.

BRIGHTEN BONUS SPACES

■ **BRIGHTEN WITH SKYLIGHTS.** Without tampering with the roofline, skylights increase natural light and add head room. Opt for energy-saving glass; control light with blinds or shades.

■ **STREAMLINE YOUR FURNITURE.** Built-ins make the most of knee-wall space. Sleek freestanding chests can line a hallway. Tuck low-slung seating and shorter chests under the eaves.

■ **CONTOUR YOUR SPACE.** Visually shorten and square up a tunnel-like attic with a fireplace or a bookcase built in across one end. Widen the space with diagonal rugs and furniture groupings. Raise the ceiling with vertically striped wallcovering. Or square it up with paint. Darker hues on end walls visually shorten the room; lighter hues on the sidewalls make it look wider.

TO FIND OUT MORE ONLINE, VISIT US @ www.bhg.com/bkdecoratingcenter

A Place for Hobbies

How can you find space for hobbies without adding a room? Here's where a home's out-of-the-way places—a laundry, basement dead space, or even a walk-in closet—can save the day. Not every space will work for every hobby. Only you know the demands of your favorite pastime, so analyze your needs before designing your space.

CRAFTING CRAFTY SPACES

■ **STEAL SOME SPACE.** Have a laundry or utility room waiting to do double duty? Great! If not, check out a main room—even a living or family room—for a corner that can cater to your passion. How messy is your activity? Will it be a maintenance nightmare on a polished wood floor? Will clutter quickly stow away, or do you need to conceal the hobby corner with a folding screen? Is quiet important? If creative writing is your avocation, find an out-of-the-way space with a door, even if that means refitting a guest room closet with a desk or replacing your nightstand with a writing table.

■ **CHOOSE HARDWORKING FURNISHINGS** that play along with your leisure pursuits. How important is storage? What kind do you need—deep drawers for bulky items, wide flat drawers for artwork? Do you or other household members prefer open or closed storage for your hobby gear? For work space, will a portable folding table suffice, or do you need to leave projects spread out? Will you need special task lighting for sewing or tying fishing flies? Or is natural light from windows better for, say, oil painting?

ABOVE: To get a railroad buff's retreat on track, walls were painted a deep coral to showcase a prized collection of O-gauge Lionel trains dating from 1946 to 1956. Display racks accent dormer angles in this over-the-garage bonus room furnished with comfy seating for reading and researching railroad history. **RIGHT:** Plunked down in a lush garden, this studio/shed doubles as a nap-time getaway and a quiet work place for the home's artist in residence. Casual open shelves and humble containers keep painting supplies within easy reach.

ABOVE: Although this storage-packed studio was designed for a potter, it could be adapted for sewing or painting by switching the potter's wheel for a center worktable. A hammered-copper sink handles cleanup, and the floor gets double protection with vinyl-coated grass matting and a floorcloth.

Landing a Job

Call them leftovers, those spaces in your home you pass by every day without a second glance. Next time you walk past, consider whether you might be passing up a good thing. That landing, the corner beneath the eaves, the sliver of wall space at the top of the stairs, or the odd, good-for-nothing nook or cranny could be just the extra space you need. Just put them to work one by one.

OLD SPACES, NEW ROLES

■ **TO FIND THESE HIDDEN TREASURES,** do your own space exploration. Tour your home as if viewing it for the first time. Look for blank walls, dead-end nooks, or little junk rooms or pantries with doors that are always closed. Then recast them to expand your storage, sitting, or display space.

■ **ARE YOUR STAIRWAY LANDINGS UNDERACHIEVERS?** Is there room for a desk, storage chest, or bookshelves? Adding a small lamp table, a chair, and wall art can brighten the journey up and down. Turn a wide landing with a window into a mini retreat by adding a window seat and wall-hung reading light.

■ **CORNERS,** especially those with low-flying or angled ceilings, can become especially snug getaways with the addition of a chair and ottoman for reading. You could even wrap the corner in low, built-in bookshelves to keep best-sellers within easy reach.

OPPOSITE LEFT: Although the dramatic, two-story entry with an overlook landing is a typical feature of many new homes, it's often underused space. A desk, a comfy chair, and personal accessories transform this overlook into a sunny home office with a bird's-eye view. CENTER: Crafted in France almost a century ago, the hall bench with bonus under-seat storage stars on this cottage landing. The tall mirror expands space and adds vertical interest. BELOW: This roomy landing offers bonus display space. Flanked by Hitchcock chairs, the pine chest is the stage for miniature pine furniture, Cole pottery, and silhouettes of the family's children.

CHAPTER 10

Kitchens

Be it galley or open-plan, today's kitchen has become a true "living" room, a hub for family gatherings, entertaining, cooking, and dining.

No wonder it's so important to outfit and decorate a kitchen to reflect your personality and suit the way you live. What's your goal? Energizing your room with spunky colors like the ones here? Banishing clutter with efficient storage? How about an easy-does-it redo with paint, fabric, and a few of your favorite things? This chapter helps you plan and pick design elements for a kitchen that will delight your eye and your taste buds.

Spice with Color

Wood or white? Kitchen trends come and go, but the crisp appeal of white cabinets and appliances never dates. White sets a timeless mood and makes the room seem more spacious. It also makes the most of natural or artificial light—a real plus in small kitchens or those with few windows. If you adore color—and your white kitchen—count yourself lucky: White makes the perfect backdrop for colorful, downright happy accents.

White exists in myriad variations, so carefully choose wall paint that matches your cabinets. Some whites have undertones of blue, pink, yellow, gray, or brown. Lighting and surrounding surface materials can make a tint look different. Take home paint chips in different tones to see how natural and artificial light changes the look of them throughout the day and evening.

WARM UP A WHITE KITCHEN WITH COLORS AND TEXTURES

When versatile white dominates your kitchen, the accent colors, wallcoverings, fabrics, artwork, and accessories that make kitchens friendly and comfortable can vary with your tastes.

■ **PAINTED FURNITURE,** stenciled borders, and decorative paint finishes on walls introduce color to help personalize a white kitchen.

■ **SOLID COLORS**—a sky blue ceiling, delicious peach-hued walls, or forest green stain on the island—add contrast. Again, consider the effects of natural and artificial light when making color choices.

■ **SURFACES ADD WARM-UP TEXTURE** and color too. To cut the monotony of an open kitchen with lots of white storage, vary countertop materials and cabinet hardware; introduce color, motifs, and texture in backsplash tile; and accent with rich woods and more color.

OPPOSITE: White cabinetry pops against chartreuse walls, bold-patterned vinyl flooring, and mixed textures in this remodeled Victorian-era home. A trio of leather-and-chrome barstools conjures a retro feeling, and dishes in glass-front cabinets echo the wall color. LEFT: Inspired by its coastal setting, this cottage brought the colors of sun and sea into its kitchen with a lemon yellow countertop and backsplash. Chandelier shades, ceramic accents, and the coffeemaker and teakettle fit the yellow and blue scheme.

Choosing Cabinetry
Every kitchen needs it, but beyond its obvious function, cabinetry is your kitchen's main style-

setter, whether you are buying new or updating the old. Crisp white cabinetry with beaded-board doors and open shelves sets a well-scrubbed cottage mood. Natural woods and chrome hardware convey modern style. Antiqued, raised-panel doors and features such as plate racks convey classic style. Dark-stained woods with stone countertops feel warmly rustic, and clean-lined laminates are beautifully contemporary. To restyle existing cabinets, replace door panels with glass, punched tin, or beaded board, create a raised-panel effect by applying molding to door fronts, or remove some doors to create open shelves.

OPEN OR SHUT CASE

Do you want open or closed storage, or a mix of both? Open storage lets you show off bright-hued pottery and collections and

gives a kitchen an airy look, but neatness counts when cabinets are open to view. Opt for the best of both worlds and remove only a few upper doors, then paint the cabinet interiors in the wall color. Or have sections of solid doors cut out and replaced with glass for a fresh, airy look.

SHOW YOUR COLORS

Stock and custom cabinetry comes in a range of hues: solids, two-toned or antiqued, glazed pastels and naturals, and opaque color over wood grains. Colors can be as dramatic as barn red, French blue, and black or as classic as glazed yellow or creamy white. Transform old cabinets with paint, colored semitransparent stains, or decorative paint techniques such as sponging, antiquing, or stenciling. Choose durable enamel paints.

OPPOSITE: The alabaster light fixture helped set the color scheme in this new kitchen with old-world flavor. Tuscan yellow cabinets with a rubbed, painted finish and the distressed, russet-hued hutch feature furniture details, such as columns and bun feet. CENTER: Against a deep-green granite wall, two inexpensive wooden étagères—a sculptural and functional alternative to upper cabinets in the kitchen—keep everyday dishes handy by the range. Wall cabinets with lead-glass doors are recessed to free up counter space. BELOW: Cubbyhole-style upper cabinets, made of plywood and maple veneer to match the stock maple ones below, give this modest-size kitchen breathing room. The stacks of dishes and the baskets for holding smaller essentials provide a "view" that is all color and texture.

TO FIND OUT MORE ONLINE, VISIT US @ www.bhg.com/bkkitchenguide

One Great Piece

Like other living spaces, every kitchen needs a focal point, and if it boosts function, character, and style, so much the better. In open-plan kitchen/family rooms, create focal points for special areas, such as the breakfast spot. For example, dress the range in a hearth-style hood for a dramatic view from the family room. A handsome piece of furniture brings instant distinction to a bare wall. By mixing old design sensibilities with modern function, some kitchens today achieve a warm "unfitted" look with furniture-style cabinets that temper the typical sweep of utilitarian cabinetry.

PAST-PERFECT GALLEYS

In past centuries—before cookie-cutter cabinetry—furniture pieces formed the kitchen. A dresser or hutch held dishes and utensils. Ingredients lined the countertop, other freestanding cabinets, and wall-hung shelves. The ancestor of today's islands was an old table for food prep and dining. Buy new cabinet designs to replicate the look or use these tips:

■ **USE FREESTANDING HUTCHES** to add vertical interest and display space. If you can't squeeze in a big wood piece, use a slim wrought-iron baker's rack for charm in small spaces.

■ **IF WALL SPACE IS AT A PREMIUM,** look for antique corner cupboards, wall-hung shelves, or plate racks. Beneath windows, tuck a small chest for linens or a table for baskets of apples, potatoes, and onions. Don't forget pot racks for storage and character.

■ **INCLUDE FUNCTIONAL ACCENTS.** Old spice and tea caddies, distressed wood boxes, small iron shelves, and even antique glass milk bottles add character while slowing kitchen necessities.

OPPOSITE: Measuring 9 feet long, this 18th-century French pastry table made such a spectacular addition to the kitchen that the homeowners extended a wall several inches to fit it in. It stores and displays various items and holds casual buffets on its marble top. **ABOVE LEFT:** Some of a collector's favorites roost on this enchanting antique hutch that's a focal point for the kitchen and dining spot. The transferware is vintage 1830s. Rare Staffordshire casseroles featuring chicken, duck, and egg-basket covers also are on display. **ABOVE RIGHT:** A hutch doesn't have to be a massive piece of pine and centuries old. This red stair-step beauty is right at home with the lively colors and playful mobiles that a professional chef mixed up for this kitchen redesign.

Cooking
Light and Bright

BEFORE

Bringing a new attitude to an aging kitchen doesn't always translate into a to-the-studs remodeling. Decide which elements to change to make your kitchen more efficient and fun; then pour on the color. With mauve walls, a sheet vinyl floor, and dark-stained cabinets, this kitchen was a 1980s fossil. Now—with a few cosmetic additions and subtractions—it's a lively family hub.

■ **DELETING A RAILING** and three upper cabinets over a peninsula opened the kitchen to the dining spot and family room. The peninsula is now an eating bar with a new green granite countertop. A reproduction hutch moved into the dining area to take up storage slack and add character.

■ **WALLS WERE PAINTED SUNNY YELLOW,** and for about one-fifth the cost of new cabinets, old ones were painted a delicious lemon chiffon hue. Artfully painted pulls and traditional moldings on the cabinetry capture a French Country look,

■ **THE DECADE-OLD DINING SET** spiffed up with new cushions, and overhead, the cast-iron chandelier has hand-painted linen shades.

■ **NEW TERRA-COTTA TILE** in 17×17-inch squares covers the backsplash and the floor. The ceiling and eating bar wear farmhouse-style beaded-board paneling.

■ **A DESK BESIDE THE REFRIGERATOR** keeps counters free of clutter. A magnetized message board on the refrigerator and a wall-hung cabinet use vertical surfaces for storage and display.

RIGHT: The refresher course for this once-dark kitchen started with lively colors, some new surfaces and lighting, and gallons of paint. But the country charm of the space comes from the thoughtful details, such as new moldings on cabinetry, hand-painted motifs on new lampshades, and inexpensive ceramic cabinet pulls.

SoftTouches

Instead of a total redesign, give your kitchen a facelift

and a beautiful new future. Paint, fresh fabrics, and a change of accents may be all you need. Updating color and design elements creates an instant change of mood—and guarantees big decorating impact on a small budget.

PAINT IT

Nothing renews a kitchen faster than fresh color on the backdrop, cabinetry, and even the floor. A broad brush of the same crisp white or light hue over cabinetry and walls makes a small kitchen seem bigger. In large kitchens, conjure coziness and intimacy with darker colors. Decorative paint finishes and special effects such as stenciled borders add depth and texture to walls and unify space. Before you paint, sand and use a deglazer to remove all the old finish so the final look will be as fresh as the new hue you choose.

TRY NEW "SOFTWARE"

Fabric softens the hard-edged look of appliances; it also absorbs sound. New curtains, softly shirred valances, sink skirts, seat cushions, rugs, table linens, and other fabric accents may provide the soft style statement your kitchen needs. Use fabric to carry color and pattern around the kitchen and link the kitchen with a breakfast area or adjacent family room. In addition to the softness that billowy fabric itself provides, look for romantic or curvilinear patterns that will break up the boxy look of a wall of cabinets. Florals, botanicals, or modern graphic designs with soft shapes will do the job.

OPPOSITE: Garden-fresh fabric and artful painting infuse this lighthearted kitchen with New England charm. There's no need to wash the dishes in these upper cabinets because they're painted-on "trompe l'oeil"—French for "fool the eye"—designs. The floor's diamonds are done in paint and stain.

BELOW: Childhood memories of a family's 1950s beach cottage inspired this kitchen's easy-does-it update. Beneath a salvaged countertop, drawer fronts on the laminate cabinets are clad in galvanized tin secured with construction adhesive, and washable linen skirts replace doors for a softer look.

Collected Works
The best kitchen warm-ups come right from your heart when you decorate with what you love.

Display your favorite collections in your kitchen to turn on a little design charm—and to tell your personal story.

COLLECTOR'S PARADISE

■ **EXPAND DISPLAY SPACE** by replacing cabinet door panels with glass or by simply removing doors on one or two upper cabinets. Paint, wallpaper, or add beaded board to cabinet interiors before arranging Grandmother's china or boldly colored Fiestaware.

■ **LOOK HIGH AND LOW** for display space. Glass shelves attached to a kitchen window frame become a showcase for bright-hued bottles sparkling in the sun or a fragrant array of herbs in terra-cotta pots. Turn wall space under upper cabinets into your own art gallery.

■ **ADD COLOR, TEXTURE,** and more storage with wicker baskets, fabric-covered boxes, hand-painted tins, and interesting old jars. Allot open-shelf space for colorful cookbooks. Instead of lining objects at the back of the countertop, group them in artful vignettes.

ABOVE: When a big new refrigerator moved into this older-home kitchen, it yelled "modern" and stood out awkwardly until the wall was built out around it and shelves were added for more display space and practical storage. **RIGHT:** Things don't get lost behind doors in the deep corner cabinet in this collector's kitchen. Rounded pitchers called "ball jugs," made by Hall Pottery in the early 1900s, join funky salt and pepper shakers in the colorful, open-shelf display.

■ DISPLAY THE UNEXPECTED. Bring out your quirky flea market finds or heirlooms—art, framed letters, dishes, old or kitschy kitchenware, and other treasures. If it's fragile or especially valuable, place it on a high shelf or under glass. Use a sliver of wall to hang a small antique shelf for display.

ABOVE: Boring no more, the painted backsplash in this small kitchen is cast in a new role as a gallery. On exhibit, a mix of old prints, photos, and flea market finds delivers color, texture, and charm.

Instant Islands

In newer kitchens, built-in islands often take center stage. Jam-packed with appliances, storage, and counter space for efficiency, they also reroute traffic and shorten distances within the work core. No island? Take heart. In many small to midsize kitchens, you still can add function with a freestanding island. That is especially true in some U-shape kitchens, which can offer too much open area in the center of the room. A small table or a butcher block 18 to 24 inches across can make all the difference when you need extra counter space. An antique baker's table or a farm table in the center of a kitchen also can handle food preparation, buffet service, and even informal dining in warm style. For comfortable movement, plan on at least 3 feet around all sides of an island.

■ **IN SMALL KITCHENS,** draft a console or drop-leaf table, a roll-away cart, or a freestanding butcher block on legs.

■ **PICK A TABLE,** old or new, that's sturdy enough for daily use. Even a chunky old sideboard can be customized to work as an island.

■ **AGE A NEW ISLAND** with vintage-look hardware and crown moldings. New cabinetry lets you customize the height and features, such as eating counters and inset cutting boards.

ABOVE: Reminiscent of old trestle tables, this charming new island is a functional addition to a small kitchen. It's a quick turn from island food prep to the range; when it's time for reading cookbooks or paying bills, pull up a stool. **CENTER:** Cutting travel time from one side of the kitchen

to the other, this trim console table directs the kids around the work core when cooking is under way. It's roomy enough for a lineup of ingredients; rings keep dish towels within reach. RIGHT: Two roll-out toolboxes, one topped with a butcher block for chopping and the other with granite for rolling dough, give this island ample storage. The island top is made from a solid-core door wrapped in copper sheeting.

CHAPTER 11

Decorate with a pamper-yourself attitude, and getting away can be as easy as walking into your bathroom.

Where better to soothe away the stress of the day and rejuvenate your spirits? But what takes a bath beyond practical and makes it luxurious? A sparkling crystal chandelier and sconces and an artist's mural, copied from real landscape photographs, transform this Victorian-era bath into an elegant retreat. This chapter offers more decorating and pampering ideas.

Bath Basics

A well-organized, well-appointed, and well-lit bath can jump-start your day

and become your round-the-clock oasis. Whether you are designing a new bath or updating an old one, turn up the comfort and convenience by paying attention to the bath's design elements and fixtures.

■ **FIXTURES COME FIRST.** For sinks, tub, and shower, buy high-quality faucets—the most frequently used device in the bath. If the bath layout works well, upgrade to a whirlpool or oversize tub or steam shower without moving plumbing lines. Add a double-sink vanity to cut traffic jams in a shared bath.

■ **MAKE A BIG SPLASH WITH SURFACES.** Set the mood with dramatic hand-painted tile, a run of colorful cabinetry, marble or granite vanity counters, elegant wallcoverings, or painted faux finishes. Let your bare feet choose flooring—water-loving tile or stone can be softened with warm carpet or nonskid area rugs.

■ **BANISH SHADOWS.** Warm incandescent lighting provides true and flattering bath light. For a shadow-free makeup spot, flank a vanity mirror with lights; for mirrors wider than 36 inches, a strip-light fixture over the mirror works best. For better general lighting, substitute track or recessed lights for a single, glaring ceiling fixture. Add a dimmer for leisurely after-work soaks.

■ **PRIVACY PANES.** Soften lines of a utilitarian bath and guard privacy with window treatments. Choose Roman shades, decorative valances teamed with blinds or shutters, or drapery panels fashioned from easy-care fabrics. Honeycomb shades that rise from the sill up can provide privacy while admitting a treetop view or exposing a decorative round-top or transom window.

■ **THINK WASHABLE.** So you don't have to perch on the tub to put your socks on, bring in a cushy upholstered chair or ottoman. Dress it in a quick-dry and easy-wash slipcover stitched from prewashed terry cloth toweling or lightweight cotton fabric.

■ **MAKE IT SAFE.** Add a telephone, childproof latches on cabinets and medicine chests, tub-and-shower grab bars, and ground fault circuit interrupter (GFCI) plugs on outlets.

LEFT: Designed around a sleek center island for storing clothes and accessories, this dramatic bath is a natural beauty with limestone flooring and white oak cabinetry, a lush view, and an oversize skylight. The yellow hue of the stone tile mimics the sun, and walls are painted and glazed in pale periwinkle blue for a sky-and-clouds effect.

ABOVE: Warmed by a clever interplay of textures, this master bath juxtaposes the unexpected old with the minimalist new. Sculptural glass sinks and expansive sconce-topped mirrors create the vanity wall. A circa-1920 French chair upholstered in skin-pleasing velvet in an Oriental warrior pattern carves out a nearby sitting spot.

Add a Little Luxe

Your aging bath may be short on square footage, but you can indulge it— and yourself—with style, quality fixtures, and touches of luxury.

■ **SPLURGE ON MATERIALS.** A small bath is an advantage here. It takes fewer marble floor tiles to add luxury to a diminutive bath. A new countertop does wonders for an older vanity.

■ **FREE UP SPACE WITH FIXTURES.** Replace a boxy vanity with a pedestal sink. Or, if you need lots of countertop space, shop for a slim 18-inch-deep vanity instead of a standard 24-inch-deep model.

■ **PAINT IT.** Visually expand space by keeping everything in the same light color family. Add depth to walls with finishes such as combing or sponging, and use semigloss or gloss paints instead of flat paints. Bathroom facelift specialists can repaint wall tile.

■ **REFLECT THE GLORY.** Mirrors work magic in small baths, reflecting space and light. Run mirrors from wall to wall and countertop to

ceiling, or for vintage character, frame a large mirror to hang like art over the vanity.

■ **ADD PERSONALITY WITH FABRIC** and pattern. For romance, consider gathered curtains and replace undersink doors on a newer vanity with a softly shirred sink skirt on a tension rod. Consider scrubbable vinyl wallcoverings, or for just a touch of pattern, add a border at the ceiling or chair-rail line. Use a ready-made wallpaper border or be playful and stencil or stamp on your own painted designs in the colors that you love.

■ **DELIGHT THE SENSES.** Create a personal paradise—inexpensively— with scented candles, sachets, small bouquets of fresh flowers, and an over-the-tub rack or tubside basket filled with soaps, oils, and loofahs.

OPPOSITE LEFT: Trailing ivy, fresh blooms, and a trompe l'oeil garland painted on the wall turn this romantic bath into a garden spot for primping. The vanity's vintage linen accents and a distressed mirror propped in the window turn back time. **OPPOSITE RIGHT:** A comfy upholstered chaise and a timeworn table and chair add the relaxed ambience that this simple bath needs. Flower-strewn fabric links the Roman shade and chaise pillow. The dressing table displays antiqueware. **BELOW LEFT:** Blue ticking and a floral sheet were fashioned into this charming shower curtain; a false beam with molding defines the tub area and hides the curtain rod. Paint-grade, beaded-board wainscoting delivers farmhouse flavor. **BELOW RIGHT:** This powder room had two things going for it—a strip of black-and-white checkerboard tile that inspired a new palette and a charming corner sink. The sink skirt's toile repeats on the wall. The black-painted mirrored medicine cabinet enhances the crisp color scheme.

Getaway Baths
The decorating options for a grand-size master bath can make you feel like royalty.

A steam shower, sauna, exercise area, whirlpool tub, audio/video systems, and other amenities can add up to a true bather's utopia if you have the space.

LUXURY ON TAP

■ **WARM UP AN OVERSIZE BATH.** Add decorative touches so sweeps of porcelain, tile, stone, metals, and mirrors don't make a large space feel cold or cavernous. Break up a large bath into zones for bathing, grooming, dressing, exercising, and relaxing. Fresh color, textured fabrics and accents, and rich woods (in a vanity, a chaise longue or chair, or cabinetry) will turn up the heat in a chilly bath. If your countertop is large enough, plug in a shaded lamp to add a warm, mood-enhancing glow.

■ **GO ALL OUT.** How about replacing a window with French-door access to a terrace or deck so that you can lounge with the morning newspaper and a cup of coffee? How about adding an overstuffed chair and ottoman for après-bath relaxing? If lounging in the whirlpool is your thing, why not set the scene with a master-bath fireplace?

■ **INDULGE.** Treat your bath to heated bars for toasty towels, lighted makeup mirrors, a television, or a massage table. Wire in speakers and let yourself get carried away by music. For safety, position a television, a radio, or a sound system away from any water source.

RIGHT: Adding a shapely slipcovered chair (or a chaise if you have room) makes a big bath feel more like a cozy sitting room. Scented with candles and flowers, this relaxing spot has a garden view and a table handy for a teacup. **OPPOSITE:** Bathed in sunbeams and stay-awhile comforts, this serene yet upbeat master bath marries vintage elements, such as the claw-foot tub, with a contemporary marble-clad shower that has a sleek, frameless glass door. Linen Roman shades mounted at the ceiling line visually heighten the windows.

Splash
On Color

BEFORE

If your bath is aging, but not gracefully, apply the lipstick principle—without the lipstick. Revitalize it with clever cover ups and splashes of color. Here, an old saccharin pink wallcovering, which no longer suited the owner's style, disappeared, and inexpensive fixes stepped in to provide fresh style. Adapt these ideas to your bath.

■ **PAINT THE WALLS.** Here, a soft lavender soothes the mood and provides contrast that makes the mosaic floor tile come to life. Painting the tub nook green accents the arch over the tub and adds a punch of unexpected color.

■ **GIVE THE CABINETRY A FACELIFT.** Replace metal door inserts with ribbed glass panels to allow colorful towels and toiletries to shine through. It's a less expensive option than having new glass-front doors made. A stained-glass store cut the panels to fit.

■ **DECORATE WITH SHEETS.** Print and gingham sheets provided fabric for the shower curtain, studded with grommets at the top, and the Roman shade that's easy to make with a kit or patterns from the fabrics store. The big surprise? The cushy bath mat is actually made from a pillow sham stuffed with thin batting. All are trimmed in red grosgrain ribbon.

■ **DON'T FORGET THE KNOBS.** Daisies were painted onto these wooden knobs, but you could stamp or stencil yours instead. Changing hardware is one of the quickest and easiest ways to update an old vanity.

TOP RIGHT: For a new view without removing the expansive vanity mirror, a smaller framed mirror hangs on grosgrain ribbon. Twin light fixtures over the sit-down makeup spot and the sink make the bath bright enough for two. CENTER RIGHT: A custom Roman shade, sewn from print and gingham sheets and trimmed in ribbon, underscores the new palette. BOTTOM RIGHT: A brush of fresh paint, textured glass door panels, and handpainted knobs give outdated cabinetry a bright new look. OPPOSITE: Despite its natural resources—ample cabinetry, a charming bathtub nook, and a sunny window—this bath needed a punch of color. Paint and sheets, sewn into accents, filled the bill.

TO FIND OUT MORE ONLINE, VISIT US
@ www.bhg.com/bkbathguide

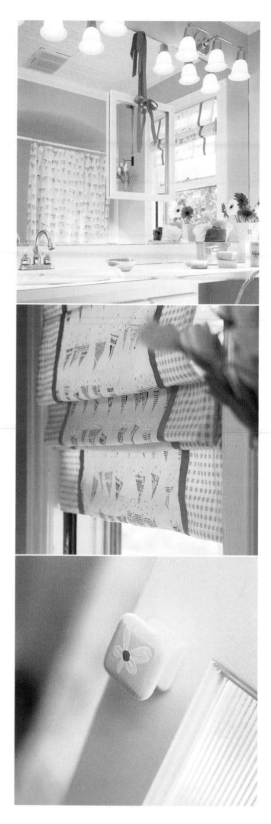

Accent Personality

Surround yourself with things you love. It's a decorating maxim that applies in the bath too. Favorite colors, motifs, and objects on display soften the bath's utilitarian elements and take the edge off cold tile and metal fixtures.

■ **CREATE EYE-CATCHING GALLERIES** of favorite photos or framed art, but consider the humidity. With no tub or shower to add humidity, a half bath makes a wonderful showcase for a treasured painting or limited-edition print. In a full bath where steam could damage fine art, however, it's best to stick with lower-cost prints.

■ **ADD COLLECTIBLE CHARACTER** with wall-hung displays or arrange treasures on shelves or atop the vanity.

■ **WARM UP WITH CONTRASTING TEXTURES.** Weathered flea market finds and antiques in rich woods play off beautifully against slick porcelain, ceramic, and glass.

■ **LOOK FOR SHAPELY VARIETY.** Soften a bath's hard edges with rounded accents: curvy hampers, plant stands, and softly gathered curtains.

■ **DECORATE IN UNEXPECTED AREAS.** Put framed prints and good-looking racks, shelves, and small cabinets above toilets, between windows, over doors, or on neglected walls.

OPPOSITE: Outfitted with modern-day spa amenities such as the whirlpool tub, this bath honors its farmhouse roots too with timeless botanical prints in antique frames. A medley of textures—wicker baskets, an old wood shelf, and a pail for sponges—warm this comfort zone. BELOW LEFT: Although its dimensions are small, this powder room squeezes in personality with a gallery of black and white photos above the boxcar wainscoting. Attached to the wall with brass upholstery tacks, family portraits mix with "ancestors" adopted at flea markets and antiques malls. BELOW RIGHT: Dramatic against the high-contrast backdrop of red walls and cream trim, the display of antique tole trays adds folk art punch and pattern to this cozy powder bath without taking up much space. Highly collectible, the elaborately decorated metalware dates from the late 1800s.

Character Vanities

All vanities are not created equal. They all do the job, but some do it with personality—and an admirable dash of the unexpected. As long as there's room to nestle in a sink, a vanity can be anything from a pair of chunky corbels to an elegant antique sideboard. Even adding stylish new hardware to a ho-hum vanity can boost its character. These one-of-a-kind vanities are the personal master-pieces of homeowners who wouldn't settle for the ordinary.

LEFT: The distressed finish on this old dresser gives it more character and charm as it assumes its new role as a vanity. Instead of occupying the usual middle position, the sink is set to one side so the drawers can open. **BELOW:** Stylewise, these movable wooden storage towers are a perfect fit for this bath in an open, contemporary attic space. In addition, they provide invaluable stashing space beneath the concrete countertop. If more storage is needed in the future, there's room to add another tower or two.

ABOVE: Gracefully carved pine corbels from France were attached to the wall to create the base for this vanity, as artistic as the gilt-framed gallery in this master bath. The corbels are topped with an all-in-one sink and counter and a mirror in a fittingly old-world frame.

OrganizeYourBath

If you've ever rummaged under the sink to find the hair dryer or lost tweezers in a cluttered drawer,

you know that efficient bathroom storage belongs on the luxury list with whirlpool tubs and scented candles. First, take an inventory of the items you frequently use in the bath; then consider these ideas for getting organized.

■ **USE VERTICAL SPACE.** Stack a corner with wedge-shape glass shelves or stow grooming supplies on a trim étagère. Install shelves above the toilet, stow rolled towels in a wall-mounted wine rack, or wall-mount the hair dryer.

■ **RETROFIT CABINETRY** with pullout hampers, tilt-out waste cans, and drawer organizers for cosmetics. Beneath the vanity, add stacked pullout trays.

■ **ADD A NARROW LEDGE** to the wall behind the sink if yours is a sleek new wall-hung or pedestal sink. (Before opting for pedestal sinks, decide if you can sacrifice under-vanity storage.)

■ **TAKE ADVANTAGE OF SPACE** between wall studs; carve out shallow recesses for shelves to hold toiletries and makeup.

■ **FILL A TUBSIDE WICKER BASKET** with rolled towels, sponges, bubble baths and oils, and fragrant candles.

■ **ADD A WINDOW SEAT** with storage below and a cushion on top for relaxing.

■ **STEAL SPACE.** Consider sneaking a few extra square feet for your bathroom by annexing space from an adjoining closet, hallway, or room.

OPPOSITE: The star of this bath is a multitalented antique dresser that is recast as a charming vanity; the sink was inset in a cabinet to the right. To expand storage, lower doors were removed and shelves added. New lighting replicates the beauty of the past. BELOW LEFT: Adding to the character of this bath with thick wainscoting and a salvaged tub, the green medical supply cabinet was purchased for $5—a storage bargain for towels and necessities. BELOW RIGHT: With trim styling and a mix of glass-front cabinets and colorful cubbyholes, this bath built-in has an open, airy feel. Hidden hinges enhance the slick design. Before hiring a craftsman to make built-ins, list and measure what you want to store so you can size the storage to suit your needs.

outside

Americans love to live in the great outdoors on sunny porches, decks, patios, and patches of garden barely big enough to slip in a chaise. With a city view beckoning, the owner of this Manhattan home created a top-of-the-world retreat with a lush rooftop garden that's ready for alfresco dinner parties and hours of leisure. The inspiring garden "rooms" in this chapter also welcome with furnishings as comfortable and beautiful as those found inside the house.

Living on the Porch

Decorate your railed Victorian porch, screened gazebo, or corner-of-the-yard retreat like any indoor living space. First, decide how you will use it. Think beyond just relaxing and barbecuing, because whatever activities you include can determine the furnishings and arrangement. Is it an entertaining spot with a table and chairs for sit-down dinners and buffets? How about hobby space? Outdoors, nobody frets about paint fumes or spills. If you like model building or decoupage, set up a worktable on a covered porch. Transform an upper deck into an observatory with patio chairs and a telescope for stargazing. Whatever's on your porch agenda, plan for privacy. Consider folding screens, container plants, and even draperies, roll-down shades, or shutters.

BELOW: On the porch of this 1930s cottage, new and vintage fabrics cover a daybed. A cup rack—hung upside down—holds garden tools. Look for water-resistant fabrics and pillow fillings, but plan to take cushions and pillows inside and cover larger upholstery with plastic when the rain comes.

ARRANGE FOR FUN

■ **CREATE SEPARATE BUT EQUAL HALVES.** A central door often divides two porch groupings. For balance, anchor one half with a single large piece, such as a porch swing or settee. On the other half, group lounge chairs or place a dining table with similar visual weight. Link the halves with a center rug or runner, or define the separate groupings with individual area rugs.

■ **RESCULPT THE TUNNEL.** Add a look of width to long, narrow porches by placing a sofa or settee cross-wise or on the diagonal; if possible, squeeze in a chair at one or both ends. Arrange three or four chairs in an on-the-bias cloverleaf for increased width, and lay rugs on an angle to play up the space-widening diagonal.

■ **LEAVE ROOM TO MOVE.** Arrange seating close enough for easy conversation and allow a minimum of 3 feet between furniture for the path from the steps to the front door.

OPPOSITE: New weatherproof wicker seating, cushioned in bright hues, teams with an easy-care natural sisal rug to bring living room style and comfort out to the front porch. An artisan-crafted pierced-metal screen and plants add touches of needed privacy and block the view to the neighboring house.

Weather the Elements

Neither gentle rain, nor gusty winds, nor blazing sun will keep you and your guests

from enjoying your porch, patio, or deck as long as you plan cover-ups. Awnings, umbrellas, tented roofs, and big shade trees can keep capricious weather from spoiling your day in the great outdoors. Plan ahead to protect your open-air space.

THE RIGHT LOCATION

Build an outdoor structure where it will get indirect light or shade for at least part of the day. A grove of trees makes the perfect spot for a gazebo or a detached pavilion. Look for a spot that's shaded by the house, by a detached garage, or even by a garden shed for part of the afternoon. To add bistro charm, shade your patio with an adjustable market umbrella, the kind used for years to shade vendors' stalls in Europe. (With an umbrella stand that does not require a dining table for support, you can create instant shade virtually anywhere.) Deflect sun and rain with a retractable awning or stitch simple curtains or roll-up blinds from new, weather-resistant fabrics.

OUTDOORSY FABRICS

Newer synthetic materials simulate the look and feel of natural fibers, but they weather the elements beautifully.

- **WOVEN VINYL-COATED POLYESTER**—a popular material for cushions, slings, and colorful umbrellas—is waterproof and resists fading.
- **ACRYLICS** sew up easily into soft furnishings and curtains. They dry quickly, don't mildew, and look and feel like indoor fabrics. Check tent, awning, and fabric stores for acrylics.
- **LAMINATED COTTON** yard goods are made for outdoor use. Or waterproof your own fabrics with iron-on vinyl available at fabric stores. Natural fabrics fade and mildew with time, so reserve them for sheltered areas.

LEFT: Defined by columns and protected from rain and sun by a covered pergola, this off-the-kitchen patio encourages after-dinner relaxing on cushioned teak and wicker seating; it can host dinner itself on a table that winters indoors. OPPOSITE: Most of the bad weather comes from the south here, so the clever builders of this home added a south-facing "window" to the covered porch to protect wicker seating—dressed in country-print fabrics—from wind and rain.

ABOVE: Cool green with crisp white trim, this cottage porch has roll-down shades to fend off glare and comfortably slipcovered chairs for settle-back ease. The inviting grouping is anchored by a leafy area rug and a round oak dining table that was cut down to tea-table height and painted white. Lamps invite lingering long after the sun has gone down—on mosquito-free spring and fall evenings, that is.

Fresh-Air Style

Once you've settled on how you want your outdoor room to function, translate the "how" into what furnishings you'll need. If you want to sink into a lazy afternoon, a cushioned chaise is a must. Conjure simpler times with an old-fashioned porch swing or glider; or create a sleeping porch with a daybed or futon sofa that doubles as daytime seating. Even little luxuries—a fan for sultry summer nights, a quilt for crisp fall evenings, a waterproof lamp for reading—add up to a peaceful oasis.

PICK PORCH-FRIENDLY FURNISHINGS

Consider indoor furniture for protected outdoor areas. An extra coat of paint or varnish and fresh slipcovers and cushions made of washable, mildew-resistant fabrics and fillings can make these pieces weather-hardy. If your furniture is a jumble of flea market finds, paint all the pieces in a single hue to create unity. Keep accent colors flowing with fabrics on cushions, pillows, shades, table linens, rugs, and also on collectible accessories.

THE GREAT INDOORS

Put porch-friendly furnishings and nature-inspired accents in reverse, and create a garden room indoors. When cold weather chases you off your real porch, you'll still have your place in the sun. Well, almost. Set the indoor mood with outdoor standards, such as Adirondack chairs, wrought-iron tables, and wicker pieces. Add slipcovers and cushions with washable covers so you—and Rover—won't be afraid to put your feet up. Choose bright accents and botanical-print fabrics for summery color and style, rugged textures that speak of wild places, and painted woods with comfortably worn surfaces.

ABOVE: An iron bed sets the scene for this romantic sleeping porch. Piled with comforters and set on a painted wood floor, the bed makes an irresistible fair-weather sleeping or lounging spot. A great temporary guest room as is, the porch would need roll-down shades to fend off rain and a waterproof cover for the mattress and box spring if the bed was to be left out all summer.

GetAway to the Garden

Whether you head for the deck or create an outdoor room for relaxing

in your lush shade garden, you'll naturally want to bring along the comforts of home—at least cushioned seating and a table for books and the lemonade pitcher. A fireplace, fire pit, or chimenea warms guests on cool nights, and burbling fountains always add a relaxing touch.

A LASTING OASIS

Outdoor furniture can be as big an investment as indoor pieces, so here are some tips to help you choose wisely.

- **ALUMINUM** is lightweight, durable, and rustproof. It comes in wrought or cast forms with a baked-on enamel or textured finish. Cast-aluminum pieces are more expensive. Look for thick, heavy-gauge alloys and smooth seams on welded parts.
- **IRON** is good for windy climates. Made from cast or wrought steel, it's heavier and less expensive than aluminum, but it rusts and may need more upkeep.
- **WICKER** must go under cover unless it's synthetic all-weather wicker. On new wicker, look for aluminum frames and baked-on polyester finish.
- **MOST WOODS** require at least a yearly coat of paint or varnish.
- **PLASTIC** lasts for years. PVC (polyvinyl chloride) furniture is made of plastic piping joined together. Resin furniture can be molded into various shapes.
- **CUSHIONS** need to weather the elements. Pick waterproof and mildew-resistant fabric covers; covers and fillings should allow water drainage. It's always best to take cushions indoors during storms.
- **PAINT** designed for outdoors protects furniture. Exterior enamel paints last longer than flat finishes. Industrial paints contain more binders to adhere paint to surfaces, and they're more fade-resistant. For bright colors, ask for industrial safety paints.

ABOVE: Stepping into this outdoor "family room," created with salvaged brick and cement-walled planters, is like taking a quick trip to Provence. The garage is dressed in lattice to improve the view. The flea market table and metal chairs serve up dinner. **OPPOSITE:** This 700-square-foot home grabbed extra living space from the garden, where inexpensive lattice creates privacy for an intimate sitting spot. Weathered collections and salvaged finds such as the marble slab atop the console accent the space.

Homegrown Hospitality

When you fire up the grill and set the table outdoors, serving even the simplest fare becomes a special occasion. With an orchestra of birds and cicadas providing the background music, you can settle back and savor good food and good friends.

ENTERTAINING OPTIONS

This rambling, two-level terrace located in a steeply sloping backyard offers a choice of seating and dining options, depending on the time of day, and it boasts an outdoor kitchen too. Here are some entertaining ideas for your next alfresco party:

■ **INVITE GUESTS INTO THE GARDEN,** or bring the garden to them by accenting your outdoor "room" with intriguing and colorful containers filled with plants and homegrown bouquets.

■ **ADD NIGHT GLOW WITH SUBTLE LIGHTING.** Set candles in windproof hurricane chimneys; bring lamps from the house or buy new waterproof ones that can live outside; and line a fireplace or porch railing with votive candles. Tiki torches make practical and festive outdoor accents; when filled with citronella oil, they help fend off mosquitoes.

■ **SOFTEN WITH FABRIC.** Plump up seating with pillows or borrow accent pillows from inside. Frame a porch with tieback curtains in gauzy fabric or with cabana-striped cotton duck hung from grommets and hooks.

■ **SUIT YOUR MOOD.** Feeling casual? Ice beverages in galvanized tubs and let new terra-cotta pots offer napkins and utensils. In the mood for formal? Set a porch table with china, crystal, and linens from the formal dining room.

RIGHT: Indoor amenities—comfortable seating, a coffee table, lots of candles, and even a lamp—make gathering at the fireside under the stars a fair-weather ritual. The brick fireplace was designed with multiple levels for displaying antique accessories and potted plants.

LEFT: In the lower-level dining spot, votives in blossom-shaped holders encircle the iron table's centerpiece bouquet. The birds miss their evening scrub because chunky, scented candles cluster in the birdbath. **BELOW:** With made-for-the-shade cover-ups, such as the table's big market umbrella and a vine-draped pergola over the outdoor kitchen, this terrace hosts casual meals on the sunniest days. Container plants blur the boundary between terrace and garden.

Deck Out
A Ho-Hum Deck

Like an empty room awaiting furniture delivery, this 15-year-old, five-sided deck was anything but a dream oasis for alfresco parties and lazy summer afternoons. Easy, affordable fixes changed all of that, and now this slice of the suburbs has a countrified air.

■ **SEMITRANSPARENT DECK STAINS** in evergreen and cream hues create the checkerboard "area rug" on the pressure-treated floor. A bedsheet was used to determine the size and position of the painted rug, 93 inches square and composed of 15-inch painted diamonds within a 9-inch-wide border. The design was plotted with a T square and chalk line, starting at one 90-degree corner. Starting at the center, cream diamonds were stained first and dried before staining green diamonds.

■ **ARCHITECTURAL SALVAGE** adds instant age, structure, and color. Four shutter panels, hinged together, create a portable privacy screen with country flavor. Simple painted doors act as wallcovering. Finials stained to match the floor hang from the soffit by wire and cup hooks. Spandrels screwed atop deck rails add a porch look. If you can't find salvaged elements, use new and affordable machine-milled trims.

■ **DECK SIDES GAIN PARK-BENCH APPEAL** from stained porch boards punctuated with X-shape cutouts and nailed to the back of the deck's built-in wraparound bench.

■ **RUSTIC SEATING,** a potting bench, container plants, and weather-hardy accents add function and set the new mood.

BEFORE

ABOVE: Portable furnishings and accents, such as the shutter screen, folding chair, and lightweight table, give this deck flexibility. The furnishings can be rearranged to fit entertaining needs or easily toted indoors for the winter. **OPPOSITE:** Surrounded by blooming plants and timeworn accents, rustic twig seating invites all comers to sit a spell and survey the deck redo and garden. Adding the painted potting bench gives this gardener's retreat additional work and display space.

BrushOnOutdoorColor

A mix of old or new furniture under a broad brush of white or colorful paints gives any outdoor space a fresh air.

For wicker, use stain-blocking primer and spray paint. Use rust-preventing primer and paints on cleaned metal furniture. For wood pieces, clean and sand the surfaces, prime, and apply paints designed for outdoor use. Here are two projects to make your outdoor living area more comfortable—and more fun.

COLOR-BLOCK ROCKERS

Pretty pastel paints put a fresh face on these classic rocking chairs, giving them a lighthearted spin. The color-block approach turns unfinished or second-hand slat-back rockers into artful seating anywhere. Use the same color blocking on Adirondack chairs or wooden benches, painting slats and trim details in different shades. Before painting rockers, work out color combinations for each chair and select several hues—here it's pale yellow, blue, green, and purple—of semigloss paint suitable for outdoor use. Sand and prime chairs. Paint the body of each chair one color and use accent hues on slats, finials, and stretchers. Use an artist's brush to apply bands of paint to finials and trim. Seal with exterior paint sealer.

REFURBISHED WOOD TABLE

This easy-to-make table is made with an old wood table base from a secondhand store. It's a perfect project for making use of a table with a solid base but a badly damaged top. Remove the tabletop; sand the base. Prime it with exterior primer and let dry; apply exterior paint. Top the base with a bevel-edge round of glass. Look for glass tabletops at crafts and import stores, or have one custom-cut at glass shops. (Plate glass tops are fine for a covered porch like this; on an exposed deck or patio use tempered glass.)

ABOVE: Brighten sturdy painted or stained chairs with your own color blocking. To re-create this kind of color play, choose chairs with ornate finials, trims, and turnings that you can detail with contrasting exterior paint colors. OPPOSITE: This easy-to-make table teams old and new. A round glass top (some import stores have several sizes of glass rounds in stock) reshapes a painted farm table for stylish outdoor dining. The table is also handy for letter writing, crafts, and games.

CHAPTER 13

Beginnings

Empty rooms can be intimidating. Where do you start decorating? What style story will you write for your space? Filled with decorating strategies, this chapter begins with the tales of two homes: One is a dark, dated cottage that yearned to be pure and simple. The other home is a brand-new, blank-canvas townhome longing for color and character. Warm, welcoming spaces, like this sunny living room, all start the same way—with a plan.

Finesse for Less

Finesse for Less

KATHY AND TOM SOHN OF SAN DIEGO, CALIFORNIA

PREVIOUS PAGES: Fresh paint turned Kathy's mom's old kitchen table into a new-generation occasional table pretty and functional enough to serve living room love seats. Paired with a trio of insect prints that Kathy framed, the vintage console table creates an "entry" for the tiny cottage. Accents are pared to a few favorite white and silver pieces. **BELOW:** After making their rooms warm and bright, Tom and Kathy Sohn took their style outside, flanking the front door with potted privet topiaries and perennials. **OPPOSITE:** Instead of a large sofa, twin love seats make friendlier, more flexible seating in the small living room; slipcovers guarantee easy care. The coffee table is a new wood bench that can double as extra seating when the couple entertains.

First came love. Then, for Kathy and Tom Sohn, came marriage and a few raids on her mother's garage to shop for cast-off furniture for their first home. They added a few secondhand and unfinished pieces, but the crucial stop was the paint store. Color by the gallon made the furnishings mix a family and their 1,200-square-foot beach cottage feel larger. "The big thing was lightening it up and making it airy," says Kathy, who takes cottage style beyond plain white. "I definitely have color, but it's a clean feeling, kind of refreshing."

EASY, BREEZY BEAUTY

After they whitewashed the original pine ceiling, removed wooden blinds, and rolled soft yellow color over the walls, the stage was set for their spray-painted oldies and a few functional splurges.

Decorating on a newlywed budget, Kathy and Tom prioritized for function, spending the biggest chunk of their dollars on a pair of small sofas. "I like that shabby chic kind of feel that's really comfortable," says Kathy. To fit the beachy look and lifestyle of the cottage, she intentionally picked slipcover fabrics in prints and solid hues that hide a little dirt. "My parents' house has everything white, and it was hard as a kid in a white-white house," she says.

The couple learned at least one major decorating lesson: Pick fabrics before the wall color. They didn't, and finding the perfect yellow for curtains took a while. Instead of pricey hardware, the curtain rods consist of two wood poles screwed together and painted white. Restraint and patience are keys to accessorizing their small space. Kathy bought cheap framed pictures, then substituted fruit prints from an antiques store. An old metal magazine rack, a carved wooden tray, or any fitting accent is fair game for a shot of white paint. They buy bargain lamps separately, then have fun searching for cool shades.

"This is the perfect first house for us," Kathy says. "It's manageable, nothing too daunting." Tom says he's learned a lot about decorating: "It's a process, and I'm the mover. I love it. I'm such a believer in what she can do." Their next project? It's the rosebud-wallpaper bath.

ABOVE: The couple finds that the whites they love are a perfect foil for a tactile mix of weathered and natural woods, including the dining table and chairs. Whether new or old, character-rich light fixtures, such as the chandelier, are a priority. **OPPOSITE:** When they painted the old green cabinets white, they removed the doors to let open shelves visually expand the small kitchen. Simply designed pottery bowls, dishes, and glassware create artful displays.

Pale paints, pale fabrics, and a pure and simple touch turn the ordinary into extraordinary.

OPPOSITE: One great find from Kathy's mom's garage is this hand-me-down dressing table. With a little paint and a soft skirt, attached with hook-and-loop tape, it doubles as a guest room nightstand. **1** Kathy tacked inexpensive sheers at the guest room window, leaving the ties to flutter in the breeze. **2** Glass knobs

from an antiques store and spray paint give this basic chest from an unfinished furniture store a cottage look. The picture frame was a gift, but it's easy to make using spray paint and painter's tape to mask off stripes on a plain wood frame. **3** In the master bedroom, embroidered and eyelet-trim linens are a mix of old and new. The flower-filled garden window becomes the headboard. **4** Tucked between a new arbor and rose-covered wall, weathered secondhand furniture creates a private backyard spot for relaxing and entertaining friends and family.

Take the New off New

Take the New off New

SANDY HAYES AND DAUGHTER KIT OF TAMPA, FLORIDA

Sandy Hayes will always be a gardener at heart, but she's downscaled to a new townhome with no flower patch she can call her own. Her past homes overlooked water and woods, but her best "view" now is the patio where she's coaxing lush bougainvillea up the lattice. "With no yard or garden, I wasn't going to have Mother Nature to help me," she says. "The eye had to be entertained inside." That's where her garden grows with the color, fabrics, and art she loves.

CHARACTER ON CALL

Did she want walls painted white, eggshell, or cream, the builder asked. None of the above, she said. What about kitchen cabinets? Pop the door panels, and ship just the door frames, she said. "I had a relatively clean slate, and I was determined to put my mark on it," she explains.

Sandy and her daughter, Kit, were eager to get cheery color on the walls before moving in, but Tampa interior designer Debbie Perez advised them to wait and experiment after the furniture arrived. "We bought pint-size cans of greens and yellows and decorated our walls and looked at it morning, noon, and night," Sandy says. The winning green for their open-plan living room, kitchen, and breakfast spot reminds her of watermelons.

After living in "serious traditional homes," mother and daughter decided they'd go casual here. Purchasing a modular, twin-chaise sofa ended one dispute. "We had been fighting over who got the

sofa for the Saturday afternoon snooze," says Sandy, who had the three pieces upholstered in two fabrics—a whimsical topiary-and-bumblebee print and a coordinating plaid to accent curves.

New crown moldings, a fireplace, and built-ins add architectural character. Sandy found ways to include touchstones of the outdoors, including a pantry screen door, screening on built-ins, chicken wire over fabric on kitchen cabinetry, sea-grass area rugs, and roosters and roses on the chandeliers. "The pantry door catches everybody's eye, and they love it," she says.

As you move through the home, the mood changes with color, toile wallcovering, and faux finishes, but there's always a touch of black. "It's my anchor for the other colors," Sandy says. She browses antiques shops and art fairs, looking for old French posters, original art, and pottery. She can't pass up a treasure, so she changes what she displays when new items catch her eye. "I have to work at editing," she says. "I'm still guilty of 'it's not done until it's overdone.' It's the sense of homeyness that gets me right to that edge."

PREVIOUS PAGES: Although the living room is small, sacrificing 3 feet for a new fireplace and furniture-look built-ins is a smart trade-off. Silver-screening inserts look airier than solid doors. Original artwork above the mantel features the colors used throughout her home. With scant gardening space outside, a weathered planter on the mantel satisfies the owner's green thumb. RIGHT: Decorating their new townhome was a team effort for Sandy Hayes and her daughter, Kit, who collaborated on a wish list and made casual, colorful comfort their priority. OPPOSITE: From the fresh green walls to plaid and topiary-print fabrics on the modular, double-chaise sofa, design elements draw the outdoors into the living room. Old painted shutters were out on the patio and waiting to be made into a coffee table when Sandy came up with a better idea: To give a blank wall in the living room more focus, she paired the shutters with one of the French advertising posters from her collection and then pulled in a 1700s pine hall bench to supplement seating.

By adding color to a plain-vanilla builder home, Sandy stamped her style all over it. Now it's a wow!

ABOVE: Clad in green paint and new copper screening, an old screen door replaces the pantry's solid door to give the breakfast room down-home appeal. The table has a junk shop base, repainted and topped with distressed maple. Down-filled cushions make seating extra soft. **OPPOSITE:** The original cabinet doors created a boring living room-to-kitchen view, so Sandy perked up the doors and the view with chicken wire inserts over checked fabric.

OPPOSITE: A peaceful neutral palette romances the master bedroom. A dramatic, hand-forged iron bed is dressed luxuriously in toile curtains and custom linens. Faux paint finishes age the new bed and give walls the look of aged plaster. **ABOVE RIGHT:** Others might have turned this off-the-foyer space into a living room, but Sandy and Kit wanted a homey home office they could share for business and homework. With plenty of pattern in this small room, they kept furniture, such as the pine desk and ladder bookshelves, leggy and light in scale. **BELOW RIGHT:** Portieres in gingham-trimmed cotton duck soften the entry. When the sofa couldn't squeeze up the stairs, it moved in and donned a slipcover. An heirloom blanket chest serves as the coffee table. The area rug is sea grass banded in black.

Decorate Step-By-Step

Homes are creative works in progress because change happens to everyone.

Families grow, jobs switch, tastes evolve, you downscale, you upscale, or you move. That's why instantly decorating an entire room isn't wise, and it's hard on the budget. Satisfy basic comforts and functions first; then phase in other design elements. Depending on your priorities, you may find it's best to invest in a great bed before bedroom carpet, or in living room seating before a formal, holidays-only dining table.

SET PRIORITIES

Wish lists are a good start, but go a step further: List your practical

needs and set a realistic budget. What are your priorities? What are your room's natural resources—a fireplace, a bay window, great built-ins? What furniture do you need now? What can wait? You may want an interior designer's help in planning and in providing access to designer-only products. Fees vary from hourly to a per-project basis; some furniture stores and home centers offer free design services.

TAKE YOUR TIME

For fun, leave space for special future finds—a bargain antique rug, Grandma's rocker, or that sleek new table you find online.

■ **ADOPT AN EASY-DOES-IT APPROACH.** Add elements little by little so you don't obscure a room's character. Prop framed art on the mantel before deciding where to hang it; let a settee settle into its surroundings before choosing a cushion fabric.

■ **KEEP IT SIMPLE.** Instead of patterned upholstery, complicated window treatments, and trendy colors, consider solid fabrics and neutral backdrops if you're unsure of your taste; they're easy to change as your confidence grows.

■ **KNOW WHEN TO STOP.** Leave breathing room. Take a periodic inventory to see if furnishings are meeting your needs or if they need editing.

■ **MIX PRICE POINTS.** Use budget-priced fill-ins as you slowly acquire high-quality pieces. The bonus? With an old or unfinished piece or two, you'll create a more interesting furnishings mix.

LEFT: A classic sofa and bamboo tables make a great start. Skirted chairs from the dining room are money-saving fill-ins. **BELOW:** As the room evolves, new armchairs and toss pillows add bolder color and pattern—a look enhanced by red candles. Tall, slim curtain panels frame the sheers, adding vertical drama that's played up by a fence-board screen aged with dabs of red paint.

ABOVE: Anchored by a space-defining rug, major seating pieces gather around the fireplace. A secondary sitting spot at the window serves as a place for reading and one-on-one conversation. A tall, full ficus tree balances the height and heft of the combined fireplace-mantel-painting focal point.

Plan on Paper

Space is a coveted commodity in the home, but it's how you arrange and furnish your rooms—not square footage—that creates comfort and convenience. Even small rooms live big if you put the right pieces in the right places. But how to decide? Forget tugging furniture here and there to see how it looks. Measure your room and furniture, pull up an easy chair, and explore your room's options on paper. Or use our interactive room arranging kit at bhg.com. Get started with the following tips. *(Turn to the "Arranging" chapter, pages 260–285, for more advice and a Better Homes and Gardens room-arranging kit.)*

MADE TO MEASURE

■ **DRAW A PLAN TO SCALE.** Transfer your room's measurements to graph paper. Make one square (¼ inch) equal to 1 foot. Using the same scale, draw your own templates of furniture on paper; note the height, depth, and width of each piece. Or photocopy our templates on plain paper and cut them out. Because color carries visual weight, shade templates with colored markers.

■ **NOTE ARCHITECTURAL FEATURES.** Mark closets, built-ins, fireplaces, electrical outlets and switches, lighting, and heat sources. Note the clearances and opening directions of doors and windows.

■ **SITE MAJOR PIECES FIRST.** Seating was the priority for the family living room here. It's focused toward the fireplace and wicker coffee table with room to move comfortably between pieces.

■ **ZONE FOR TRAFFIC.** Allow a 4-foot-wide path for traffic in entries and at least 30 inches for other walkways. For conversation areas, group sofas and chairs a maximum of 8 feet apart. Leave 14 to 18 inches between a sofa and coffee table and at least 3 feet of pullout space behind dining chairs.

■ **MAKE A LIFE-SIZE PLAN.** If it's difficult to visualize your room from tiny templates, tape newspaper sheets together to create full-size templates to place on your floor, or stack empty cardboard boxes to approximate your own furniture sizes.

ABOVE: Backed up to the sofa, this slim table is a high-function addition that takes up little space. It holds lamps, stores books, and displays an array of personal accessories. LEFT: To make furnishings fit, arrange your own cut-to-scale templates on graph paper, use computer software, or use our room-arranging kit, which begins on page 280.

TO FIND OUT MORE ONLINE, VISIT US
☞ @ www.bhg.com/bkhousehome

Smart Shopping

Take your time when exploring the dizzying array of retailers, discount stores, custom shops, online

businesses, and catalogs. Browse first, buy later. Peruse books and magazines to study styles and construction; then comtrast items in all price ranges. Compare when buying high-ticket items. Here are tips for buying quality furniture:

UPHOLSTERY AND WOODS

■ **BE SURE YOUR FURNITURE WILL FIT.** When you shop, take along your to-scale floor plan, a tape measure, and fabric and color samples.

■ **TEST-DRIVE UPHOLSTERED SEATING.** Sit on it, lean on it, lift it up, and turn it over to check comfort and construction. Frames should be kiln-dried, seasoned hardwood joined by dowels or interlocking pieces, not butted together. Tempered-steel springs are coil or sagless; eight-way, hand-tied springs denote good quality. Polyurethane foam is the most common filling; down is softer and more costly. *(Consult the "Fabrics" chapter, pages 336–357, before selecting upholstery fabrics.)*

■ **KNOW YOUR WOODS.** When shopping for case goods, the industry term for chests and cabinets, check hangtags and labels to learn which woods or veneers are used in them. Look for strong construction where pieces bear the most weight—legs, shelves, braces, drawers. Check that doors and drawers open and shut easily and that finishes are hard and smooth with no visible imperfections.

■ **BONE UP ON HISTORY.** If you're buying reproductions, know period details and craftsmanship. Reproductions are exact copies of antiques, usually made with the same materials and detail; adaptations are loosely based on original pieces; visual reproductions are made with modern shortcuts to hold down costs.

OPPOSITE: When buying upholstered furniture, find the best value by balancing the quality of the fabric with the inside construction. Some furniture lines come with optional wardrobes of slipcovers, such as the cleanable cover-up on this chair.

WAVE SPRINGS Used on the sofa back, they're covered with a thin layer of padding when loose back pillows will be used.

PILLOW BACK When the pillow is a part of the back construction, the wave springs are topped by individually pocketed coil springs or foam.

SPRING CUSHIONS In high-quality sofas, seat cushions are made from individually pocketed coil springs or from latex foam. Budget sofas use less dense foam.

HARDWOOD FRAME Hardwoods such as oak are the most durable, but semi-hardwoods in 1¼- to 1½-inch dimensions are good too. Low-quality frames use softwoods or plywood.

DOWEL AND SCREW JOINTS Good sofas use dowels at the joints; cheap ones don't. All frames should use glue, screws or staples, and corner blocks.

EXTRA PADDING Every surface of the sofa should be padded, including the front rail; padding makes fabric last longer. You shouldn't be able to feel wood anywhere—even on the outside back.

CUSHION PADDING Spring cushions are covered in foam, down, cotton, or polyester fiberfill.

EIGHT-WAY, HAND-TIED SPRINGS are the longest-lasting. Coil springs are each tied with cording to surrounding springs and the frame.

Mix In Some Character

Antiques, quirky-but-sturdy flea market finds, and vintage handcrafted pieces lend unrivaled character to your home. A few aged pieces—whether curvy Victorian or sleek Heywood-Wakefield—can give rooms a burst of personality. Scout secondhand stores, online auctions, and local dealers, keeping these shopping tips in mind:

■ **KNOW YOUR DEALER.** If you're looking for antiques, generally defined as

objects more than 100 years old, consult a reputable dealer. A piece is more valuable if it has a known maker and date, fine design, original hardware and finish, and no damage or repairs. Antiques are a major investment; you don't want to pay top dollar and then discover you bought a reproduction, not an original.

■ **KNOW THE MARKET.** Whether you want Louis XV, Shaker, American primitive, or mid-century modern, study up on history, construction details, and recent auction and retail prices.

■ **CHECK THE CONDITION.** Wood frames should be sound with no sign of termite damage or dry rot. If legs are wobbly, finishes are marred, or upholstery is worn, factor repairs into the total cost before you buy.

■ **IS IT TRUE LOVE?** The antiques market is mercurial, so buy for love, not money. Whether its price is high or low, you'll always find a place for something you love. And don't worry about mixing woods, finishes, even eras; variety builds character.

OPPOSITE: Mixing new pieces with sentimental favorites, such as a turned-leg table and a butternut chair from two grandmothers, adds charm and preserves family ties. CENTER: Vintage chairs and a bench—all linked by golden tones—gather around a rugged table. The server? A worn chest. Beaded-board paneling covers the back of the open bookshelves for more character. BELOW: Leaving kitchen duty behind, an antique pie safe moves to the living room to stow audio gear and bring rich texture to the bright white setting.

Investment Dressing

You've got some of the best decorating inspiration
in your closet. There's the little black dress or classic navy blue blazer that, dressed up or down with accessories, goes anywhere and always looks great. Start collecting your home's wardrobe of versatile, well-designed basics to mix, match, and move around today and in future homes. To nail down your decorating style, clip magazine photos of rooms and design elements you love; then spread them out and see what they have in common.

VERSATILE PICKS

Whether your home is large or small, build on classic, adaptable pieces, such as modular shelves and bookcases, daybeds, armoires, storage ottomans, sectional sofas, armchairs, parsons chairs, folding screens, and flip-top, round, and sofa tables.

■ **CHOOSE SIMPLE UPHOLSTERY.** If you're starting out and unsure of your future decorating taste, consider neutral fabrics for classic seating; you can add colorful toss pillows or slipcovers later.

■ **RETHINK THAT LONG SOFA.** Love seats and upholstered chairs, instead of conventional long sofas, offer room-arranging versatility. They can face off around a coffee table, form a right angle in a corner, float inward to define a conversation spot, or split up to serve two rooms.

■ **GIVE EACH ROOM A FOCAL-POINT PIECE.** Armoires, superstar beds, and oversize art offer grand scale, impact, and character, and they become flexible centerpieces of future homes and redesigns.

■ **RELY ON EASY MIXERS.** Whites, wood, wicker, and brushed metals make congenial companions.

■ **BUY WELL-DESIGNED PIECES** one at a time, instead of matched suites. It's OK to mix pieces of all price ranges. If you're timid about mixing, let one mood (formal, cottage, modern, whatever you love) dominate. Feeling braver? Mix in a style surprise—a modern coffee table with that traditional sofa, for instance.

ABOVE: No matter where you put a handsome armoire, it's bound to steal the show, and it neatly stows everything from a tangle of electronics gear to clothes. This cherry wood beauty with frosted-glass inserts blends contemporary and Shaker spirit. **OPPOSITE:** Even the quirkiest floor plans welcome sectional sofas, because the pieces can be reconfigured to fit the space. Simply styled and comfortable, this versatile seating hugs the right angle of corner windows and frees up floor space.

A Built-In Reborn

Like it or not, this built-in behemoth was the small living room's focal point, but its dark, looming presence almost scared off the home's buyers. Measuring in at about 8 feet long and 6 feet tall, the stained walnut cabinet with 1970s colonial details didn't fit the new homeowners' light-and-airy style. They planned to tear out the intimidator, but a design-savvy friend came to the rescue with reasons to save it. The wood

was good, as was the construction, and the homeowners needed display space. Besides, a small home can't afford to toss out storage. Let this redo inspire you to turn your own dark storage piece into a focal-point star.

- **REMOVE CABINET CONTENTS.** Remove any glass shelves, doors, and hardware. Then wipe down and sand.
- **PRIME, THEN PAINT.** Apply two coats of linen-white semigloss paint. The white-out disguises dated colonial styling.
- **RESTYLE FOR DISPLAY.** Here, some glass shelves were discarded to create taller display slots. The glass doors were not replaced; hinge holes were filled with putty before painting.
- **REFRESH HARDWARE.** Matte metallic paint gives old hinges on the lower doors a brushed-nickel look. Inexpensive metal pulls replace drawer handles; old handle screw holes were filled with wood putty before painting.
- **LIGHT YOUR TREASURES.** This cabinet's interior lights were retained. No lights? Buy shelf strip lights at the home center; they simply stick on and plug in.

ABOVE: Dark and overpowering, this built-in was worth saving. Besides offering storage space, the unit creates a focal point for the small living room. **OPPOSITE:** Removing the busy glass doors streamlines the storage piece, making more of its crown and dentil molding. Paint turns the built-in into a gallery-white showcase for the owners' favorite things. *(For fun, see these shelves accented in different styles on pages 308–309.)*

CHAPTER 14

Arranging

Arranging easy-living spaces is like assembling pieces of a puzzle so rooms can flow smoothly, welcome comfortably, and look oh-so-inviting.

But which furniture pieces go where? Are there options beyond the typical sofa, chairs, and coffee table grouping? Radiating like spokes of a wheel from the center table, this quartet of sink-in seats says, "Yes!" Use the ideas in this chapter to explore other options and consider how you might reshape your own spaces. Then get to work with our room-arranging kit.

Wide-Open Style

Wide-Open Style

ED SARGENT OF HOUSTON, TEXAS

HOMETOUR

There was plenty of room to roam around Wichita Falls, Texas, where Ed Sargent grew up, but the wide-open spaces that intrigued him were pure fantasy. What would it be like to live in a rambling, New York-style place—slick, sophisticated, and all skyline views—like those in the movies and on television? With a divide-and-conquer plan and scaled-up comfort, Ed turned his fantasy into reality—a new Houston loft.

"I was always fascinated with movies where they have these wonderful lofts and big open spaces," Ed says. "You think 'I could never live that way,' but you take that as a starting point, then improve on it to suit your personality and your space."

A LIFT FOR THE LOFT

Ed wanted the new loft to look like an old, renovated space, so he artfully aged textured walls and stained concrete floors to mimic leather. Slick, modern finishes—stone, concrete, metals, and glass—lose their cold, warehouse character juxtaposed against the warm beige walls, mellow woods, and rich primary colors, including Ed's favorite cobalt blue. Expanding an upper-level "loft

within a loft" created more privacy for a master suite. When your ceilings soar 21 feet high, off-the-rack furnishings look puny, so Houston interior designer John Robinson created massive pieces—a 12-foot-long sofa and 14-foot-tall bookcases—as modulars so they would fit into the building's elevator.

"There's a side of me that likes that minimal, industrial look, but it's a home, and you want to soften it up and feel warm and comfortable," Ed says. He used an unexpected and stylish mix of commercial fabrics for upholstered seating and covered an upstairs wall in the fabric used for office cubicles.

He also reupholstered the Eames chairs that he used as a kid. His father, he recalls, thought they were pricey when his mother bought them for $40 apiece in the 1950s. "No one knew they were classics—they weren't then," he says.

Ed tempers the sleek furnishings with collections of primitive wood pieces and eclectic sculpture, art, and pottery from his travels and a Peace Corps stint in Micronesia. "It's sort of a dream come true. It turned out much better than I anticipated," Ed says. "It's absolutely the best for entertaining. I've had 200 people here, and it's wonderful. Nobody is isolated."

PREVIOUS PAGES: Stepped three-tier bookcases anchor one side of the living room and offer plenty of display space for mementos, art, and sculpture along with an extensive library. The bookcases are standard black metal units encased in a custom mahogany shell. On the opposite wall, sheetrock and stacked granite create the stepped effect around the fireplace and entertainment center behind doors. BELOW: Ed Sargent relishes both the open, relaxed ambience of loft living and his high-rise view of the Houston skyline. OPPOSITE: With no defining interior walls, furniture arrangements create "rooms" within the loft and make the space ideal for entertaining. Guests can move from the stools around the kitchen bar to the railed media room upstairs and still be connected to action in the living room below. Extensive track lighting on dimmers manages the mood and accents. Structural columns emit an ambient glow from lighting hidden around the bases and capitals.

Color, texture, and a think-big attitude warm up lofty spaces. "You want to feel comfortable," Ed says.

ABOVE: The dramatic view of Houston's skyline is "incredible at night" and always the unrivaled focus of the living room that draws its bold palette of primary colors from the Russian rug. Against a backdrop faux-finished to mimic aged plaster, the extra-long sectional sofa and towering bookshelves offer comfort and function on a grand, Texas-size scale. **OPPOSITE:** Beneath the upper-deck living spaces, the kitchen is defined by an eating bar; its mahogany cabinetry echoes the palette's warm tones. Diamond-pattern aluminum covers the backsplash, refrigerator doors, and columns. The dining area floats in a space furnished with classic 1950s Eames chairs placed around a glass table with a stainless-steel base.

OPPOSITE: The upstairs "loft" is a music lover's retreat, complete with a built-in entertainment center that has pullout drawers, a mini-bar, and a refrigerator. Track lighting accents a collection of Acoma pottery from New Mexico. **1** Ed commissioned this original painting that honors the creativity of man and

machine. It hangs high on the stairway wall so both levels enjoy a view of it. **2** In the master bath, light flows through the shower's curved glass-block wall, and the chrome-accented vanity seems to float between the slate floor and countertop. **3** A triangular wall-hung desk turns a potentially useless corner in the master bedroom into an office with a view. Mail racks hang on a wall of metal screening on an aluminum frame. **4** Incorporating a structural column for impact, the master bedroom's headboard is upholstered and slightly concave for comfy lounging. Side shelves hold books and other treasures.

FloorPlan Basics

What's your definition of comfort?

Do you like to curl up, stretch out, or rest your feet on the coffee table? Do you prefer a room that accommodates hobbies or one with plenty of seating for family movie nights? Do you usually entertain a crowd or only a few friends? Before you arrange your furnishings, decide what you want your room to do and how your family lives. *(For more on floor-plan basics, see pages 70–73 in "Living Rooms," pages 100–101 in "Dining Rooms," pages 118–119 in "Bedrooms," and pages 250–251 and 256–257 in "Beginnings.")*

ARRANGE TO SUIT YOURSELF

Successful arrangements don't depend on the style or status of your furnishings. What matters is how your pieces work together and relate in the overall space.

■ **FIND A FOCAL POINT.** It's the cornerstone of your arrangement. A fireplace or a spectacular view can fill the bill. (Need to focus on both the fire and the view? Angle major seating pieces accordingly.) In rooms without a natural focus, group furnishings around a bold painting, free-standing shelves, a tall cupboard or armoire, or a wall artfully hung with collectibles.

■ **SUBTRACT TO ADD; DIVIDE TO MULTIPLY.** Could you open up floor space by deleting some nonessential furnishings? Would the room be more livable if you added more furniture to divide the space into activity centers?

■ **BEND THE SO-CALLED RULES TO CUSTOMIZE YOUR SPACE.** The sofa doesn't need to be anchored to a cocktail table. Dining tables don't need to be centered, and beds don't have to hug walls. Different plans might be more comfortable and convenient for your lifestyle.

■ **MAKE ROOM FOR PERSONALITY.** Surrounding yourself with the furnishings and collections you love is the key to making a room satisfying, so factor in display space for the treasures that will make the room truly yours.

> **TO FIND OUT MORE ONLINE, VISIT US**
> @ www.bhg.com/bkarrangearoom

1 **A HAND-PAINTED WALL** in the entry, wrought-iron accents, and sculpture enhance this home's fresh take on Spanish style.

2 **AN END TABLE AND LAMP** tuck into the corner between the sofa and chairs. The coffee table is large enough to serve the wing chair, which has its own floor lamp for an on-the-side reading spot.

3 **TRAFFIC PATHS** are marked by furniture. A fireside wing chair and demilune table flank the route to the terrace, and high-back dining chairs and the back of the sofa define the path between separate seating and dining areas.

4 **ON THE SEA OF DIAGONALLY SET FLOOR TILE,** an antique Oriental carpet defines the conversation island and leads the eye to the hearth.

5 **MULTIPLE ENTRYWAYS** in this expansive Mediterranean-style great-room minimize wall space available for furnishings. As a result, the sofa and paired chairs float mid-room at a right angle, focused on the fireplace. The curvaceous sofa was chosen because it looks beautiful from the back as well as from the front.

6 **AN ORNATE IRON CHANDELIER** illuminates the dining area; it matches the visual weight of the fireplace to maintain balance in this soaring space.

Direct Traffic

When the party's over, notice the messages your guests left behind. Did they pull chairs and an ottoman off the beaten path and into a corner for undisturbed conversation? Did they edge modular seating closer to the television so they could watch the game without people traipsing by the screen? These are clues to how you can make your everyday furniture arrangements more comfortable and convenient. After all, entertaining is the best test of the suitability of the traffic patterns in your home.

GO WITH THE FLOW

Convenience means grouping your furniture to promote traffic flow and encourage whatever activities you've planned for your rooms. Use furniture as curbs to funnel traffic around seating or a hobby or homework table or to channel traffic through a family room/dining spot to the backyard.

■ **HALT CROSS-TRAFFIC.** If pedestrians interrupt conversation by constantly cutting through the main sitting area, rearrange your room. The open-plan family room/kitchen (opposite) uses seating to define the "living room" and to take in the three focal points—the fireplace, the big-screen television, and the view beyond French doors.

■ **ELIMINATE SPEED BUMPS.** Position secondary sitting or work spots so they don't impede across-the-room traffic. Keep electrical cords from underfoot and secure area rugs along routes with tape or nonskid backing.

■ **CREATE AN ENTRY.** If your front door opens directly into the living room, create an entry with a love seat or tall screen backed up to the boundary.

■ **CONSIDER LANE WIDTHS.** Allow about 2½ to 3 feet for major traffic lanes. *(For other measurements, refer to pages 250–251 in the "Beginnings" chapter.)* Custom-size certain pathways, if needed, and widen the space between the sofa and cocktail table for long-legged comfort.

LEFT: A wraparound breakfast bar and boundary-setting furniture arrangements for conversation and dining areas divide and conquer open space in this new great-room. A wide passage defined by an area rug directs traffic behind the sofa and out to the terrace.

Create Equilibrium

The artistic secret ingredient that makes a photograph or a painting intriguing also makes room arrangements successful and pleasing to the eye. The secret is composition—a well-balanced mix of large- and small-scale furniture, accessories, accent colors, and patterns throughout a room. Coax the eye around the room with interesting furniture and art placed high and low. Give the eye a rest now and then with breathing room— not clutter—around furnishings. With good composition, spaces avoid that uncomfortable, listing-ship feeling. *(For more on balance, scale,*

and proportion, see pages 302–305 in the "Elements" chapter.)

FORGE GOOD RELATIONSHIPS

Balance works on the teeter-totter principle. If a large seating group at one end of a living room lacks a counterweight—built-ins, an armoire, or even a weighty painting hung above a table—the room seems lopsided. You needn't match a chunky sofa pound for pound with another hefty piece. Instead, group a couple of chairs, a table, and an area rug; together they will match the visual weight of the sofa. To maintain a room's balance:

■ **STUDY YOUR SCALES.** The scale of individual pieces contributes to a room's overall balance. Next to massive upholstery, a delicate tea table with slender legs looks spindly, but a heavy marble-topped coffee table holds its own. A small lamp gets lost on a large table, and an oversize painting overwhelms any small furniture beneath it.

■ **COUNT COLOR IN.** Dark upholstery grants importance to seating, but covering a sofa to match the wall color blends the sofa into the background. If you anchor an area with strong, dark colors or bold patterns, scatter colorful accessories around the room for balance.

OPPOSITE: At one end of this serene bedroom, a cottage-style bed is the main attraction. Together with the natural wicker seating, it creates casual counterpoint to the more-formal arrangement of elements. A filmy canopy adds vertical interest to the bed. BELOW: Balancing furnishings in this high-ceilinged space is a challenge, but the chunky armoire opposite the bed does the job, along with a collection of straw hats that perks up the plain wall. An area rug defines the bedroom's beauty spot, a charming vanity.

Tame Your Space

One is sleek and modern and the other is traditional—but they're still identical twins. These two new townhomes have floor plans, high-rise windows, grandly vaulted ceilings, and built-in features in common, but that's where the similarity ends. In style, furnishings, and arrangements, they comfortably go their separate ways. Take the focal-point fireplace, for example. It's a logical magnet for seating in both spaces, but in the pared-down room (above) the hearth wall functions like stand-alone art, thanks to its deep, rich paint color. Instead of a sofa, an angled pair of chairs takes in the fireplace and the

park view. An Oriental rug defines the seating area. A tall plant at the windows balances the fireplace and built-ins. A low-slung chaise allows a full outdoor view. The casual haven (above) cozies up with collections, warm woods, and seating for a crowd. (Here's where the break-the-rules principle comes in handy: Knowing they need lots of seating, the owners created a grouping that allows traffic to move through the conversation area to the deck.) A trio of neutral-hued sofas in a U-shape faces the fireplace, where a framed piece and folk art accent the hearth wall. A sofa table adds a functional surface for a lamp and display, and as a visual counterweight to the fireplace and built-in entertainment center, a lofty hutch displays a plate collection near the windows.

A New Angle
A Better View

Most spaces have a few architectural eccentricities.
Built-ins, fireplaces, and a view give spaces personality,

but they also can put your seating pieces in a quandary: Which way to turn? How to embrace more than one focal point? How to choose which to snuggle up to, the view or the fire? In such cases, placing a sofa with its back to the wall just won't do. Instead, for comfort, float your furnishings, as shown in this living room.

■ **THE SOFA AND FIREPLACE FACE-OFF** (see opposite page, inset) was comfortable enough. But pulling the sofa away from the wall and angling it toward the leaded-glass windows in the corner doubles the viewing pleasure. It also widens the room visually and puts loungers closer to the fire.

■ **FOOT TRAFFIC CAN NOW FLOW** around—not through—the conversation area. The newly opened space behind the sofa allows for the addition of a sofa table with a pair of reading lamps, family photos, and a pot of greenery.

■ **THE COFFEE TABLE MOVES CLOSER** to the sofa because the side chairs now flank their own occasional table and lamp.

■ **THERE'S A FLIP SIDE** to this versatile furniture arrangement. If the angled sofa and side chairs switch places, the sofa still embraces two focal points: the fireplace and a garden view through the bay window. Plan flexibility into your own seating arrangements.

Upholstered Furniture and Bedding Templates

Symbols

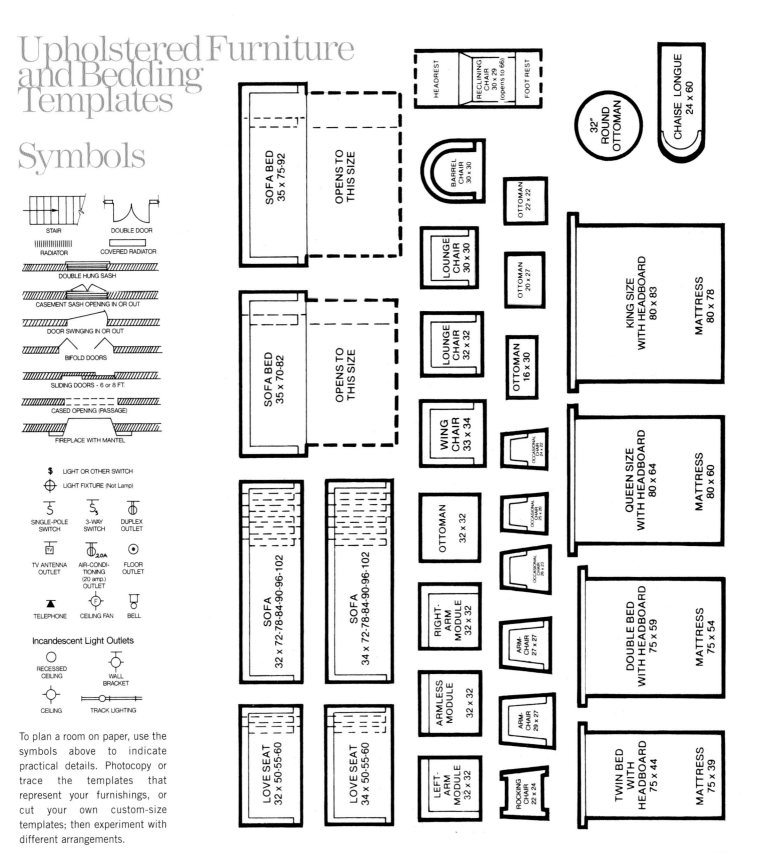

STAIR

DOUBLE DOOR

RADIATOR

COVERED RADIATOR

DOUBLE HUNG SASH

CASEMENT SASH OPENING IN OR OUT

DOOR SWINGING IN OR OUT

BIFOLD DOORS

SLIDING DOORS - 6 or 8 FT.

CASED OPENING (PASSAGE)

FIREPLACE WITH MANTEL

$ LIGHT OR OTHER SWITCH

LIGHT FIXTURE (Not Lamp)

SINGLE-POLE SWITCH

3-WAY SWITCH

DUPLEX OUTLET

TV ANTENNA OUTLET

AIR-CONDI-TIONING (20 amp.) OUTLET

FLOOR OUTLET

TELEPHONE

CEILING FAN

BELL

Incandescent Light Outlets

RECESSED CEILING

WALL BRACKET

CEILING

TRACK LIGHTING

To plan a room on paper, use the symbols above to indicate practical details. Photocopy or trace the templates that represent your furnishings, or cut your own custom-size templates; then experiment with different arrangements.

SOFA BED 35 x 75-92

OPENS TO THIS SIZE

SOFA BED 35 x 70-82

OPENS TO THIS SIZE

SOFA 32 x 72-78-84-90-96-102

SOFA 34 x 72-78-84-90-96-102

LOVE SEAT 32 x 50-55-60

LOVE SEAT 34 x 50-55-60

HEADREST

RECLINING CHAIR 30 x 29 (opens to 66)

FOOT REST

BARREL CHAIR 30 x 30

LOUNGE CHAIR 30 x 30

LOUNGE CHAIR 32 x 32

WING CHAIR 33 x 34

OTTOMAN 32 x 32

RIGHT-ARM MODULE 32 x 32

ARMLESS MODULE 32 x 32

LEFT-ARM MODULE 32 x 32

ROCKING CHAIR 22 x 24

OTTOMAN 22 x 22

OTTOMAN 20 x 27

OTTOMAN 16 x 30

OCCASIONAL CHAIR 24 x 22

OCCASIONAL CHAIR 25 x 26

OCCASIONAL CHAIR 26 x 23

ARM-CHAIR 27 x 27

ARM-CHAIR 29 x 27

32" ROUND OTTOMAN

CHAISE LONGUE 24 x 60

KING SIZE WITH HEADBOARD 80 x 83

MATTRESS 80 x 78

QUEEN SIZE WITH HEADBOARD 80 x 64

MATTRESS 80 x 60

DOUBLE BED WITH HEADBOARD 75 x 59

MATTRESS 75 x 54

TWIN BED WITH HEADBOARD 75 x 44

MATTRESS 75 x 39

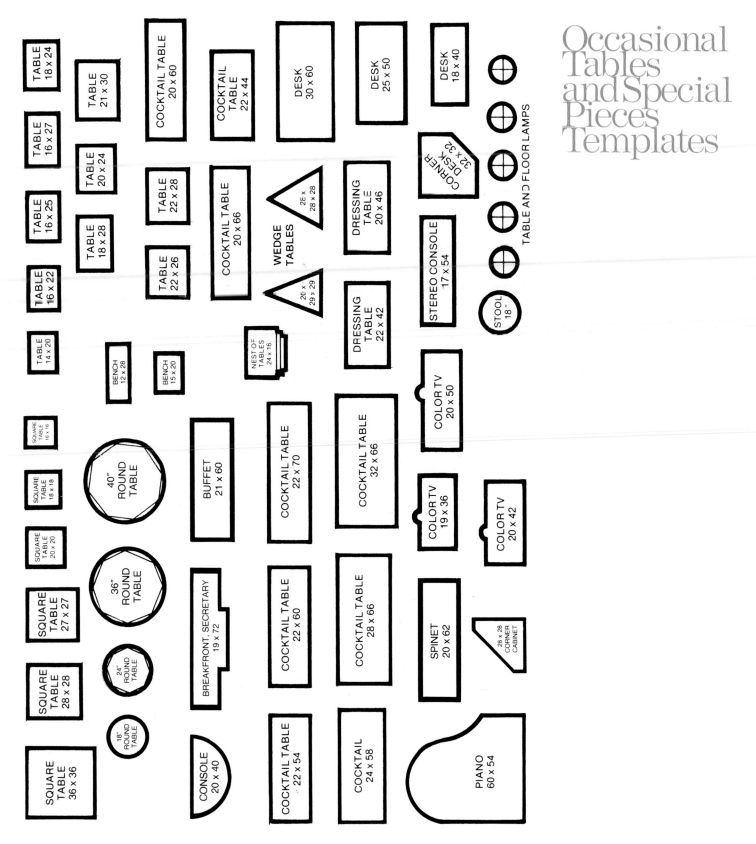

Occasional Tables and Special Pieces Templates

TABLE 18 x 24

TABLE 21 x 30

COCKTAIL TABLE 20 x 60

COCKTAIL TABLE 22 x 44

DESK 30 x 60

DESK 25 x 50

DESK 18 x 40

TABLE 16 x 27

TABLE 20 x 24

TABLE 16 x 25

TABLE 22 x 28

CORNER DESK 32 x 32

TABLE 18 x 28

COCKTAIL TABLE 20 x 66

WEDGE TABLES

28 x 28 x 28

DRESSING TABLE 20 x 46

STEREO CONSOLE 17 x 54

TABLE 16 x 22

TABLE 22 x 26

20 x 29 x 29

DRESSING TABLE 22 x 42

TABLE AND FLOOR LAMPS

STOOL 18"

TABLE 14 x 20

BENCH 12 x 28

BENCH 15 x 20

NEST OF TABLES 24 x 16

COLOR TV 20 x 50

SQUARE TABLE 16 x 16

40" ROUND TABLE

BUFFET 21 x 60

COCKTAIL TABLE 22 x 70

COCKTAIL TABLE 32 x 66

COLOR TV 19 x 36

SQUARE TABLE 18 x 18

SQUARE TABLE 20 x 20

36" ROUND TABLE

COLOR TV 20 x 42

SQUARE TABLE 27 x 27

BREAKFRONT, SECRETARY 19 x 72

COCKTAIL TABLE 22 x 60

COCKTAIL TABLE 28 x 66

SPINET 20 x 62

SQUARE TABLE 28 x 28

24" ROUND TABLE

28 x 28 CORNER CABINET

18" ROUND TABLE

CONSOLE 20 x 40

COCKTAIL TABLE 22 x 54

COCKTAIL 24 x 58

PIANO 60 x 54

SQUARE TABLE 36 x 36

Dining Tables and Chairs Templates

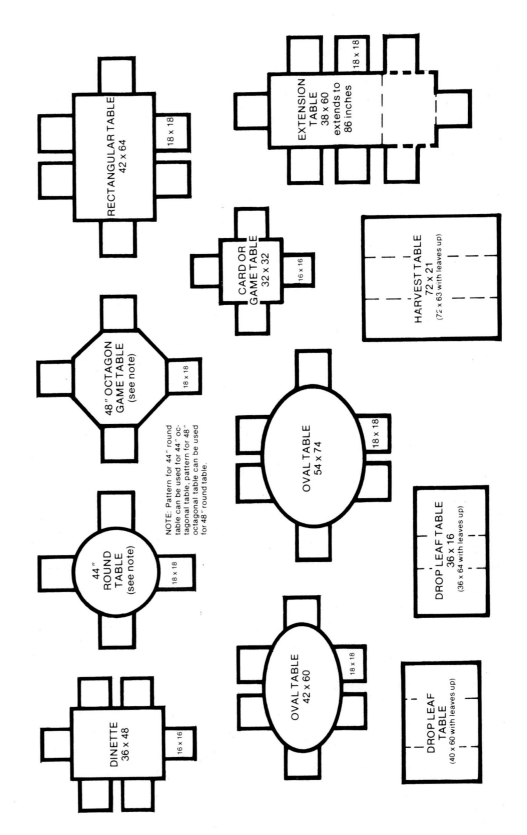

RECTANGULAR TABLE
42 x 64

18 x 18

EXTENSION TABLE
38 x 60
extends to 86 inches

18 x 18

CARD OR GAME TABLE
32 x 32

16 x 16

HARVEST TABLE
72 x 21
(72 x 63 with leaves up)

48" OCTAGON GAME TABLE
(see note)

18 x 18

OVAL TABLE
54 x 74

18 x 18

NOTE: Pattern for 44" round table can be used for 44" octagonal table, pattern for 48" octagonal table can be used for 48" round table.

44" ROUND TABLE
(see note)

18 x 18

DROP LEAF TABLE
36 x 16
(36 x 64 with leaves up)

DINETTE
36 x 48

16 x 16

OVAL TABLE
42 x 60

18 x 18

DROP LEAF TABLE
(40 x 60 with leaves up)

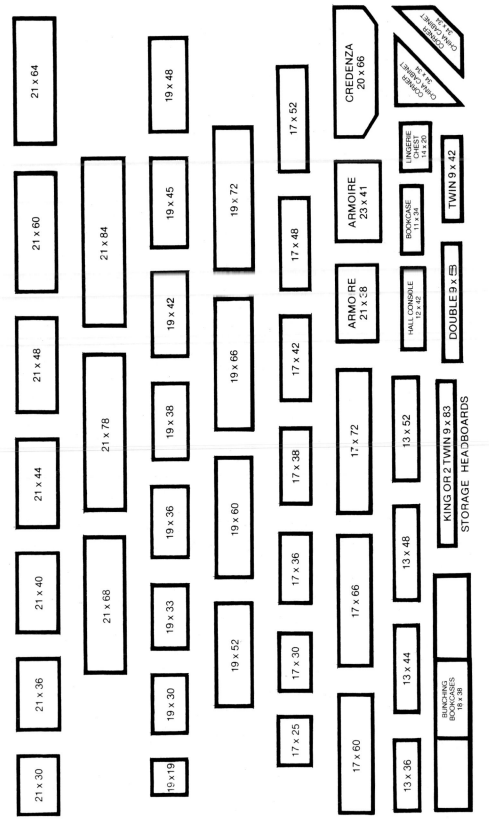

Interchangeable Storage and Special Pieces Templates

Room Arranging Graph Guide

1 square equals 1 square foot

These templates can be used for charting chests, dressers, serving carts, buffets, china cabinets, credenzas, consoles, hutches, tea carts, bars, stereo cabinets, hope chests, window chests, secretaries, and many other pieces of furniture.

CHAPTER 15

Elements

You already know more about the principles and elements of good design than you may realize. That's because you play a designer's role every day when you get dressed. When you mix and match the pieces in your clothing wardrobe, you blend patterns, cozy up with texture, and keep scale and balance in mind. Those same principles were used to create the well-designed room shown here. In this chapter, you'll learn how you can use design principles to dress your rooms with personal style.

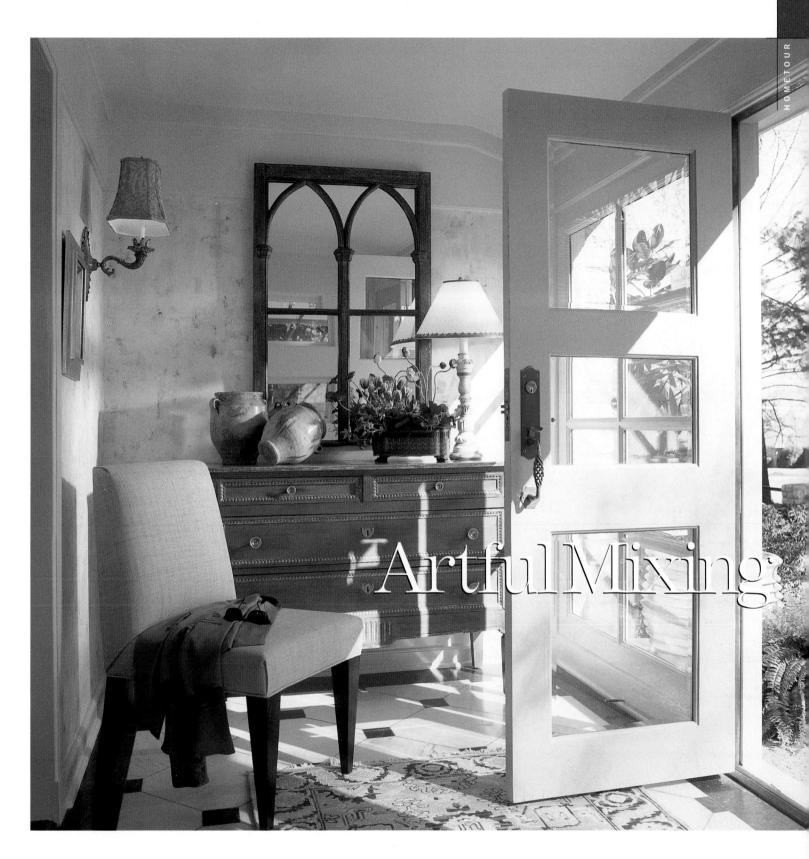

Artful Mixing

Artful Mixing

BETH AND ROBERT SACHSE OF TULSA, OKLAHOMA

PREVIOUS PAGES: Travel is a rich source of design inspiration for Beth, who admires the graphic drama of an African kuba cloth she hung in the breakfast room. The reproduction gateleg table is made from old wood. Decorative and functional, antique French doors hide a wet bar. The entry, set with a mirrored Gothic window, a contemporary chair, and an 1860 French chest, introduces her penchant for mixing styles and periods. **BELOW:** What makes a room homey? It's books and pets, says Beth, relaxing with her husband, Robert, and the family's boxers, Diego and Freda. **OPPOSITE:** This art lover honors a William Hook landscape painting by hanging it center stage. Colorful glass balls that catch the light echo the luminescence of the painting. Functional art, heirloom Imari porcelain, and vintage leather-bound books fill shelves.

If there's one constant in the elegant rooms of interior designer Beth Sachse, it's change, and she wisely designs for it. Static looks and labels don't last, she says. How can they when true personal style reflects one's changing life experience? To prove her point, Beth creates rooms that are movable feasts of furnishings and collections. "I really love moving things around, and you'll see positions changing year to year," she says. "That's something I grew up with. Moving furniture around was part of the entertainment when Dad was out of town, and he was always pleasantly surprised."

FINE LINES AND TIME LINES

Why do sleek, red leather chairs work as beautifully with a rustic table in the dining room as they do next to African art in the kitchen? If a piece is designed well, it mixes well, she says, so she picks each element to stand on its merits. "I like a layering mix of artistic influences. It makes more interesting design," Beth says. "The table looks kind of primitive and the chairs are real modern, and I love that combination."

Neutral backdrops set a flexible stage for the links of color that her furnishings and accessories carry from room to room. "I'm big on 'less is more.' I like to have a feeling of space...so your eye has time to focus on each thing as something important," she says. That requires editing when rooms start feeling too busy. She looks beyond the sentimental in assessing each element, asking: Why do I want to keep that? Her collection of antique Chinese and Japanese Imari porcelain always makes the cut. "I can't live without that Imari red color," she says. "There are certain colors I am always comfortable living with— those colors I use in the fabrics. And they can move around."

When it comes to rearranging elements, never fear, just experiment, she advises. In tabletop vignettes of metal or glass, she tucks in a wood element for warmth. If a grouping needs sparkle, she adds an object that catches light. "You've got to get personality in there. That's what accessorizing is all about," she says. "It's saying, 'I've got a sense of humor, I like an element of surprise, and I like certain colors'." What is the most important element in her rooms? It's artwork. "To me, it's like poetry," says Beth. "Make sure it means something to you. Never buy a piece of art to fill a hole because the wall is boring."

Pattern and color—always with a dash of Beth's favorite Imari red—flow throughout the home, creating harmony.

ABOVE: In the open-plan dining and living area, sleek Italian chairs clad in red leather present a striking contrast to the reproduction English table with its double gate legs. Flanking the French walnut buffet, 1930s chairs upholstered in a botanical print provide extra seating for the table. OPPOSITE: Sentimental objects give a room meaning, says Beth, who displays her mother's collection of tea caddies, miniature musical instruments, and tiny tortoiseshell pieces from the 1800s on the buffet. The lamp is fashioned from an antique hand-painted water jar. The circa-1820 chinoiserie clock is English.

Into her traditional-modern mix, Beth blends Oriental and Asian-inspired elements. The sofa's gold upholstery is sprinkled with scarlet Chinese characters, the bamboo bookcase is English, and the lamp is made from a tin Chinese jar. **1** On the terrace, neutral colors and natural finishes set a serene

mood for fireside dining and relaxing. **2** Antiqued cabinets and sleek stools echo the home's traditional-modern mix. Robert, a gourmet cook known for his pies, appreciates the efficiency of concrete countertops and high-tech cable lighting. **3** Botanical-print draperies, woven shades, and relaxed slipcovers enhance the master bedroom's casual "treehouse" ambience. The white Tizio lamp adds a stylish modern surprise. **4** Once a garage, the guest suite uses the textures of fabrics and primitive African stools (used as coffee tables) to warm sleek elements, including low-profile shelves and a modern LeCorbusier chair.

Layer on Texture

How touchable is your room? Texture is one design element that can make the difference between a merely pleasant room and one that welcomes with warmth and richness. Although texture isn't as dramatic as bold color or lively pattern, an interplay of contrasting textures—weathered wood beside fuzzy chenille or wrought iron against buttery leather—subtly delights the senses of sight and touch.

DIVERSITY IS THE KEY

■ **LET OPPOSITES ATTRACT.** Pair hard and soft, nubby and smooth, rough and slick, fuzzy and silky, coarse and fine for design interest. Forget matching and mix things up. Encircle your smooth wood- or glass-top table with rippled wicker chairs or rugged log- or twig-frame designs. Pull a rough-hewn iron lamp and nubby throw close to a petal-soft sofa. Experiment with textiles of different feels, from crisp chintzes to feathery velvets, and toss in a few rugged weaves as wake-up calls for your senses.

■ **SET THE MOOD YOU WANT.** Certain textures are mood-setters. Grouping soft, fine textures casts a romantic, feminine spell; rugged, hard surfaces create a more masculine mood. When planning your mix, pick the mood you want and rely on the textures that will express that feeling for a majority of the room's materials. Then spread other textures around with accessories.

RIGHT: This collector's sun-washed foyer plays a favorite country air. Guests can't help but slow down to enjoy the weathered and worn textures of garden topiaries, an antique rhubarb press, down-on-the-farm art, and other treasures gathered around the handsome console table. **OPPOSITE:** From the rough sisal carpet and sun-bleached seashells to hard metal accents and a soft leather "daybed" coffee table, a touchable—and unexpected—textural mix warms the clean lines and serene neutral palette in this living room.

■ **TEXTURE THE BACKGROUND.** Play rough against smooth, shiny against matte when planning floors and walls. Plop a shaggy flokati rug atop a smooth hardwood or tile floor to intrigue the eye. Contrast a rough brick or stone wall with a shiny framed mirror, or warm a flat painted wall with a textured-plaster dado.

PatternPower

Ah, love! Picking one pattern you can't live without is the easy part. The process of decorating can begin to get complicated, though, when it comes to deciding how to use the pattern in your room—or what patterns to mix with it. Simple guidelines can eliminate the guesswork of pattern mixing and restore the fun. *(For more on pattern, see pages 352–353 in the "Fabrics" chapter.)*

PATTERN POINTERS

■ **MAINTAIN A ROOM'S BALANCE** by distributing pattern evenly around it. The exception? Place all your pattern in one part of a room—say, to draw the eye to a seating grouping—but balance that pattern cluster with weighty furnishings or architectural features elsewhere.

■ **CONSIDER A ROOM'S SIZE** and how the patterns will be used. Small prints may look insignificant in a large room; a large print sometimes can overpower a small room. When mixing patterns, use prints that vary in scale—large, medium, and small.

■ **KEEP THE REPEAT IN MIND.** A large-scale print can repeat its pattern on a sofa or draperies, but it won't work on a little cushion. Similarly, an especially intriguing pattern may be lost on gathered curtains, but it can show off on flat, tapestrylike panels.

■ **KNOW YOUR GEOMETRY.** Mix in a fail-safe geometric check or stripe. For example, wake up a floral sofa with a couple of striped toss pillows or romance a striped sofa with an array of floral pillows.

■ **SELECT PATTERNS WITHIN A COLOR FAMILY** for pleasing harmony. Patterns don't have to be the same color (it's often more intriguing if colors don't match perfectly), but a thread of color continuity will pull the whole look together.

■ **MAINTAIN A CASUAL OR FORMAL ATTITUDE.** It's generally best not to mix a formal silk damask with a country gingham. Do mix damask with moiré stripes, or gingham with ticking.

■ **STILL TIMID?** Look at premixed collections sold by wall-covering stores, fabrics centers, and interior designers.

OPPOSITE: A large-scale plaid on the largest furniture piece—the sofa—forms a strong visual anchor for this seating group. A related midsize print carries color and pattern to the windows.

BELOW: Always congenial mixers, stripes and florals enliven this romantic sitting spot. The antique needlepoint pillow inspired the room's soft hues and garden motifs. Shells echo the fabric's stripes; the screen's decoupaged roses repeat the pillow's palette.

Set a Tempo

Is your eye "sitting this one out" because your room isn't inspiring it to get moving? Liven things up with a little rhythm. The way you arrange colors, patterns, and shapes can create new visual rhythm that grabs the eye and dances it around a room.

AND THE BEAT IS?

Create the feeling you want: You may want a lively, playful tempo in some rooms and a slower, more graceful pace in others. The rapid repeat of big, friendly checks creates lively energy in the room below. Note how your eye can't help but move from the blue sofa with its red and gold accents to the accessories in the background. In the room opposite, dashes of blue lead the eye down the wall, across a sofa, and out to the terrace. Using the following tips, distribute colors or shapes around the room to create the beat you want.

GO FOR THE FLOW

■ **SCATTER A DOMINANT HUE** throughout the room; color repetition keeps the eye moving along and weaves the space together. Use color and pattern on walls and floors, as well as on furnishings.

■ **PUNCTUATE WITH ACCENT COLORS** in spots anywhere you want the eye to pause and linger. Use such colors to draw the eye to a forgotten nook.

■ **USE PATTERNS** to link windows and upholstery. Consider the natural rhythm of geometrics or viney florals to bring a dull room to life. Toss pillows in several patterns add staccato rhythm to a sofa.

■ **LET TEXTURE DRAW THE EYE.** A rough-hewn stone urn displayed in a corner grabs attention in a room with soft textiles and cushiony seating.

■ **GROUP OBJECTS FOR IMPACT.** Small objects strewn around a room lack visual focus. Displayed together, however, small items can captivate the eye.

■ **WHEN IN DOUBT,** subtract patterns, colors, or objects to slow the tempo.

LEFT: As lively as a rousing rendition of "Yankee Doodle Dandy," this living room's All-American palette begins with the artwork, then marches around the room in fabrics and accents. The repeat of shapes also creates rhythm: Curvy bowls carry the eye up the wall in a corner. **OPPOSITE:** White board-and-batten paneling and shutters set the stage for blue and white artwork and pillows that lead the eye in a lively two-step dance from living room to deck. Large-, medium, and smaller-scale fabric patterns vary the tempo.

Practice Your Scales

Who hasn't seen a lamp much too large for its tiny table?
Or who hasn't noticed a willowy chair that seems to disappear beside a chunky sofa? Such negative examples are an easy way to understand proportion. In furniture design, proportion is about the relationship between the parts of a piece—how the shape and size of chair arms look compared to the shape and size of the legs and seat. In room design, proportion refers to how furnishings look in relation to each other and to the room itself. Getting proportions right means working out relationships among your furnishings—choosing and arranging pieces so they appear compatible in scale.

RELATIVELY SPEAKING

- **GROUP SMALL FURNISHINGS** to keep them from getting lost in large-scale spaces. In petite rooms, don't limit yourself to small-scale furnishings: A single oversize piece—a lofty armoire, a wall-to-wall bookcase, or a fat sink-in sofa—can make a small room feel more generous.

- **FORGET MIRROR IMAGES** when you're balancing the proportions of furnishings at sofa ends. Tables and accessories don't have to match; a lower table at one end could have a taller lamp.

- **CHECK THE VISUAL WEIGHT** of furnishings; it matters as much as the height. Even if chairs are the same height, a reed-thin one looks awkward beside a hefty one.

- **COMPOSE TABLETOP DISPLAYS** that span at least one-third of the table diameter. For impact, make groupings a few inches taller than one-half the table's height.

- **THINK BIG,** starting with your largest piece of furniture—usually the sofa. Then add other furnishings that visually fit. A table and lamp may be proportionate to each other, but placed next to a sofa, they may look too large or too small.

ABOVE: This living room feels more cozy than cavernous because its owners paid attention to scale. The vintage cupboard measures up to the tall window. Conversely, a gracefully draped swag and a partially lowered window shade re-scale the window so it better suits the low seating pieces. **OPPOSITE:** A quartet of architectural drawings climbs the wall to bring this bed in scale with the room's large and lofty windows. A statuesque accent light also is appropriately scaled to the high-ceiling space.

Watch Your Balance

If you have carefully chosen furnishings with good proportions but find that the overall effect isn't quite right, check your equilibrium. Think of your room as a see-saw; the eye won't be content and you won't feel at ease unless furnishings and accessories are comfortably in balance.

JUGGLING THE ELEMENTS

■ **FORMAL SYMMETRY IS CREATED** with mirror images on either side of an imaginary line running through the middle of a space. Objects don't have to be identical on either side—only close enough in size and shape to look like a perfect match. Symmetry soothes the eye, but it can lapse into boredom unless you add an off-center item. For example, a symmetrical grouping of fireside sofas will be more interesting if the mantel display has an off-center painting or a mantel scarf that dips gracefully off one side.

■ **ASYMMETRICAL ARRANGEMENTS** don't pretend to be mirror images. Instead, they evenly distribute visual weight in an informally balanced way. Five

RIGHT: Natural woods and white, punched up with colorful print fabrics, freshen this small living room. A wall shelf for collectibles was added behind the sofa to balance the heft and height of the fireplace. On the mantel, a candlestick grouping offsets a chunky finial. OPPOSITE: Classic and comfortable with a sofa slipcovered in brushed denim and a mix of tables and textures, this room takes a formal approach to balance. Wall-hung mirrors and window-framing curtains create symmetry, as do end tables that balance without matching.

objects grouped on one side balance a massive piece on the other. A fat, squat object makes a pleasing counterpoint to several tall, thin objects.

■ **RADIAL BALANCE MIMICS** the dial on a clock. To balance an angular painting, for instance, hang a circle or a half-circle of plates in orbit around it.

COLOR CARRIES WEIGHT

In designing a well-balanced room, remember that color wields great influence. Warm colors and bright patterns advance toward you, visu-ally consuming more space than their cooler counterparts. A heavy seating grouping on one side of a room, for example, can be balanced by a boldly painted wall or a large bright canvas on the other. Balance colors on the walls themselves too. When using two paint colors on one wall, anchor the lower part with the warmer or brighter hue and apply the lighter, receding color on top. Otherwise, the space will look top-heavy.

HappyEndings

DON'T super-size it. As an end table, the traditional carved pedestal, **ABOVE**, looks too tall and too spindly alongside the low-slung, soft-arm sofa. At that height, it's awkward to stretch for a drink if you're sitting on the sofa. (Beware of those sharp pedestal corners if you do.) **DO make access easy.** Substituting stacked wooden boxes, **LEFT**, for the pedestal lowers the table surface to a comfortable sofa-arm height. Now you're not as likely to bump into things if you grab a book or adjust the lamp from the sofa. Stylewise, the rustic table complements the relaxed seating.

Creating a comfort zone means more than pulling in a plump sofa or a comfortable reading chair. Seating needs a supporting cast. End tables store the books, hold the lamps, display the family photos, and give your guests a place for drinks, so choose sofa sidekicks that measure up physically and visually. If a table is too tall, watch those elbows or you'll topple the lamp as you raise your entire arm to attempt to pick up or set down a glass or a teacup. If the table is too short, your tea can slosh in midair as you look down for a safe landing spot for your cup.

Don't

DON'T skimp on inches. The drop-leaf table, ABOVE, is too short to serve the high-arm sofa. Imagine settling back and having to reach around or over the tall arm to grab a book or a drink. Getting the pharmacy lamp in proper reading position is a full stretch too.

DO take a cue from your sofa. The high-arm sofa and chunky pedestal, RIGHT, make a perfect pairing. The pedestal is the right height for the arm, and it also has the visual weight to stand up to the big sofa. Consider the role of your end tables. This pedestal is for accessories only; a coffee table handles beverages.

Do

Practice, Practice

Now it's time for you to put design principles to work. If you want more practice
before tackling a whole room, start small by rearranging shelf groupings. We created these examples to help you visualize your own groupings. For an asymmetrical informal look, use a one-third/two-thirds guideline; start with the tallest object one-third of the way in from one side of your display, then work down and out with smaller items. Let some objects overlap.

SHELVES TWO WAYS
What clues do your shelf displays and tablescapes reveal about your personal style? Although these two arrangements reflect different design styles, they're built on these principles of good

ABOVE: Bright accents and pattern create a clean, contemporary look. Three boxes at the lower right balance a trio of lime pots at the upper left. Note how groupings of smaller objects balance larger single items. **RIGHT:** This new retro clock delivers focus—and fun, because clocks in the display are set for different times. Instead of boring bookends, a straw bag displays old volumes in an unexpected way. *(See another variation of this built-in on pages 258–259.)*

design—ideas you can adapt to your own taste and objects.

■ **CREATE A FOCAL POINT.** Prop a framed print, or cast a tall or patterned object as the vignette's star; then build around it.

■ **PICK A COMMON DENOMINATOR.** The shelves on the opposite page celebrate color and form with collectible clocks mixed with fun and funky finds. The shelves above have a textural theme, layering objects in wood, wicker, metal, iron, glass, and paper.

■ **VARY THE HEIGHTS OF OBJECTS FROM SHORT TO TALL.** Then arrange items in overlapping triangles to keep the eye moving.

■ **USE AN ODD NUMBER OF OBJECTS.** A display of two objects can be static and formal; add a third for more visual appeal.

■ **BE REPETITIOUS.** Pairing curvy candlesticks and shapely ceramics softens inherently angular shelves. For easy mixing, choose items that share the same color and material.

■ **ADD DEPTH.** Instead of a flat lineup, stagger glassware, framed photos, or candlesticks in a front-to-back zigzag pattern.

■ **LEAVE SOME BREATHING ROOM.** Instead of cramming too many objects together, leave space between them so shapely pieces can show off their curves.

ABOVE: Mother Nature's riches—a twig wreath and airy greenery—create a well-balanced mix of textures. The brown-tone objects also create rhythm that leads the eye from one end of the bookcase to the other. The large clock and message board in the center sections serve as anchors for groupings of smaller items that orbit around them. RIGHT: A wicker-and-wood message board creates a backdrop for smaller items up front. The board echoes the natural-texture theme while also adding a display spot for colorful wine labels, old photographs, and cards tucked behind crisscrossed ribbons.

CHAPTER 16

Color

Somewhere over the rainbow is that one color or magical mix of hues to make your room pop, sizzle, soothe, or charm. This chapter is designed to help you find it. Ready to be adventurous and dip into something bold? Consider the tangy citrus hues and hot-pink bamboo used in the sitting room here. For a high-energy but low-risk start, contrast one or two solid hues with lots of white. This chapter builds confidence with basics on choosing and mixing colors.

Inspired by Color

Inspired by Color

PAM PANIELLO OF TAMPA, FLORIDA

PREVIOUS PAGES: It's only natural that the bounty of cheerful hues inside this vintage home would spill out onto the terrace when it's time for entertaining. A quilt dresses the old iron table set with artisan-crafted dishes bearing fruit and vegetable motifs. Pam Paniello's collection of dishes includes designer pieces and art fair finds; all share vibrant blues, yellows, oranges, and greens. BELOW: Pam enjoys the tropical greens of her landscape, so she pulled those calming hues inside. The greens also provide a refreshingly cool counterpoint to the Florida sun, which floods the home. OPPOSITE: Generously sized and clad in fabric that is bold in color and scale, an array of sink-in seating pieces cozies up the oversize family room. For sit-down meals, chairs pull up to a farm table behind the sofa. The green ottoman is ample in size—just right for snacks when the family gathers to watch television.

Pam Paniello's palettes start in her tote bag, because she always takes color inspirations with her to the paint store. For the perfect purple, she pulled out an eggplant. For "grown-up primaries"? A piece of majolica. Banana-tree leaves inspired her home's peaceful greens. Melon hues came from hibiscus blossoms. "Find something you love—pottery, fabric, art, flowers—and there's a reason you love it, and it's usually color," Pam says.

COLOR STRAIGHT FROM THE HEART

With high, arched windows and French doors overlooking the terrace, the large family room and kitchen in Pam's 1930s home was a sun-catcher thirsty for a drink of cool color. The cool palette Pam chose also sets just the right relaxing mood for a room where friends inevitably congregate. Color inspiration came from the dishes in her cupboard. The refreshing green backdrop cozies the large space, plays up the windows' crisp trim and curves, and visually links the room to the backyard's leafy, tropical greens. On the sofa, the farmer's market print offers a hint of green in that restful blue hue.

Once Pam laid her family room foundation of cool blues and greens, she notched up the heat with lively accessories and fabrics in luscious yellow-greens, yellows, and oranges, from melon to pumpkin.

"I wanted it fun, colorful, and relaxing, not staid and stiff," says Pam, who mixes her greens to soothe and open up her home. "This is a pretty serious house, but I pushed it as far as I could push it."

Recalling that traditional homes of the past often sported bold colors of their own, Pam says "bold colors contemporize tradition and bring it back to its roots." She notes that George Washington is said to have found his small dining room's verdigris wall color "grateful to the eye."

In choosing colors for the rest of her home, Pam follows her heart. She carries the signature reds, blues, and yellows of her beloved majolica collection through the living room. In the master bedroom, chinoiserie on an antique armoire inspires colors and fabric. When in doubt about color choices, she says, "Nature provides the best inspiration. We couldn't come up with those gorgeous colors."

She understands the fear factor. "People are afraid of making mistakes and choosing colors they'll tire of," she says. "Look up and down the hues. You can make any color work in some way. You may think you don't like pink, but fuchsia can be dynamite." If not, repaint.

1 Inspired by the real thing just outside her windows, Pam chose a tropical banana-tree green for the walls and for the fabrics on the banquette and the windows in the kitchen eating area. **2** Rich, dark glazes over marigold yellow paint age this reproduction Welsh cupboard, which displays pottery and gives the kitchen a colorful, functional focal point. **3** Pam borrows the organic colors she loves from collections, such as the charming Limoges vegetable boxes arranged like fresh produce on the window sill. OPPOSITE: Pam's vintage home calls for traditional cabinetry; her personality calls for color. Green walls back up the French blue cabinetry and a yellow island. She favors glass-doored cabinets and plate racks so her old pottery and bright dishes can color every view.

OPPOSITE: The jewel tones of majolica inspired the wall color, new upholstery fabrics, and the hand-painted mirror in Pam's Florida living room. The tilt-top, gateleg table is an antique—a portable picnic table once used for lunching in the French vineyards. **1** With regal purple walls, the dining room is an elegant

and intimate entertainer, especially in the evenings when the rich woods and crystal accents glow in the candlelight. **2** Used to cover an antique bench in the dining room, this 18th-century French tapestry inspired the backdrop color. **3** The mellowed hues and floral motif on this 18th-century French armoire launched the master bedroom palette. Crisp red and white linens and accessories tone down the all-over pattern. **4** Extravagant use of the same floral fabric on the upholstered walls, seating, and window treatments diguises the master bedroom's asymmetrical features, such as an off-center fireplace.

What Colors Speak to You?

Painting a room in your favorite color is an easy start. But is it enough? For the visual tension that makes rooms interesting, a single color needs some company. Mixing colors to create your own palette takes some skill, but it needn't be an intimidating task. Begin—always—with your favorite color; then use the color wheel lessons on the next few pages to find compatible accents for it. You can prevent color clashes by choosing a palette from one of four color groups: primary, secondary, tertiary, and monochromatic.

PRIMARY COLORS

SECONDARY COLORS

A STRONG FOUNDATION: PRIMARY COLORS

To design a room that feels strong and solid, consider using a classic primary color scheme—red, blue, and yellow. Each is a pure color that can't be created by mixing other hues. Use primaries in pairs or combine all three; they work well with all decorating styles.

THE NEXT STEP: SECONDARY COLORS

Secondary colors—green, orange, and purple—are created by mixing two primaries in equal amounts. Green is made from blue and yellow, orange from yellow and red, and purple from red and blue. Like all colors, each secondary hue can be tinted with white or shaded with black for variations. If you can't envision a bold orange and green room, pair up their paler tints of peach and sage. The primary and secondary colors illustrate that you can make a compatible triadic scheme by choosing any three colors equidistant from each other on the wheel.

INTERMEDIATE PLAYERS: TERTIARY COLORS

These colors are created with an equal mix of a primary color and its closest secondary color: blue-green, yellow-green, yellow-orange, red-orange, red-purple, and blue-purple, for example.

ONE-SHOT COLOR: MONOCHROMATIC

A monochromatic (one-color) scheme works when you vary the intensity of a single color. For instance, orange, coral, and peach offer variety within the same family.

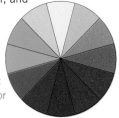

RIGHT: A color wheel is simply a rainbow in the round. Before you decorate, look at the wheel and think about the color or colors to which you are most drawn; then use our tips to find color companions for your favorite hues.

TERTIARY COLORS

MONOCHROMATIC COLORS

How Does Color Affect Your Mood?

You respond on an emotional level to the colors that surround you. Some palettes lighten and brighten your mood; others calm or purify. We respond to color with our hearts, not just our heads. Colors behave in three basic ways: They are active, passive, or neutral. Knowing those color characteristics and the intended use and mood of your rooms, you'll be able to match palette to purpose in each space.

ACTIVE COLORS

On the warm side of the color wheel, active colors include yellow, orange, and red. Extroverts, these advancing hues step out into the room to greet,

ACTIVE COLORS

PASSIVE COLORS

but they sometimes dominate. They inspire conversation and an upbeat attitude. Red pumps the adrenaline like no other color. The fire-engine hue can wake up an entry or turn up the heat in a hearthside den. Yellows—good for home offices and kitchens—unleash creative juices. Beware: Active colors can be too energetic for bedrooms, where a restful mood is needed.

PASSIVE COLORS

These cool colors—blue, green, and purple—pacify, staying quietly in the background to calm and restore depleted spirits. They're ideal for bedrooms or private retreats. If yours is a cold climate, however, you may want to work in some decidedly sunny color accents for warmth and contrast.

NEUTRAL COLORS

Neutralizers are the "uncolors"—browns, beiges, grays, whites, black, and taupes. They neither energize nor pacify but combine and cooperate, bridging together different rooms and colors. They make good transitions on woodwork and trim and in hallways, kitchens, and baths; even living rooms can benefit. Darker neutrals tone down other colors; crisp white intensifies them.

THE LANGUAGE OF COLOR

PINK soothes, acquiesces; promotes affability and affection.

YELLOW expands, cheers; increases energy.

WHITE purifies, energizes, unifies; in combination, enlivens all other colors.

BLACK disciplines, authorizes, strengthens; encourages independence.

ORANGE cheers, commands; stimulates appetites, conversation, and charity.

RED empowers, stimulates, dramatizes, competes; symbolizes passion.

GREEN balances, normalizes, refreshes; encourages emotional growth.

PURPLE comforts, spiritualizes; creates mystery and draws out intuition.

BLUE relaxes, refreshes, cools; produces tranquil feelings and peaceful moods.

NEUTRAL COLORS

Energize or Relax?

Know the mood your psyche needs when you pick a room's color palette.

Draw a line through the color wheel. On one side, you see nature's cool, refreshing hues—watery blues, restful greens, and dreamy-sky violets. On the other are warm colors—reds, oranges, yellows, and yellow-greens—that warm the mood like the sun itself. With a change of paint, this room demonstrates the mood-altering effects of both. What mood do you want your room to have?

KEEP YOUR COOL

Cool colors visually recede, so they're ideal for making small rooms feel more spacious and for any room in which you want to relax. Cool

colors conjure tranquility and dissolve indoor-outdoor barriers when spaces open to the outside. In sunny south- or west-facing rooms, cool colors keep the visual temperature from overheating.

FIRE UP YOUR ENERGY LEVEL

Warm colors visually step toward you. Use them to warm an entry or add sunshine to a breakfast room. Or "remodel" a long, narrow room the easy way: To help square up the space, roll a warm hue onto an end wall to make the wall visually advance. Warm colors are a good choice for spaces with minimal natural light, a northern exposure, or rooms over which an expansive woodsy view casts a cool greenish light. When entertaining is the main function of a room, warm colors deliver a high-energy mood.

Neighborly Hues

No wonder they mix so well; neighborly analogous
hues live next door to each other on the color wheel.

Compatibility is guaranteed when you choose two or three analogous colors—blue and green; green and yellow; blue, green, and purple, for example. Use colors of roughly the same intensity.

PICK YOUR FAVORITE COLOR

Analogous schemes can be created from any point on the color wheel. A palette can be warm, cool, or both. Start with your favorite color; then look on either side of it on the wheel. I like both colors? Include them. If you only like the color on one side, select that one and use the color next to it as your third hue. Finally, pick a dominant color; then use the other two as accents. Let your favorite color dominate, or choose a color that best fosters the mood you want your room to have. *(Refer to pages 322–325 for information on the emotional impact of colors.)*

RIGHT: Accent an analogous scheme for more punch. In this charming cottage bedroom, oranges, orange-reds, and yellows gain intensity when paired with complementary accents of fresh green and blue. OPPOSITE: Exuberant orange joins analogous mates yellow and green to create a playful scheme for this kitchen. The colors share the same intensity, so they don't drown each other out.

A PARTY OF THREE—OR MORE

Why limit the kindred colors to only two next-door neighbors? The true spirit of an analogous scheme is best expressed using three or more adjacent hues. Don't get too carried away. Use no more than half the colors on the wheel for your palette.

Opposites Attract

In color as in love, embracing the adage "opposites attract" can be the start of a beautiful relationship.

Known as complementary colors, hues opposite each other on the color wheel make dynamic duos, creating stimulating, high-energy spaces. When you choose complements, including red and green, blue and orange, and yellow and purple, the warm and cool hues play off each other, producing palettes that enjoy the best of both worlds.

Opposites are eye-catching. When warm and cool colors are viewed together, they intensify each other and bring out the best in both. That means red is redder and green is greener—more so than when each is used alone or in combination with another hue. When working with complementary colors:

■ **CHOOSE A STAR.** That's the only real rule when you're working with complements. Let the other color serve in a supporting role as an accent. Otherwise, the complements struggle for attention or even neutralize each other.

■ **PROVIDE SOME WHITE SPACE** or any neutral to prevent overkill.

■ **RELAX.** Complementary schemes are among the easiest to implement because you're dealing with only two colors. Such a scheme provides instant drama.

LEFT: Complementary blue and orange of similar medium intensity accent these dining chairs. Vintage barkcloth draperies yielded enough orange-coral print to cover the backs of the chairs, so the slipcovers incorporate two accent hues, a vibrant blue to complement the exuberant print and white to cool things down. OPPOSITE: In this inviting suite, yellow dominates. The yellow fabrics, hand-painted striped walls, and painted yellow and white chest play beautifully against cool complementary purple accents. Lavish use of white keeps the high-energy scheme from overpowering the sleeping spot.

Neutrals Soothe
Mix them, vary them, build a room around them, or cast them as grounding accents

in any scheme. Whatever you do with earthy neutral hues—grays, whites, beiges, taupes, and black—they're easy to work with and soothe the eye and psyche. Although they aren't on the color wheel, neutrals enjoy more popularity than their flashier chums, because they blend into any palette and serve as quiet backdrops. In fact, there's such a wide range of white variations that the hue could have a color wheel of its own. You can create an all-neutrals room when a soothing retreat is your goal. Or create a neutral, barely there backdrop to highlight colorful collectibles.

THE NEW "NEUTRALS"

In understated and elegant room schemes, neutrals have an expanded definition. Although one usually thinks of whites and beiges as neutrals, a neutral can be any color that mixes easily with other hues and allows those colors to dominate. Soft mauves, greens, and peaches can play a neutral role. Surprisingly, bolder red or purple also work with most other colors.

WARM UP THE MOOD

When invited center stage, non-colors relax.

Consider the romance of a white-on-white cottage-style bedroom or the snug appeal of a den in tranquil beiges and taupes or grays. To keep neutrals from becoming boring, create drama by varying the tonal range of furnishings and accessories from light and medium to dark. In addition, consider an accent in black or white as a grounding influence. Finally, always layer on textures for warmth and visual interest in neutral schemes.

ABOVE: White comes in many "colors." This living room mixes creamy and crisp whites, then layers on warming texture with wicker, carved woods, fabrics, and carpet. Washable slipcovers are a wise choice in this all-white scheme. OPPOSITE: In this serene bedroom, "cafe au lait" walls set a cozy mood. Particleboard tables covered in fabric add softness and plenty of storage space. The mix of textures, from rough to smooth, plus additions of white, keep the colorfree space interesting to the eye.

GoodMorningColor

LEFT: A palette-pleasing plaid fabric now dresses the bay window in crisp color. The colorful cafe curtains afford the breakfast room more privacy without sacrificing the coveted morning sun.

Even if your room is rich in natural and architectural resources, a splash of color can boost its personality dramatically. This gallery-white breakfast room had a lot going for it—abundant natural light from the big bay window, beautiful built-ins, and charming farm-style dining pieces. The room only needed paint and pattern to jump-start the day.

■ **TO SOFTEN THE HIGH CONTRAST** between white walls and red-toned woods, walls got a sunny gold base coat; then a mix of darker gold paint and glaze was wet-sponged over the base coat. To create the 30-inch-tall faux wainscoting, the diamond grid was lightly penciled on the wall. Dark gold glaze highlights the stenciled squares and diamond outlines; the black accents were painted freehand.

LEFT: Against a freshly painted backdrop of warm gold, the wood in the focal-point built-ins looks richer, making the whole room feel warmer. Although it's only paint, the faux wainscoting adds architectural interest and visually shortens the wall to create a more comfortable, intimate feeling.

■ **THE ONCE-BLANK WALL NOW DISPLAYS EASY ART** made with 8-ounce artist's canvas, vegetable stencils, and paints. Each canvas was primed, given a dark brown base coat, crackled, lightly painted again to let some base coat peek through, then stenciled. Canvases have grommets and hang from picture wire.

■ **THE DINING SET AGED GRACEFULLY AND COLORFULLY,** with everything but the tabletop and chair seats painted green. When the paint was dry, a black glaze was rubbed into cracks and turnings for depth and a hint of age.

■ **THE LIVELY PLAID FABRIC,** fashioned into cafe curtains, valances, and chair cushions, cued the color scheme. When in doubt, let a fabric set your palette.

Recycled Color

Decorating materials can come from surprising places—even the trash bin.

All the time you've spent mixing and matching at the paint and tile displays and all that energy expended in hauling a multitude of color chips and tile samples home is about to yield a surprising bonus. To cash in, get out those stacks of old paint cards, tile samples, and dabs of leftover paint. Then adapt one of these projects to turn your colorful leftovers into unique, personality-adding decorations for your home.

RAINBOW-TILE WALL
What you'll need:
Sheets of ceramic tile samples,
tile adhesive, grout, and tiling tools

Here's a brilliant idea for a small powder room with scant space to squeeze in color accents, a backsplash for a mudroom sink, or any sliver of wall that needs a shot of fun-and-funky color. These tile samples still have the color-code numbers on them. Apply adhesive; apply tile; when set, add grout.

CHIPS-OFF-THE-BLOCK BENCH
What you'll need:
Paint, paint-chip cards, spray glue, polyurethane, and sandpaper
Give an old coffee table or unfinished bench some snap with a topping of paint chip cards. A bench works best for large color-card strips that display several hues. Alter this project to suit your tastes and your favorite palette. Give the bench or table two to three coats of paint for the base color, sanding lightly between coats. Arrange cards in a pleasing sequence, butting them together. Trim cards as needed to fit; then spray-glue cards in place on the top. Finish with a coat of polyurethane.

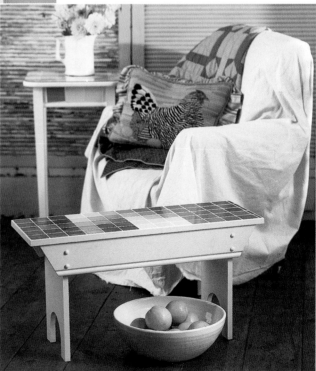

COLOR-BLOCK ARMOIRE
What you'll need:
Primer, paint, painter's tape, and brushes
Colorblocking is a great way to dress up unfinished furniture—always a budget-wise addition to any room—and use up leftover paint. The technique works on walls too. For an unfinished armoire, prime and let dry. Paint the armoire door borders, interior, and back glossy white. Tape off door insets, paint in different colors, and let dry. Paint each drawer a different hue too. For a long-lasting finish, use oil-base paint.

CHAPTER 17

Fabrics

Think of fabric as personality you buy by the yard. When you mix fabrics creatively, you can set any mood you choose, from elegant to exuberant. In this dining area, a cheery red plaid on the walls and chair backs puts a casual spin on the yellow floral that dresses the chair seats and fronts. In this chapter, we'll help you pick and mix fabrics and give you tips on where to put them for beautiful results that reflect your own decorating personality.

Style by the Yard

Style by the Yard

JANE OSBORNE OF HOUSTON, TEXAS

Jane Osborne's search for "software" leads just about anywhere if she suspects the perfect fabric awaits in a forgotten attic, a farm-field flea market, or the discount store down the block. Never mind a few worn spots in that old paisley shawl; it will look smashing tossed over an easy chair. Never mind the sofa's elegant upholstery; a new bargain-priced tea towel will stitch up into a pretty pillow for it because the color's just right. "I love the hunt," Jane says. "I love to find that perfect thing."

FOR THE LOVE OF PATTERN

To Jane, fabrics are friends, so when she and her daughter, Eden, moved to their new home, some old "friends" naturally came along. "Refresh, not re-cover" was the plan when Jane hired Houston designer Daily Howard to pull things together.

From the stylized, landscape-print linen on club chairs, they pulled out snappy reds and friendly blues and yellows for new upholstery and pillows to perk up the checked sofa. "That chair fabric is so memorable," she says. "It has lots of colors, so it was easy to go from there."

Jane loves to mix heirlooms, antiques, and flea-market finds, so layering on more fabrics only adds to the homey, collected-over-time look. "You can have beautiful furniture and wonderful old pieces, but if you don't dress it up with fabrics, it goes unnoticed," she says. "This is a labor of love. So many things have come from different places— antiquing, flea markets—and they fit."

Threads of rosy red color and floral pattern run

through the old and new fabrics from the living room to the kitchen and upstairs to the family room, tying the spaces together. With accents of green throughout, Jane says,"It's a wonderful house to decorate for Christmas."

Golden yellow pulled from the living room wing chair is the dining room star. "I needed lots of color because I have four different sets of china that I use in that dining room," Jane explains. As another color link, the dining room draperies are trimmed in floral bands cut from the same striped fabric used on the wing chair.

In a worn piece of paisley or a snippet of old needlepoint, Jane sees possibilities. Needlepoint embellishes a new pillow; paisley makes a hand-some throw for the sofa. "Great old fabrics have such character," she says. "I wouldn't drape a new piece of fabric over a chair. It has to mean some-thing to me."

PREVIOUS PAGES: Classic Chippendale chairs seemed too formal for the country French mood Jane wanted for the dining room, so she relaxed them with provincial print slipcovers in the golden yellow of the walls. Illustrations from an Italian calendar look like vintage botanicals in elegant new frames. Since the living room's checked sofa and print-upholstered chairs were keepers from a previous home, Jane added color, pattern, and character with an infusion of old and new accent fabrics. RIGHT: Jane Osborne and her daughter, Eden, feathered their new nest with furnishings of various vintages for easygoing comfort and a sense of history. OPPOSITE: With larger scale patterns on the sofa and club chairs, small-scale prints dress the other seating. An antique French Voltaire chair is clad in red, sprinkled with what Jane calls "tiny green Christmas trees." The new mantel has a faux-stone finish. The coffee table is a salvaged firescreen atop a new hand-forged base.

Creamy white walls create a refreshing playground for an earthy, rich palette of toile, gingham, paisley, stripes, and friendly florals here and there. Threads of personality and color weave it together.

ABOVE: Fragments of vintage needlepoint and paisley combine with new trims and fabric on an elegant, one-of-a-kind pillow in the family room. Mixing is a creative way to use old textiles that are often found in less than perfect condition. OPPOSITE: Red accent fabrics echo the toile Jane chose for the family room chaise; all of the toss pillows and cushions on the wicker seating are mix or match. After the table and ottoman skirts were stitched up, remnants of the checked fabric were used as trim for the window shades.

OPPOSITE: Because family and friends linger in the kitchen, Jane wanted comfort, not more cabinetry. She created a mini-family room at one end with a sofa tucked between built-ins. Prints of varying scale dress the walls, sofa, and a sheaf-back chair Jane got "for a song" at a flea market. She stitched a cover for the accent pillow from a plaid tea towel.

1 No one's quite sure what happened to the rest of the French armoire, but Jane found just the face frame and doors at an antiques shop and installed them as the facade of a recessed entertainment center in the living room. Color links pillows in a mix of fabrics to the club chairs' upholstery. **2** In the guest bath, plain but functional cabinetry hides beneath a new curved countertop. A fabric skirt repeats the floral fabric used as an accent in the bedroom. **3** Jane recycles fabrics. In the guest room, the multicolor stripe fabric came from her daughter's college dorm room. She painted her own childhood bedroom furniture in honeydew green; then she mixed in new coordinating fabrics, including the fanciful hot-air balloon print on the upholstered headboard and quilted shams.

Fabric Basics

Fabrics, like people, have distinct personalities—
some refined, some easygoing, some the life of the party. Brocade and damask convey classic elegance; gingham connotes country. Some fabrics—nubby chenilles or crisp stripes—get along with virtually any style. Take samples of carpet, wallcovering, paint, and other fabrics along when you fabric shop. Take fabric samples home to see how light changes their look. Buy durable decorating fabrics, not garment fabrics; decorating fabrics are typically 54 inches wide. Order all fabric for a project at once.

SOME TERMS TO KNOW

■ BROCADE, with a raised pattern resembling embroidery, is used in fine, formal upholstery.

■ CHENILLE, with thick needle-punched designs, is suitable for casual upholstery.

■ CHINTZ, a plain-weave glazed or unglazed cotton, often has a traditional mood and floral motifs.

■ DAMASK comes in various fibers and weights and features textural contrast between satiny and dull. It makes durable formal draperies and upholstery but goes casual in loose-fitting slipcovers.

■ MATELASSÉ has a double weave and an embossed look; use it for elegant bedcovers and throughout the home.

■ MOIRÉ, with a shimmery finish resembling watermarks or wood grain, sets a traditional mood.

■ PLISSÉ looks like overscale seersucker with wide puckered stripes; it can feel casual but suits traditional rooms too.

■ TOILE DE JOUY, a tightly woven fabric with a pictorial print on a neutral ground, shows off best on large seating, walls, and flat drapery panels. It can look formal or casual.

■ STRIÉ, a good casual and formal mixer, has subtly varied warp-thread colors and irregular streaks.

■ TAFFETA is a crisp, plain-weave fabric that works well for more formal window treatments because it retains shape with little support.

■ TAPESTRY, with thick weaves and pictorial designs, suits simple upholstery and flat window panels.

■ TWILL is tightly woven with a diagonal ridge; two types, denim and herringbone, are ideal for casual upholstery.

■ VELVET creates a mood of formal elegance with lush cut pile that shimmers in the light.

LEFT: It's the fabrics that give this window and settee their upbeat personalities. The oversize plaid brings new life to the traditional setting. Crisp leaf prints soften the seating and balance the bold curtains. The pillows wear a touch of vibrant pink and yellow to echo the plaid. OPPOSITE: Flowing portieres, or door curtains, create an air of intrigue and intimacy because they afford only a glimpse of the living room beyond. The curtains' floral fabric echoes the red hues in the upholstered seating beside the fireplace.

Choose the Right Fibers

Different areas of your home get different types of use, so consult this handy guide to determine which fabrics are smart choices for your space and lifestyle. For example, you may want to veto linen for a sofa in a high-traffic family room or silk in an everyday dining spot. Instead, upholster the sofa in a sturdy cotton blend that will stand up to stains, spills, and hard wear; cover dining chairs in a durable nylon fabric. Once you've finished this short course on fibers, you'll be ready to head for fabric shops, furniture stores, drapery and upholstery workrooms, or an interior designer's studio.

RIGHT: Sturdy cottons make long-wearing seating and drapery fabrics. Because it takes color well, cotton can bring deep, crisp color to a room. A classic blue and white plaid trims windows and reappears as a mat for whimsical framed sculptures of children's clothing. Yellow walls and a large-scale yellow floral print give the room sunny ambience, even on cloudy days.

THE NATURALS

	COMMENTS	ADVANTAGES	DISADVANTAGES	CARE/COST
COTTON	Creases easily; absorbent; breathes well; easily treated; highly flammable; fair resilience and elasticity.	Strong fiber; takes color well; blends well with other fibers; versatile.	Wrinkles easily; affected by mildew and sunlight; shrinks and stretches unless treated; yellows.	Machine-washable; must be ironed. Inexpensive.
WOOL	Very elastic and resilient; good absorbency; does not burn easily.	Strong fiber; insulates; takes color well; handles and drapes easily.	Attracts moths unless treated; needs careful cleaning; weakened by sun; shrinks unless treated.	Must be dry-cleaned. Moderately expensive.
LINEN	Low resilience and elasticity; natural luster; burns easily; absorbent.	Very strong fiber; nice texture; somewhat resistant to sun and mildew.	Wrinkles easily; inconsistent in quality; somewhat stiff; shrinks unless treated.	Needs special cleaning to preserve appearance; colors may run; must be ironed. Expensive.
SILK	Lustrous; elastic; resilient; good absorbency; does not burn easily.	Strong fiber; drapes beautifully; resists mildew; colors have jewel-like tone.	Weakened by sun; water spots show unless treated; colors may run or change with age.	Dry-clean unless label indicates it can be hand-washed. Very expensive.

THE SYNTHETICS

	COMMENTS	ADVANTAGES	DISADVANTAGES	CARE/COST
RAYON	Creases easily; versatile; high absorbency and moderate elasticity; not flammable.	Drapes well; blends well with other fibers; takes color well; can be made to look like natural fibers.	Weak fiber; shrinks and stretches unless treated; weakened by sun; needs special care.	Dry-clean unless label indicates it can be hand-washed; must be ironed. Usually inexpensive.
ACETATE	Moderately good resilience and elasticity; fair absorbency; burns readily and melts.	Appears lustrous and silklike; drapes well; resistant to mildew; somewhat wrinkle-free.	Weak fiber; weakened by sun; colors fade from atmospheric fumes.	Dry-clean unless label indicates it can be hand-washed; use a cool iron. Moderately inexpensive.
ACRYLIC	Low absorbency; good resilience and elasticity; does not burn easily.	Wool-like in texture; resists mildew, moths, and sun; holds color well; fairly strong fiber.	Tends to pill; stretches somewhat; not as durable as some fibers, especially when it's wet.	Hand-wash unless labeled otherwise; hang to dry. Moderately expensive.
POLYESTER	Very good resilience and elasticity; not absorbent.	Strong fiber; resists wrinkles, moths, and mildew; blends well; doesn't stretch or shrink.	Slick to nubby textures; difficult to dye; sun exposure causes gradual loss of strength; melts in high heat.	Most items can be machine-washed and dried. Moderate cost.
NYLON	Very good resiliency and elasticity; low absorbency; melts under high heat.	Very strong; can be sponge-cleaned; blends well; lustrous; resists abrasion.	Tends to look glassy; fades and weakens from being exposed to sun.	Most items can be machine-washed and -dried. Moderate cost.
OLEFIN	Low absorbency; lightweight with good bulk; somewhat resilient and elastic; not flammable.	Strong; takes color well; good insulator; resistant to stains, sun, and mildew; resists abrasion.	Best as blend or lining due to appearance. Do not iron; can melt in high heat.	Machine wash; dry at low heat. Moderate cost.

Which Fabrics Go Where?
Consider whether the fabrics you've picked are right for the roles you want them to play

before you make a final selection. Are they in the mood to enhance your room's style? A lustrous moiré is unmistakably formal, a tweedy homespun more rustic, and a watercolor print more lighthearted and romantic. Is the fabric right for your application? A heavy canvas, for instance, won't have the drape required for pleated curtains, but it could make a great roll-up shade. Similarly, filmy gauze can't hold up as upholstery on the sofa, but it makes wonderfully gossamer curtains.

MAKING GOOD CHOICES

The array of natural, synthetic, and blended fibers makes it possible for you to match fabrics to individual needs. Manufacturer's labels are required to show fiber content so you can make comparisons.

■ **WHAT'S YOUR CLIMATE?** This is especially important in choosing drapery fabrics if yours is a cold or an unusually sunny climate; natural fibers trap heat, and light-hued, tightly woven opaque fabrics reflect sunlight. If humidity is a factor, look for fibers with less absorbency.

■ **DO YOU WANT EASY-CARE,** soil- and stain-resistant upholstery in the family room? Then look for cleanable fabrics that have protective finishes. You also can apply a spray-on finish yourself.

■ **WILL FABRIC BE USED NEAR A FIREPLACE** or a wood stove? If so, ask for fabrics with flame-resistant finishes.

■ **PUT THE RIGHT FABRICS TO WORK IN THE RIGHT PLACES.** Consider these guidelines: Fabrics that work well on upholstery include chintz and cotton for light upholstery; brocade, corduroy, and damask for heavier upholstery; chenille, flannel, Jacquard, homespun tweed, tapestry, ticking, toile de Jouy, twill, velvet, and wool for medium-weight upholstery. Fabrics for draperies include lightly glazed chintz, light- to medium-weight cotton, lightweight corduroy, damask, dotted swiss, faille, flannel, homespun tweed, linen plissé, silk, taffeta, and toile de Jouy.

ABOVE: Now you see it, now you don't—the rooftop terrace and cityscape beyond, that is. Hung on a sleek, room-spanning track, a floor-to-ceiling fabric "wall" controls privacy, sun, and the view. OPPOSITE: A classic toile-and-check fabric mix sets a traditional yet casually comfortable mood in this bedroom.

Pick Three for Harmony

Pattern mixing is as easy as 1-2-3. Start with one print you love: then work in color-related fabrics in two other scales. Love a narrow stripe? Mix it with a bold-scale floral and a midsize stripe. Love a miniprint floral? Mix it with a midsize gingham and a large floral. The three-scales rule remains the same, but the beautiful specifics are up to you and your decorating taste. Remember, for unity and balance, spread your chosen patterns throughout your room.

VARIETY IS THE SPICE

Too many small prints can be dull, and two or more large prints can fight for attention. A family of large, medium, and small patterns coexists without sibling rivalry. Where to start? Consider a large-scale pattern for large furnishings or walls. Successfully marry two or more disparate patterns with color. Stick to patterned fabrics of approximately the same weight, texture, and degree of formality. Feeling nervous? Use color-coordinated geometrics—a stripe or check, for instance—which always mix well with other print and solid fabrics.

MORE WAYS TO MIX

■ **TRY THE 60/30/10 APPROACH.** To balance three patterns, use your favorite fabric in 60 percent of the room, your second favorite in 30 percent, and the third fabric as an accent in 10 percent.

■ **MULTIPLY BY 3.** Use each patterned fabric at least three times. For example, your dominant pattern could be used on the window treatments, an armchair slipcover, and an accent pillow on the sofa.

■ **FOCUS ON PATTERN.** Pattern attracts the eye, so use it to reshape awkward spaces. Bold patterns in advancing colors square up tunnel-shape spaces; bright accent pillows placed on a sofa in a long, narrow living room visually pull the sofa toward you, making the room seem shorter.

RIGHT: Pulling coordinating fabrics around this spacious kitchen warms the stretches of creamy cabinetry and links the different areas. For perfect balance, the patterns vary in scale: Bold checks cover the breakfast banquette, toile dresses the window, and a smaller plaid appears on the chairs.

ABOVE LEFT: If it's in good condition, one wonderful piece of old fabric can be an accessory gold mine when fashioned into pillows, cushions, and trims. In this country bedroom, a vintage peony-strewn bedspread creates the pretty dust ruffle beneath a crisp coverlet. **ABOVE RIGHT:** At a Paris flea market, a creative collector found some old monogrammed linen sheets, which she stitched together to make the dining room tablecloth. She uses French tea towels from a long-ago bride's trousseau to top the chairs. **OPPOSITE:** Vintage textiles are magical mixers that cozy up beautifully with a variety of new fabric accents in nostalgic prints and patterns. This window seat is dressed in new garden-inspired florals and an old quilt; beribboned toile draperies complement the mix.

"Past Perfect" Fabrics

Vintage textiles remind people of childhood and simpler times.

You can re-create either a colonial or a Victorian mood using fuzzy chenilles, printed flannels, 1940s barkcloth, antique quilts, coverlets, and table linens. Or use these fabrics for a few retro accents—these oldies fit perfectly into contemporary eclectic decorating schemes too.

RECYCLE CREATIVELY

If you weren't lucky enough to inherit Grandmother's monogrammed sheets, find vintage linens and fabrics at antiques shows, estate sales, and flea markets. Buy worn textiles and salvage all you can for accents.

■ **OLD TABLECLOTHS MAKE PRETTY BEDCOVERS,** curtains, and valances; bedspreads can be fashioned into draperies, dust ruffles, and other accents.

■ **TURN DISH TOWELS INTO CAFE CURTAINS** with clip-on rings, and into valances by draping them over a rod or stitching in a rod pocket.

■ **REMNANTS CAN COVER** accent pillows of various sizes. Also use remnants to make drapery trims and curtain tie-backs.

■ **QUILTS ALWAYS MAKE APPEALING WALL HANGINGS.** If a quilt or coverlet is fragile, use it as a decorative bed topper and remove it at night.

TAKE CARE OF COLLECTIBLE FABRICS

Launder old fabrics carefully. Try a 15-minute presoak to loosen dirt. Baste delicate lace to tulle netting or muslin to support the threads, or sandwich it between fiberglass screens before cleaning. Gently hand-launder in warm water with a mild, nonabrasive pure soap. To remove stains, soak in a solution of enzyme cleaner and water. Or try the old-fashioned method: bleach in the sun after dampening with lemon juice and salt. Hang carefully or lay flat to dry. Instead of folding old textiles, roll them for storage.

PickAPerfectPillow

Does your room need a splash of color? Are your accent pillows looking a little too comfortable and worn? Are your bolsters, well, boring? It only takes a few minutes to remedy the situation with dazzling pillow cover-ups made from colorful and inexpensive table napkins. Because napkins already have finished or hemmed edges, these projects take minimal or no sewing skill. If you can sew on a button, you can "redecorate" your pillows. Look for standard-size napkins in interesting fabrics and patterns or create a seasonal wardrobe of toppers.

TIE-ON TOPPER

To mark tie positions, slide the pillow between two dinner napkins. Tack 7-inch-long, ⅝-inch-wide double-face ribbons 2 inches from each pillow corner and at the center of each side, for a total of 12 ties. Choose a pillow that coordinates with the napkin color and pattern, because it will peek out at the open edges.

1. LACE A LOOK

Many napkins have cutwork, lace, or other openwork—readymade holes for lacing—so all you need is cording. Choose cording that fits the napkin weight, design, and opening size. Dip cord ends in glue; let dry. Cut the ends diagonally for easier lacing. Tie ends in a knot or bow.

2. GROMMETS GALORE

Grommets turn two reversible dinner napkins into reversible pillow covers. Use a grommet tool and ½-inch grommets to make holes for lacing. On each napkin, place a grommet 2 inches from each corner; then evenly space three more grommets along each side. Tuck the pillow in between. Lace the napkins together with thick cord and tie the ends.

3. ZIPPY COLOR

Zip on fun and function with a contrasting-color

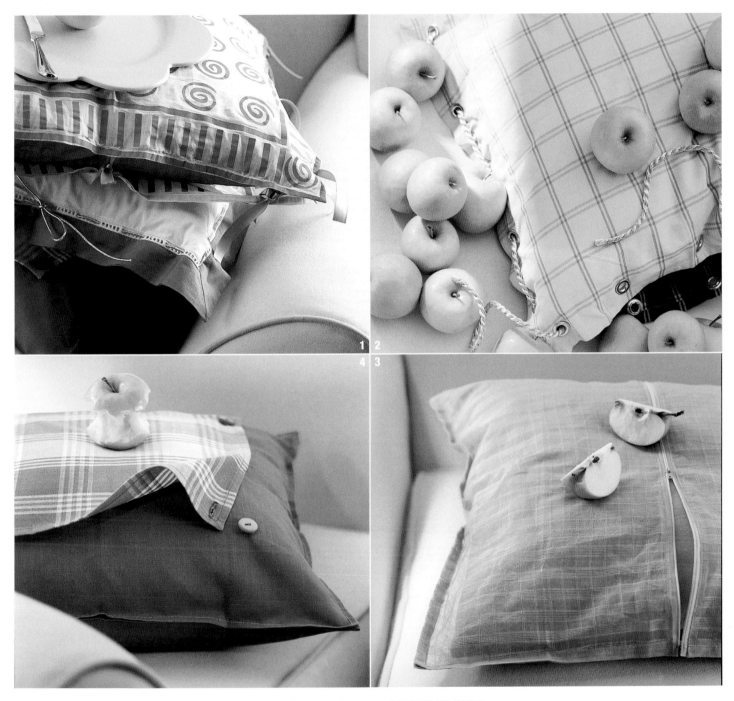

zipper that matches the napkin weight. Choose a zipper at least 2 inches longer than the napkin so you can turn under the ends. Both the zipper and tape will show to create a stripe. Cut one napkin in half. Press under the raw edges ¼ inch and baste. Pin the basted edges over the zipper so ½ inch of zipper tape shows; sew close to the basted edges. Pin the zippered napkin to the remaining one, wrong sides together, and stitch around the hemline.

4. BUTTON-UP STYLE

Button on a burst of pattern or color using a smaller napkin on a larger, plain pillow. Choose a cocktail-size napkin or one that's smaller than the pillow dimensions. Make a buttonhole in each corner of the small napkin and sew a corresponding button onto the pillow. Make several toppers for quick changes and seasonal touches.

CHAPTER 18

Windows and walls

Well-dressed windows link interiors to the light and beauty outside. Think of your walls as blank canvases awaiting your personal touch. Working together, windows and walls can express your unique style and enhance the light and views from every room. A bookish wallcovering gives the sunny space shown here its bright yet elegant mien. Use the fresh ideas and special effects in this chapter to put your windows and walls to work.

Formal or Casual?

Making a style statement in any room starts with the stage.

How you dress your windows and walls

depends on the mood you want that background to create. If walls are snowy white and windows unadorned, the scene feels swept-clean and modern. Classic swags and jabots or taffeta draperies puddled on the floor convey formality; floral-print cafe curtains, colorful Roman shades, or simple shutters are casual and relaxed.

BEST-DRESSED PANES

■ **BE PRACTICAL.** Window dressings control light, save energy, and ensure privacy. Insulating honeycomb shades can take the chill off a room. In a south- or west-facing room, louvered shutters or blinds can be tilted to block midday or afternoon glare without completely obscuring the view.

■ **SET A MOOD.** For an elegant, traditional look, consider treatments with valances and side panels, richly gathered draperies, or classic swags and jabots. Decorative details, such as rosettes and fringe, add even more elegance. Although generally considered more casual in feeling, shutters, blinds, and Roman shades, which bring linear interest and texture, are flexible; layer draperies over them for a touch of formality, or use them when you want to create a clean, crisp look. Gauzy curtains spark romance.

■ **ALTER ARCHITECTURE.** To heighten or widen small windows, extend treatments beyond the frames. Visually raise a low ceiling with ceiling-high, floor-length curtains and vertical wall stripes.

■ **PAY ATTENTION TO DETAILS.** Surprise the eye with details, such as unusual hardware or drapery linings in contrasting colors and patterns. Braids and fringes dress up plain linen draperies. Fashioning old finials, doorknobs, or even branding irons into rods and tiebacks adds personality to casual windows.

ABOVE: Traditionally furnished with a Queen Anne table and chairs and a symmetrical display on the mantel, this dining room eases up with spirited raspberry color on the walls and gathered, swag-style valances. **OPPOSITE:** With a casual checked valance and curtains over textured roll-up shades, this living room window sets the style scene for a mix of classic and fixer-upper furnishings. Floral-fabric trim softens the drapery checks and echoes colors of the needlepoint rug.

Window Solutions

Whether you swag it, shade it, shirr it, shutter it, tie it back, or let it flow,

a window treatment can be a problem solver. Fabric treatments soften angular walls, introduce color and pattern, and make eloquent style statements. The right fabric treatment can make windows look taller, wider, or more dramatic than they really are. But fabric is optional. Because clean-lined shades, shutters, or blinds tuck close to panes, they're sensible treatments in small spaces. When privacy isn't a major concern, leaded-glass and art glass window panes solo beautifully. Take a creative approach, as these homeowners did, to turn your windows into decorative assets.

LEFT: Frame a window and a wall for a focal point. Wall-to-wall swags in red toile create headboard interest for this room's twin beds and add drama to a single window. The treatment echoes bed linen patterns and heightens the overall feeling of luxury. **OPPOSITE:** Keep a low profile in tight places. Trim Roman shades are great for small spaces and kids' rooms. These limeade-green shades add more tropical punch to the cool blue guest bath, which was a screen porch before the home was remodeled. Made of easy-care canvas duck, they have cording strung through silver grommets.

LEFT: Enjoy your view and privacy too. To showcase the architecture and the woods beyond, this expansive bay window dresses light in valance-topped Roman shades that unify the panes with old-world, crewel-like pattern. The stylish yet practical treatment means there are no fussy curtains to interfere with window seat lounging. The shades are mounted low to allow the high transom windows to shine. **BELOW:** Unify a mix of window shapes with a one-for-all treatment. Crisp floor-to-ceiling draperies blend this living room's panes. As a bonus, the draperies elegantly soften walls too. The natural linen panels are studded with nickel-finish grommets that slide, shower-curtain style, along silvery rods attached to ceiling brackets.

Personality by the Roll

Why remodel when you can use wall coverings to give your rooms a dash

of colorful character? With wallcoverings that mimic the real thing, you can even wrap a den in what looks like rugged leather or logs, a dining room in faux scarlet moiré, or a living room in a trompe l'oeil mural or a cityscape "view."

WALLS AT WORK

How dominant a role do you want the walls—and wall covering—to play? In a neutral scheme, you may only want subtle texture. What are your walls up against wear-wise? Prepasted, scrubbable vinyl coverings are easy-care choices for kitchens and baths.

■ **ADD COLOR AND CHARACTER.** This is the forte of wallcov-erings. Trompe l'oeil coverings let you create an instant faux library, a plate-lined shelf—and more.

■ **REMODEL WITHOUT REMODELING.** Vertically striped wall covering visually raises a ceiling; horizontal designs help widen a narrow room. A pattern with curves and flowing lines eases boxiness.

■ **CREATE ARCHITECTURAL INTEREST.** Apply a striped wallcov-ering to a lower wall and band with chair rail molding to create a wainscot effect. Use a border as a faux molding at the ceiling line. To accentuate architec-tural features such as doors and alcoves, consider outlining them in a border.

OPPOSITE: Wallpaper mimics whitewashed wood paneling in this bedroom. The raised-panel illusion is created with large rectangles cut from a coordinating border and applied to walls. Using coordinated wallpaper and fabrics collections like these makes pattern mixing a breeze. **ABOVE LEFT:** A Victorian-inspired floral wallcovering works with a vintage-style cross-handle faucet to set a nostalgic look. A coordinating stripe adds interest to the mirrored wall niche. **ABOVE RIGHT:** Inspired by the Far East, this flowing floral wallpaper adds curves that break up a boxy bath. A window shade adds privacy while reflecting light all day.

Artful Touches
You can add architectural oomph or a new view to blank walls, dead-end hallways, and featureless

spaces with paint. The delightful fireplace on the opposite page won't warm your tootsies or toast your marshmallows, but it warms the hearts of overnight guests in the third-floor guest suite. The faux fireplace and other special effects shown here are done in trompe l'oeil, a witty decorative painting technique defined as "fool the eye." Use trompe l'oeil to add architectural dimension or imaginative accents, to make walls and ceilings disappear into painted-on landscapes, and to give plain wood floors the rich look of parquet. Investigate trompe l'oeil wallcoverings and posters. For custom touches, hire a pro.

FIND YOUR ARTIST

■ **TROMPE L'OEIL REQUIRES ART SKILLS.** If decorative painting isn't your forte, hire a professional. Or search for a skilled painter at local schools and colleges; an art teacher may recommend talented colleagues or students. Inquire about qualified artists at art supply or crafts stores.

■ **CHECK WITH INSTRUCTORS** of studio art. They may know creative students eager to add your project to their portfolios.

■ **INTERVIEW CANDIDATES.** Review artists' portfolios and references. Discuss options for your space. Do they have fresh, original ideas that fit your vision? Be sure you agree on materials, cost, and project deadlines.

ABOVE: Even a small flourish of decorative painting brings a dramatic architectural accent, vertical interest, and a treetop view to this windowless wall. An artist created the elegantly molded faux window and filled it in with a leafy scene that replicates what's outside. **RIGHT:** Until an artist stepped in, this stairwell was about the only space in the waterside home that didn't enjoy a surf's-up view. The painted-on double-hung window echoes the home's original panes. The handrail is brushed in a trailing vine to bring more alfresco ease to a once-dull passageway.

OPPOSITE: Dressed in a distressed antique mantel and real props such as the log-filled pot, this fanciful fireplace is painted onto a plain, flat brick wall. With library shelves and a butter-soft leather chair pulled up "hearthside," the reading nook is definitely cozy and almost as much fun as having the real thing.

Playful Painting

Put the "wow" in plain walls with decorative paint finishes. Even beginners can paint stripes, stencil borders, sponge finishes and brush on fabric looks, such as linen or suede. If you're a novice, start with sponging or ragging or use painter's masking tape to mark off simple stripes. Also check out new paint products and finishes in crafts stores and home centers.

ABOVE LEFT: For a den that needed subtle color and pattern, checkerboard walls created the perfect backdrop for a comfy mix of furnishings and the family photo gallery. Walls got a base coat of the lighter hue; then darker checks were done in watered-down acrylic. **ABOVE RIGHT:** Literally dressed to the nines, this remodeled Craftsman-style entry marches a parade of Roman numerals around the top of the wall just for fun and, of course, for vertical interest. The numerals were done in gold on a broad painted border of yellow.

PAINTER'S SECRETS

- **BEFORE YOU DECIDE ON THE SCALE** of your pattern, measure walls and note ceiling height, window and door placement, and the size of patterns used on furniture. Oversize designs may fit a large room but over-power a small one; vertical patterns may be too much for a tall room; a strong horizontal design can be bad news for a low ceiling. If yours is a roomful of patterned furnishings, consider a subtle washed or sponged finish versus a busy patterned one.
- **REPAIR WALLS FIRST.** Then practice your technique and try out colors on a drywall remnant or smooth plywood 3 to 4 feet square.

- **PICK A TEXTURE.** Flat, eggshell, semigloss, and high-gloss paint fin-ishes give off different auras. Gloss finishes reflect light and create a spacious look; flat paints do a better job of masking wall damage.
- **USE COLORED PENCILS** matching paint colors to mark pattern on walls.
- **PICK A PARTNER** for large or difficult projects. Factor in drying time for individual steps; complicated designs could take several days.
- **SELECT WELL-MADE BRUSHES** designed for your project. Depending on the paint job, you may need basic brushes, small artist's brushes, and specialty-finish brushes or rollers. You also may need levels, straight-edges, and painter's tape.

ABOVE: The homeowner's collection of antique quilts inspired the spring-fresh greens and soft pinks of fabrics, layered bed linens, and the walls in this charming guest room. A lacy stenciled border accents the ceiling line, and hand-painted motifs are sprinkled over the walls. **ABOVE RIGHT:** Wide cabana stripes in varying shades of green coax this sunroom into a summery mood all year round. The homeowner lightly marked stripes with a pencil, then used a straight-edge brush to fill them in with watered-down acrylic paint for a "washed-out" look.

WindowSketchbook

Browse through this sketchbook, and you'll find ideas for a variety of window and door treatments.

SINGLE WINDOWS

If you're dressing a single window (see illustrations 1–5), consider its size first. Does the window look small compared with the furnishings or the room itself? Add fullness with gathered tiebacks (4) or flowing curtains (1, 5). If its scale matches other elements, treat it simply with a shade or a top treatment (2, 3). Increase its visual size by mounting the curtain rod beyond the frame top and sides so that panels stack back over walls.

MULTIPLE/SPLIT WINDOWS

A series of identical windows (6–10) invites the light and outdoor view inside. These windows also offer numerous decorating options. First decide whether you want to treat each window separately or the series as one window. Taking a look at your room's style may give you a clue as to which approach is best. In a clean-lined contemporary setting, the geometric look of a bank of windows can be an asset. To get the full architectural impact, use a top treatment only or inside-mount identical curtain panels (6). Do you need more privacy, light control, or energy efficiency? Shades, blinds, and shutters (7, 8) mounted inside each window's molding perform those tasks and offer a tailored look. If you prefer a softer, traditional look, fabric options abound. Flowing, to-the-floor draperies (9) lend timeless elegance to spaces. Crown draperies with a sculpted cornice (10) to add height and formality, or use a cornice alone for architectural interest. For a lighter look, half-curtains can add French-cafe charm, plus privacy and sunshine; in a pared-down setting, simple side curtains add color and pattern. The all-for-one treatment applies to split windows, too, whether you treat them to shades, shutters, or swags and cascades pulled to the outer edges (11).

Window Sketchbook continued on page 372
Window Sketchbook continued on page 372

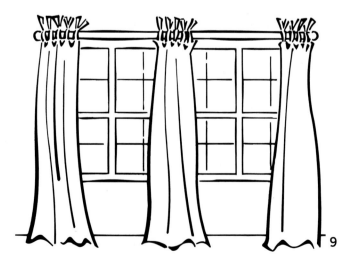

3

4

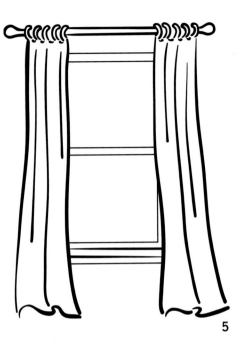

5

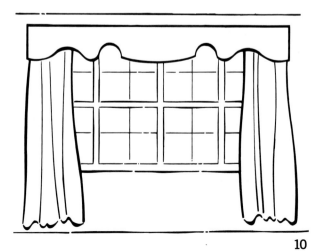

7

8

10

11

CORNER WINDOWS

Mirror-image dressings (1–5) allow you to treat corner windows separately but achieve the effect of a single design. Be sure draperies or vertical blinds draw to the outside, and blinds raise and lower without clashing. In small spaces, avoid fabrics with busy patterns and contrasting colors; instead match treatments to wall color to blend them into the background and expand the room.

BAY AND BOW WINDOWS

Like corner windows, the windows within a bay or bow may demand separate but equal treatment (6–10). Like matched series, there are many ways to treat bays. To keep things clean, stick with trim shades or blinds (6), or add a window seat and shutters (7). Outline those tailored treatments with fabric, such as a sweeping swag or a scalloped valance for eye-pleasing softness and color (9). Do you want to fabricate a formal look? Install framing draperies across the front of the window alcove (10), or for an airier look, add sheer panels that slide on cable wire (8). For a curving bow window, consider hanging curtains on a flexible rod that sweeps around the bow.

SLIDING DOORS

Treatments for sliding glass doors must allow free operation and access while also enhancing the doors' appearance and providing privacy and light control. Blinds, shades, draperies, panels that slide to one side, split panels that meet in the middle, or stationary curtain panels flanking the door are options (11–15). Mount treatments so they draw completely beyond the walkway. To control light and privacy, use individual blinds or shades; for more finesse, add a top treatment (12) or (not shown) layer draperies over blinds.

HIGH WINDOWS

The goal in treating high windows is to visually lower them with long treatments and/or by placing a piece of furniture beneath them. If you place a piece of furniture under the window, choose a fitted covering, such as shutters, shades, or blinds (16–18), that will stay out of the way. If your room is full of horizontal elements—beds, chests, and bureaus—add visual interest with a vertical, to-the-floor treatment (19, 20). To make windows appear larger, install a row of fixed shutters below the windows and operable shutters on the panes (17).

Window Sketchbook continued on page 374

1

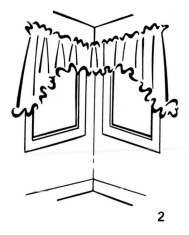

2

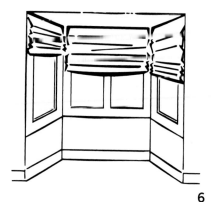

6

7

11

12

16

17

3

4

5

8

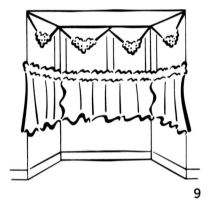

9

10

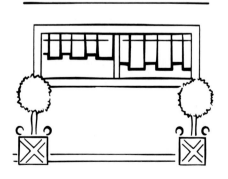

13

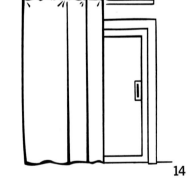

14

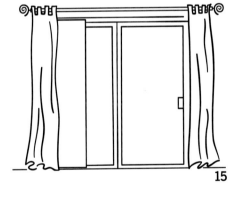

15

18

19

20

CASEMENT WINDOWS

Standard casement windows open in or out and can be treated like single windows. However, the ideal covering should mount to the outside so that it falls over the window's cranking mechanism. Swinging crane rods (1) or fixed curtain rods (3) offer good solutions, as do top/down and bottom/up fabric shades topped with a valance (2). If you choose tiebacks, dress each window in a drapery panel that draws to the outer edge of each window where tieback hardware is installed. For inward-swinging casement windows, the treatment shouldn't interfere with window operation. Inset curtains or blinds on each window (5) or inside-mount a roller shade and paint "architecture" with stenciling or freehand designs on the wall around the frame (4).

FRENCH DOORS

French doors combine the problems of outfitting inward-swinging casement windows with those of covering sliding glass doors. The solutions divide into two groups: Either affix your treatment to each door panel, or opt for a treatment that clears the doors by drawing completely to the side or top. For a look that won't interfere with the architecture, mount blinds or shades on each door (6–8). If your decorating style calls for a softer touch, consider shirred lace or fabric panels or door-mounted tiebacks. Traditional drapery treatments are viable options (9, 10). Simply make sure the rod extends well beyond the frame so draperies can be drawn out of the way of the doors.

TRANSOMS, SIDELIGHTS, SKYLIGHTS

The trick to treating windows with sculptural curves and unusual shapes is to flow with the curve or bend with the angle of the opening without sacrificing light or privacy. For windows topped with stationary transom-style panes (11, 12), leave the upper windows bare, or treat the transom panes and lower windows as one with the rod installed at the ceiling line. For doors with sidelights (13), treat the two as one whether you use curtains, sheers, blinds, or shades. Palladian-inspired half-round windows (14) are most spectacular when they're minimally dressed. For skylights, filter sunlight with stationary sheer panels (15) or remote-controlled motorized shades.

1

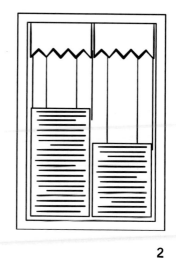

2

6

7

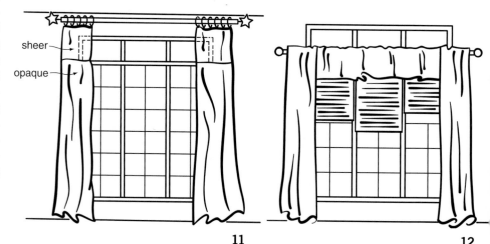

sheer

opaque

11

12

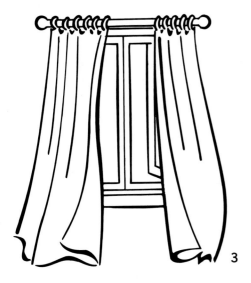

3

4

5

8

9

10

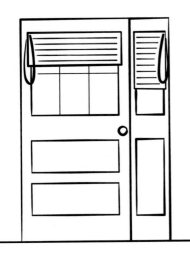

13

14

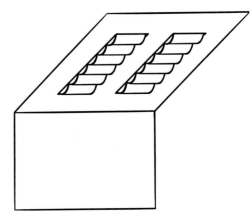

15

CHAPTER 19

Floors

When decorating, pay attention to the bottom line—the floor. It's one of your room's largest areas, so it has a major impact on how a room looks and feels. Choose floor coverings with an eye to color, pattern, transition, texture, and, of course, comfort and function. Depending on how it is treated, the floor can be a room's decorating star, or as this bathroom shows, it can create an elegantly understated backdrop. Use the tips in this chapter to help your floors play the roles you assign them in high style.

ComfortUnderfoot
Carpet and area rugs enrich the mood and turn up the comfort level in any room.

They also help you set your style, visually open or define your space, and add warm texture and color. To shop wisely, take along room measurements, fabric swatches, paint chips, and even snapshots to guide your color and style choices.

WALL-TO-WALL FLOW

■ **UNIFY WITH CARPET.** For continuity, run similar color and texture throughout open-plan spaces. A seamless sweep of floor color gives choppy floor plans a spacious feel and flow.

■ **TAKE A BREAK.** Use a change of carpet color or texture to deliberately set one area off from another. For instance, a subtle change of a carpet's shade or texture can set a bedroom hallway apart from an entry or living area.

■ **EXPRESS A MOOD.** In general, the stronger the texture, the more casual its decorating effect. For an easygoing look, choose nubby-textured berber or another loop-style carpet or sisal or sisal-look blends. For a more formal mood, consider velvety, plush pile carpet.

■ **GO EASY ON THE MIX.** When rooms have bold motifs or mixed patterns on walls and/or furnishings, select pattern-free or subtly patterned carpet.

VERSATILE AREA RUGS

■ **MAKE A RUG A PALETTE-SETTER.** Redecorating? Make the rug the first element you choose. Then use its colors and motifs in other furnishings. (Yes, it's OK to lay a rug over carpet.)

■ **ENHANCE AN EXISTING COLOR SCHEME.** Working with what you have? Use a patterned rug to liven up a room dominated by solids. Conversely, add a solid-color rug to anchor busily patterned upholstery and create a calming effect.

■ **MAKE IT A FOCAL POINT.** Choose a rug with bright colors, strong color contrast, or artful pattern when you want to draw the eye to a seating group or slow the pace in an entry hall. A round rug throws soft curves into a mix of angular furnishings.

■ **DEFINE AND CONQUER.** Use rugs under dining pieces and under seating pieces to subtly separate zones in an open-plan living-dining room or great-room. To securely anchor conversation groupings, it's best if seating pieces rest entirely on or off the rug.

LEFT: Floors covered in a wonderfully textured soft brown carpet turn this library into a luxurious retreat. Furnished with a mix of contemporary seating and antiques, including an 18th-century French console, the room gains even more mellow appeal from the rich terra-cotta hue of the walls.

WarmUp with Wood

No matter what mood your room's in—from rustic cottage style to gallery-white contemporary—nothing can substitute for the warmth of wood floors. Wood floors are a top-of-the-line investment, but should you go to the expense of installing real oak or pine planks? Would lower-cost wood veneer over particleboard or new laminated wood look-alikes work equally well? It depends on your practical needs and your budget.

ABOVE LEFT: Not every space benefits from a bold rug. This elegant bedroom needed only a dose of warm-up texture. Neutrals rule the day and pattern speaks softly here, so the rug follows suit with a subtle overall motif and border. **ABOVE RIGHT:** In this laid-back beach cottage where sun and sea set the yellow and blue palette, the breakfast room boasts an easy-care floor of blue laminated hardwood. Playful painting salvaged the old game table and chairs for dining.

REAL WOODS OR FABULOUS FAKES?

Real woods generally cost more to buy, but they pay you back with years of style and wear. Wood-look laminates generally cost less than the real thing and are easier for do-it-yourselfers to install. They mimic anything from oak and pine to maple and cherry.

■ **INVEST IN THE REAL THING** if you're planning to stay awhile in your home. It will last not only your lifetime, but also the lifetime of your home. Except when used in wet areas, wood ages gracefully, developing a deeper, richer patina over time. Unlike wood floors of the past, today's floors have polyurethane finishes for easy care. Remember, though, that real woods shouldn't be used in rooms where moisture could be a problem. Consider real wood for public or formal rooms because it's hardworking and easy to care for; lower-priced look-alikes may repel scratches but they won't go the distance of real wood. Real woods are available prefinished, but often it's less expensive to have a new oak floor installed and finished on-site.

■ **ADD FUNCTION WITH FAUX WOODS** in kitchens, baths, and family and kids' rooms where you want the wood look without worrying about potential damage from kids' spills and overflowing plumbing. Laminated "wood" planks resist scratching and staining and come in colorful stains and finishes. Prefinished planks of oak veneers over particleboard save money but won't wear as long as solid wood.

ABOVE LEFT: An artist's touch imbues the entry of this Victorian home with grandeur and a sense of place—the seaside. With a combination of stains and paints, the once-plain hardwood floor boasts a faux-parquet look. A flock of painted shorebirds hops along the baseboards. **ABOVE RIGHT:** An old wood floor needs only sanding and a couple of coats of bright enamel to bring it back to life. A change of color separates the sunny hallway from the rooms that connect to it.

Down-to-Earth Delights

Beyond carpet and wood, a separate category of flooring called nonresilients, or hard surface flooring, offers natural variety for your decorating schemes. Clay, tile, slate, brick, marble, terrazzo, and limestone, for instance, bring rich colors, textures, and natural patterns to floors. A less expensive option is a concrete floor, which can be colorized, chemically etched, or stamped to mimic tile, slate, and rough-hewn rock.

MATCH YOUR STYLE

Different materials can set a variety of decorating styles. Consider creamy travertine for neoclassic or contemporary style, veined marble in sophisticated traditional spaces, random-cut fieldstone for a rugged lodge look, saltillo tile for a south-of-the-border flavor, or brick pavers for an indoor-garden or yesteryear feel.

CONSIDER THE COST

Is real stone worth it? Aesthetically, yes. But stone floors generally require professional installation, and the materials themselves are costly. Stone also is among the coldest of all flooring choices; it's unforgiving on dropped plates and doesn't provide noise insulation. On the plus side, stone adds unrivaled texture, mood, and natural appeal to spaces; it repels water, and it's easy to clean.

HOW TO SAVE MONEY

To enjoy the beauty of natural stone without breaking the budget, think small. Enjoy a luxurious travertine floor, for example, in a half bath or a touch of marble in a small entry. Or create a border of stone or brick around the perimeter of a room; then add an inset of more affordable carpet.

OPPOSITE: A concrete floor stained to mimic aged leather beautifully complements and blends with this mahogany cabinetry. The warm tones of the floor and cabinets make a perfect foil for metal hardware and walls of diamond-pattern aluminum. LEFT: Vintage woods and natural stone bring the charm and character of an old Virginia farmhouse to this new kitchen that offers state-of-the-art efficiency. For rugged country appeal, the cabinetry is made of salvaged heart pine and vintage wavy glass, and the flooring is a mosaic of soapstone.

VersatileTile

Affordable and easier to find and install than stone
or similar natural materials, ceramic tile and vinyl flooring offer a
versatile and easy-care option for living spaces. An ever-growing range of colors, patterns, sizes, finishes, and even grout colors makes ceramic tile flooring worth considering for more than the kitchen or bath. And vinyls in a range of sophisticated styles, patterns, and custom designs are readily available.

CERAMICS STAND UP

Whether in solid colors or fresh hand-painted designs, ceramic tile offers fuss-free durability and style. An expected choice for a kitchen or bath, ceramic tile also makes sense in a high-traffic entry or in a family room that needs to look great for entertaining despite kids tracking in grime from outside. Stylewise, a clean sweep of single-color ceramic tile across a floor creates a streamlined effect that can visually expand a space. Look at other options too: Use tile to create an inlaid "area rug," add a patterned tile on the diagonal every few feet for interest, or create a patterned border. Or go for a classic approach with a two-tone tile checkerboard.

STYLISH VINYLS

Affordable vinyl flooring is another great pretender. You'll find a wide range of vinyl tiles or sheet vinyls that mimic ceramics, faux lapis paintwork, stone, natural sisal, wood, and other flooring materials. Classic checkerboard patterns are hard to beat because they fit almost any room style and furnishings mix even if the room already has a helping of pattern. Install the checkerboard on the diagonal to add pleasing depth to any room or to make a small space feel bigger.

BELOW: How do you throw a few dramatic curves into a grid of square tiles? Break things up. Creating fluid contrast to pavers in this entry, splashes of broken blue ceramic tile and glass have terra-cotta-color grout to highlight the cobblestoned look.

OPPOSITE: Showing the versatility of the classic checkerboard floor, this dining room/kitchen addition features tile laid on the diagonal. The repeating floor pattern grounds a mix of traditional and garden-style furnishings against the fresh citrus backdrop. The table is a cast-iron garden urn topped with a glass round.

FlooringFacts
Selecting the right floor covering to beautifully underscore your room's style
means looking beyond that gorgeous color, bold pattern, or rich wood grain. Will the flooring stand up to heavy traffic? Does it fit your room's style and your comfort demands? For example, hardwood or hard surfaces are better for relieving allergies and maintaining indoor air quality, and vinyls and laminates help you save money. Shop around, and you'll see that you can find a floor covering to fit nearly every job description—and, yes, you can have that gorgeous color, bold pattern, or rich wood you love too. To make the right match, check out our flooring chart.

CARPET AND RUG CONSTRUCTION

	CHARACTERISTICS	ADVANTAGES	DISADVANTAGES	CARE/COST
COTTON	Soft fiber often used for informal area or scatter rugs.	Easily dyed.	Limited durability.	Cleans very well, some rugs machine-washable. Usually inexpensive.
WOOL	Deep, warm, rich look; excellent resiliency and abrasion resistance; has a warm and natural feel.	Excellent durability; flame-resistant; crush-resistant; dyes well in a wide range of colors.	Can be damaged by alkaline detergents; needs moth-proofing; not best medium for bright colors.	Resists soil; not cleaned as easily as many synthetic fibers. Expensive.
COIR, JUTE, AND SISAL	Used for informal matting; available in colors (mainly earth tones); can be stenciled or painted.	Offers textural contrast and a variety of patterns.	Fair-to-poor durability and resistance to wear and soil; not as soft underfoot as conventional carpet.	Offers little resistance to soil; not easily cleaned. Usually inexpensive.
ACRYLIC	Of the synthetic fibers, closest to wool; nonallergenic; resists mildew, moths, and insects; comes in a range of colors.	Crush-resistant; springy; fade-resistant; generates minimal static.	May form pills, or beadlike balls of fiber, on face of carpet; not as resilient, as durable, or as stain-resistant as wool or nylon.	Cleans very well; smooth fibers resist soil. Moderate price.
NYLON	Wide choice of colors; excellent color retention; soft and resilient.	Strongest synthetic fiber; resists abrasion, mildew, and moths; nonallergenic; continuous filament fibers minimize pilling and shedding.	Static-prone unless treated; cut-filament loop carpet may pill.	Good cleanability; stain-resistant treatments offer effective stain protection. Moderate price.
POLYESTER	Similar to wool in look and feel; good color and texture selection and color retention; resists moths, mildew; nonallergenic.	Very durable, resilient; abrasion- and static-resistant; sheds moisture; available in a wide range of colors.	Does not wear as well as wool or nylon; some pilling and shedding; susceptible to oil-base stains.	Good cleanability, enhanced by stain-resistant treatments. Less expensive than nylon or wool carpet.
OLEFIN	Primarily loop and randomly sheared textures; nonabsorbent; resists abrasion, pilling, and shedding.	Fibers can withstand moisture; use indoors or outdoors; very durable in level-loop styles.	Lower grades may crush and flatten.	Excellent cleanability, especially with stain-resistant treatments; resists static, acids, chemicals. Moderate price.

RESILIENT AND HARD SURFACE

	CHARACTERISTICS	ADVANTAGES	DISADVANTAGES	CLEANABILITY
ASPHALT TILE	Porous; resists alkalies; low cost.	OK on cement floor; can be below grade.	Noisy; dents easily; needs waxing.	Damaged by grease and harsh cleaners.
CORK TILE	Handsome, sealed surface.	Warm; comfortable, and quiet underfoot.	Not for heavy traffic.	Easy upkeep; must be sealed for durability.
RUBBER TILE	Handsome, clear colors.	Excellent resilience; quiet; durable.	Expensive; slippery when wet; must be above grade.	Resists dents and stains; damaged by strong detergents and grease.
VINYL COMPOSITION	Resists alkalies; easy to install; low cost.	Durable; colorful.	Not very quiet or resilient.	Embossed surfaces trap dirt; clean with heavy-duty detergents.
CUSHIONED SHEET VINYL	Wide range of colors, patterns, surface finishes, and prices.	Superior resilience; quiet; comfortable; stain-resistant.	Expensive; lower-cost grades susceptible to nicks and dents.	Easy upkeep; no-wax or never-wax feature available
SHEET VINYL	Wide range of colors, patterns, and surface finishes available.	Good resilience.	Less expensive grades susceptible to nicks and dents.	Easily maintained; some with no-wax feature.
SOLID VINYL TILE	Often simulates natural materials.	Easy to install; durable.	Only fair resilience.	Stain-resistant; easy to clean and maintain.
WOOD	Natural or painted; wide range of patterns possible.	Good resilience; hardwoods very durable.	Softwoods less durable than hardwood counterparts.	Should be sealed with a penetrating oil sealer (with wax protector) or waterproof polyurethane; manufactured floors usually are presealed.
BRICK, SLATE, QUARRY TILE	Natural look; variety of exciting shapes.	Durable; beautiful.	No resilience.	Slate and quarry tile may need sealer; good stain resistance.
STONE (GRANITE, LIMESTONE, ETC.)	Offers a natural look.	Durable; beautiful.	No resilience.	Some types absorb stains easily.
CERAMIC TILE	Colorful; many shapes and designs.	Beautiful; stain- and fade-resistant.	No resilience; cold underfoot; noisy under hard-soled shoes.	Clean with soap and water only.
MARBLE	Costly; formal.	Beautiful.	Hard underfoot; noisy under hard-soled shoes; stains easily.	Needs waxing; stains are difficult to remove.
TERRAZZO	Smooth, shiny finish; variety of multicolor effects.	Durable; stain- and moisture-resistant.	Comes in limited designs; permanent installation.	Easily cleaned.
CONCRETE	Design flexibility; wide range of colors and patterns.	Mimics other materials, including stone and tile, at lower cost.	Porous; seal so stains don't penetrate.	Easily cleaned.
LAMINATES	Wide range of colors and patterns; wood and stone looks available.	Scratch- and stain-resistant.	Some types prone to water damage unless sealed; some need underlayment to deaden sound.	Easily maintained; avoid wet mopping.

Accent
Rugs

If your off-the-rack sisal or coir rug lies in the middle of your living room looking ordinary, turn it into a natural wonder with one of these easy-to-do projects. Fabric, paints, and powdered fabric dyes are all you need to add colorful personality and a sense of style to your ready-made rug.

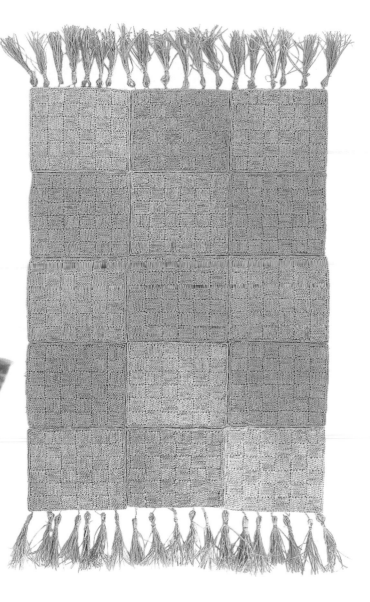

CUTTING-EDGE SISAL
What you'll need:
4×6-foot sisal rug, 3 yards of 54-inch-wide sturdy cotton fabric that will stand up to foot traffic and vacuuming (total border width is about 9 inches for 4-inch border front and back and ½-inch hems), yarn, crewel needle, spray adhesive, and fabric glue

Cut and hem the border pieces, and "baste" them in place using a small amount of spray adhesive. At each corner, fold one end under at an angle to form a mock miter; secure with fabric glue. Using a crewel needle and yarn (double strands for larger rugs), stitch a zigzag pattern around the inside perimeter of the border. Stitch diagonally in one direction around the rug, then stitch back in the opposite direction.

CHECKMATE TO DYE FOR
What you'll need:
A sisal or maize rug made of 12-inch squares, powdered fabric dye, heavy string or dental floss for reattaching squares, large-eye needle, heavy cardboard, and natural or dyed raffia for tassels

Cut rug squares apart. Mix fabric dye with 2 quarts hot water (for stronger colors, use two boxes of dye per 2 quarts of water). Soak squares in dye for 5 to 10 minutes until color is slightly darker than desired; drain excess dye, and dry squares on newspapers overnight. If more than one color is used, clean dye pan with bleach between colors. Reassemble rug with heavy, large-eye needle and string or floss. For tassels, loop one strand of raffia around a 7-inch length of heavy cardboard 15 times. Tie one end of loops together with a separate 10-inch length of raffia; slide loops off cardboard. To create tassel head, wrap a 20-inch raffia strand 1 inch from top; knot ends. Cut and trim tassel bottom ends; stitch tassels to rug, 2 inches apart.

HIGH-STEPPING STENCILS

What you'll need:

Rug, precut stencil or plastic stencil sheet, latex or high-quality acrylic paint, nonyellowing floor wax, painter's tape, 1-inch foam brushes, fine paintbrush, and paint roller and cover

Use precut stencil or cut designs from plastic sheet; cut a separate stencil for each color used. Dilute each paint with equal amounts of water. Tape and paint rug border; let dry and remove tape. Tape and paint first stencil. Because of rug's rough texture, lines and colors won't be perfectly even. Repeat first-color application in each square. Repeat with remaining stencils and colors; paint any fine lines freehand. When rug is dry, apply nonyellowing floor wax with a paint roller to protect the painted design from chipping.

PERENNIAL BORDER

What you'll need:

4x6-foot coir or other solid-woven sisal rug, 10-inch-wide fabric strips for border—4 inches front and back and 1 inch for hems (the larger the rug, the wider the band should be), hot glue and glue gun, carpet thread to match fabric, and commercial-strength glue

Cut 10-inch-wide fabric strips 4 inches longer than the rug sides. Press strips in half lengthwise and press under 1 inch hems. Fit bands over rug edges and tack with hot glue. Slip-stitch bands to rug with a double strand of thread. At corners, fold excess fabric on diagonal to make a mock miter. Trim excess fabric and slip-stitch in place. For high-traffic areas, stitch fabric to back of rug in the same way or secure back border with commercial-strength glue.

CHAPTER 20

Lighting

With the flick of a switch, you can work decorating magic with lighting. The right light can set a new mood, enrich colors, spotlight art and collectibles, and make your rooms work harder. Candle-style sconces play up this room's warm wall color, and lamps turn a part-time dining table into a multipurpose desk and reading table. In this chapter, you'll learn how to improve existing lighting to give your rooms more function and drama.

Lighting Basics

Well-balanced lighting goes beyond the ubiquitous reading lamp by the sofa or the centered ceiling fixture. Layering the essential building blocks—general (also called ambient) light, task (also called local) light, and accent light—is what makes living spaces truly inviting and functional. With the right mix of these essential illumination sources, you can bring "sunshine" to any room, create drama, visually alter a room's dimensions, and highlight your favorite things.

THE BIG THREE

■ **GENERAL, OR AMBIENT, LIGHTING** allows you to move safely through a room without running into furniture or tripping on the kids' toys. Glare-free, indirect light bounces off the walls and ceiling to add comfortable background illumination. An even distribution of light is key so that you don't end up with areas that are overly bright or hidden in shadows. Recessed canisters, track lighting, cable lighting, chandeliers, and hanging paper-shaded fixtures can be good general light sources. With the help of a dimmer control, they can change the mood of a room instantly and still light your way.

■ **TASK, OR LOCAL, LIGHTING** provides necessary illumination for reading, cooking, crafting, hobbies, and the like. As with general lighting, position lights to avoid casting shadows. A long desk or sewing table might require two light sources (one on each end). Reading lamps and undercabinet lighting also fit into this category.

■ **ACCENT LIGHTING** has a decorative function and can come from several sources. Including everything from floor-based uplights and torchères to sconces and direct spotlights, accent lighting draws attention to a room's most interesting aspects. Shine a little light on a favorite work of art or an architectural element, or add a shelf strip light to highlight small collectibles.

BELOW: Sleek and chic, a lineup of suspended halogen spotlights illuminates this dining table and echoes the clean-lined architecture of the surroundings. A ceiling spotlight flips on at night to turn artwork into a colorful focal point for dining.

OPPOSITE: Creative lighting brings sculptural form and function to this whitewashed cottage living room. This small space couldn't squeeze in bulky tables with reading lamps, so leggy floor lamps flank the loveseat. In the background, the pendant over the table was made with a vintage shade.

Balance Your Lighting

Different spaces need different kinds of illumination, and it's not just the quantity of light

sources that creates well-balanced lighting. It's the way you distribute those light sources to avoid glaring mistakes and create practical, beautiful pools to light your path.

PLAN ROOM BY ROOM

To customize your home's illumination, match each fixture to the role it will play and provide enough light sources for pleasant, safe, comfortable spaces.

■ **MIX SOURCES FOR LIVING AND FAMILY ROOMS.** For television viewing or relaxing, general lighting from indirect sources is best—wall washers, uplights, and recessed fixtures. For homework, hobbies, and reading, add task lighting—downlights, spotlights, and table or floor lamps. Remember that older eyes need more light (ideally 100 watts) for reading.

■ **GIVE DINING ROOMS FLEXIBILITY.** Tame a bright chandelier with a dimmer to soften the mood. Above a long table, consider a trio of pendants instead of a lone fixture. Supplement over-the-table lighting with buffet lamps, art lights, and plug-in shelf lights.

■ **LIGHT KITCHENS FOR EFFICIENCY.** Augment general illuminators—track, recessed, or other ceiling fixtures—with task lights beamed on counters, cooktops, and islands. The cozy trend? A small table lamp atop the counter for warm general light and a homey feel.

■ **ADD TASK LIGHTS TO BEDROOMS AND BATHS.** Put general lighting on a mood-setting dimmer. For kids' rooms, avoid halogen lamps, which produce intense heat; ceiling or wall fixtures are safer than table lamps for very young kids.

■ **IN A ROOM WITH A VAULTED CEILING,** ceiling fixtures are of little help to people below. Use torchères, track lighting, or spotlights mounted on open beams to bounce light off the ceiling for a general glow. Supplement with task lamps.

■ **PUT SAFETY FIRST IN ENTRIES,** but keep drama a priority. Up a stairway, several elegant sconces make more sense than a hard-to-clean hanging fixture on the landing. Aisle lights installed above sidewall baseboards also can light a dark, potentially dangerous stairway.

RIGHT: For efficiency and a perennially bright mood, this kitchen combines subtle and dramatic light sources. Interior lights set glass-front cabinets aglow, a lineup of pendants illuminates food preparation and casual dining on the island, and recessed fixtures cast light on countertops.

Switch On the Accents

Stars step into the spotlight at the theater, so why not borrow the same creative stagecraft for your home's featured performers? Well-planned accent lighting can play up your room's best assets—artwork, important furniture groupings, intriguing architecture, or collectibles. Just remember that lighting meant to accent objects should be about three times brighter than the room's general lighting.

AMAZING GRACE

Until a lighting redesign, this suburban living room was not equipped to give due attention to collections of classic retro furniture and modern art, such as Andy Warhol's Grace Kelly portrait. These treasures deserved the drama only accent lighting can ignite. To create a relaxed gallery mood, low-voltage halogen lights were recessed in the ceiling. They're adjustable, so varying beams spotlight specific art or furniture. Incandescent uplights tuck behind sculpture pedestals.

SPOTLIGHT YOUR FAVORITES

■ **EXPERIMENT FIRST.** If you're unsure where to put accent lights, buy inexpensive clamp-on lights with spotlight bulbs. Try them in different locations. You'll see where you want to direct extra light, and you may opt to keep the clamp-ons instead of installing fixed lighting.

■ **GET DIRECTIONS RIGHT.** Light decorative objects from the front or above, emphasizing shape and texture. Angle an art light toward a painting, not down on it, to minimize reflection and glare.

■ **TO CREATE A FOCAL POINT** for a furniture group, wash a wall of artwork with clear, soft light or focus a spot on mantel art or an important item, such as an armoire.

■ **CONSIDER ADDING ONE OR MORE LOW-VOLTAGE SPOTLIGHTS** to existing track lighting; they produce dramatic accent beams from narrow to wide, depending on the bulb.

■ **BRIGHTEN A HARD-TO-DECORATE CORNER** with an uplight behind a plant. Or turn a hallway into a gallery and spotlight paintings and the passageway simultaneously.

LEFT: Stepping into the spotlight again, Grace Kelly stars in a focal-point portrait in this retro-spirited living room. A low-voltage halogen spot in the ceiling bathes the art in the perfect beam size. Picking up the portrait's blue hues, the chest below it is vintage 1940s. OPPOSITE: With the instincts of a theater director, the collector who lives here uses well-placed accent lighting to direct the eye to his stars. Uplights in the corners showcase objects and make the room seem larger; ceiling spotlights illuminate wall art and the shapely mix of midcentury seating. Lamps double as artful accents.

Star Lights

Why merely light a room, when you—and your lamp—can make a style statement too?

Innovative lighting designs make fabulous focal points. With lamp-making kits, you can transform almost any stable, hollow object—from antique candlesticks to rustic olive jars—into lighting with true character.

SITE YOUR LIGHT

Use these tips to ensure that your light hits the right spot.

■ **POSITION SHORT FLOOR LAMPS** so they are even with your shoulder when seated; set tall floor lamps about 15 inches to the side and 20 inches behind the center of what you are reading.

■ **POSITION THE BOTTOM OF A TABLE LAMP SHADE** at seated eye level, 38 to 42 inches above the floor; for task lighting, shade bottoms need to be 10 to 12 inches below eye level.

■ **SITE THE LOWER EDGE OF A HANGING FIXTURE** 4 feet from the floor by a chair or bed, 15 inches above a desk top and about 30 inches above a table. When the ceiling height in a dining area is more than 8 feet, raise the fixture 3 inches for each additional foot of ceiling height.

■ **SPACE RECESSED FIXTURES** with flood bulbs at least 4 to 6 feet apart for general light, 15 to 18 inches apart for task lighting

■ **INSTALL SCONCES** about 65 inches from the floor, above standing eye level.

OPPOSITE LEFT: To a flea market fan's way of thinking, almost anything can become a lamp if you think creatively. This surveyor's tripod was found at an antiques store, electrified, and invited into the living room. If new shades aren't in scale, look for old shades to strip and re-cover. OPPOSITE RIGHT: Lighting lofty spaces can be challenging, but this urban retreat plays up its natural resources and mix of textures with dramatic fixtures. In scale with the high ceiling, the tall, curvaceous light over the iron dining table and 1950s chairs is as sleekly modern as it is functional. ABOVE: Lights, camera, floor lamp? Looking as if it was plucked from a photographer's studio or movie set, this adjustable floor lamp fit the design mandate—bold, clean, and masculine—for this media room. The sofa slips into gray flannel, and the chair wears paprika upholstery to echo the brick walls.

ABOVE: It's more than the raised hearth and soft seating that cozies this spot; special lighting accents add to the effect. Interior cabinet lights accent colorful plates. Fun hat shades give sconces a new personality. **OPPOSITE LEFT:** Two fixtures can be better than one if you have a long table. These chandeliers hang closer to the wall than the table to bounce a soft candle glow around the room. **OPPOSITE RIGHT:** A chest displays inexpensive items with treasures; the art light on the decoupaged print gives it an air of importance. Art lights are easy to install; angle them toward the print or painting, not down, to avoid reflection and glare.

Customize Your Lighting

Does your room's lighting plan end just where it should begin—with a couple of lamps flanking the sofa or bed? With today's array of simple plug-in fixtures, it's easy and fun to bring each room to life with light.

DO-IT-YOURSELF LIGHTING

- **STRIP IT.** In varying lengths and finishes, strip lights simply stick on to direct light up, down, or sideways. They're an easy way to highlight bookshelves and hutch displays.
- **PICTURE IT CLEARLY.** Plug-in picture lights showcase artwork after dark, and they install in minutes.
- **PIN IT UP.** Wall-mounted pinup lights are space-savers; sconces brighten halls, stairs, and entries. For aesthetics and safety, run exposed cords along a baseboard or behind furniture.
- **ADD A LAMP.** A torchère bounces a glow off the ceiling. Candlestick lamps are perfect for slim console tables and mantels. Small accent lamps brighten a sideboard, entry table, or kitchen pass-through; miniature lamps turn dark shelves into glowing assets.
- **DIM IT.** Add dimmer controls to table lamps and chandeliers to dial down the mood.

CHOOSING SHADES

- **PUT FUNCTION FIRST.** For accent or task lights, use opaque shades to cast light up and down. For general lighting, translucent shades bathe spaces in a soft glow.
- **MEASURE UP.** The distance between tabletop and the bottom edge of the lampshade should exceed shade height to avoid a top-heavy look. Choose shades that extend at least 2 inches beyond the lamp base.
- **CONSIDER STYLE.** Pleated shades fit traditional schemes; simple, non-pleated shades mix into contemporary or eclectic schemes. Choose a shade texture that complements the lamp base; for example, a gathered silk shade for a crystal base or natural linen for metal or stone.

The Right Bulb

When it comes to lightbulbs, mix them, match them, and experiment with colors, shapes, and wattages to

create extraordinary lighting and special effects. You'll be working with three basic types of lighting:

■ **INCANDESCENT LIGHTING** is provided by common, inexpensive "A" bulbs that cast yellowish light. These bulbs are not energy-efficient. They come in decorative shapes (candle flame for chandeliers, oversize globe for exposed downlights, or tubular for modern styles) and clear, white, and colored styles. White bulbs soften light to prevent eyestrain; colored bulbs are used for mood lighting. In recessed cans and track fixtures, use spotlight and floodlight bulbs; their silver coatings produce well-defined narrow rays for accents or wider beams for general lighting and wall washing. For the most natural, sunny light, look for "full-spectrum" bulbs.

■ **HALOGEN BULBS** boast a crisp white light that intensifies colors in a room. It's whiter and more sunlike than incandescent light. Halogen bulbs can screw into existing fixtures. These small bulbs cast exceptionally strong light and are excellent in recessed ceiling cans and track spotlights.

Halogen bulbs cost more than incandescents and generate extreme heat; always keep portable halogen lamps and torchères away from flammable materials.

■ **FLUORESCENT BULBS** offer true light, although it's not as warm and friendly as incandescent and can cause colors to fade. Warm fluorescents mimic natural sunlight. Fluorescent bulbs are more expensive than incandescent but can last longer, which is a plus for hard-to-reach areas. They are available as screw-in bulbs that fit many lamps and ceiling fixtures.

1 **FLUORESCENT.** Chosen for long life and energy efficiency, the bulbs are manufactured for newer lamps designed for fluorescents.

2 **TUBULAR.** With a candelabra base, these are used to highlight art and sheet music. They're also used in some small accent lamps.

3 **REFLECTOR.** Designed for ceiling or wall track lighting and recessed fixtures, these coated bulbs provide directional light.

4 **THREE-WAY.** Used for lamps with three-way switches, these bulbs are an easy way to create mood lighting without dimmers.

5 **HALOGEN.** In fixtures and lamps, these bulbs provide clear white light. Do not use in lamps in rooms for small children; the bulbs get quite hot.

6 **FLUORESCENT TUBES.** Cool, long-lasting, and energy-efficient, these bulbs are practical for overhead lighting in utility areas.

7 **INCANDESCENT.** Classic for warm, soft light or for tinted light, these easy-to-find "A" bulbs are used for lamps and overhead fixtures.

8 **COMPACT FLUORESCENT.** Designed for undercounter spaces and tight spaces, these bulbs generate less heat and last longer than incandescent bulbs.

9 **GLOBES.** Clear or white, these round bulbs are sized for lighted vanities as well as decorative indoor and outdoor lantern-type lighting.

10 **CHANDELIER.** These candle-shape bulbs, which can be displayed without a shade, are made for chandeliers and some sconces and lamps.

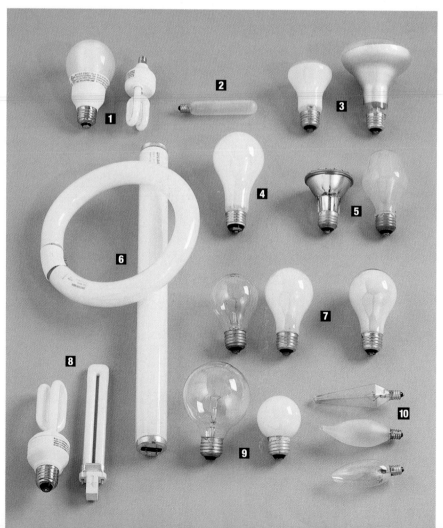

ABOVE: Kitchens are a great place to experiment with different lighting types. Use fluorescent tubes, halogen fixtures, or mini track lights under upper cabinets to create a shadow-free work area below. Ceiling cans provide general lighting in walkways using floodlight bulbs for a wide beam. Over an island, hanging fixtures can use common "A" bulbs, but spotlight halogens are a better choice when you want a defined beam for task lighting.

Lighting Sized Right

DON'T light too light. Tucked at the end of a heavyweight sofa, the leggy little table and wispy lamp, ABOVE, seem to float away. The lamp size matches the delicate table, but the sofa overpowers the table, which is too short, making it hard to reach over the sofa arm.

DO listen to your sofa. The thick-cushioned, rolled-arm sofa, LEFT, demanded some hefty accessories that could measure up in scale and balance its weight. This lamp is a perfect match; both tall and wide, it provides good reading light. The solid chest of drawers is a better choice than an open-leg table, and it provides bonus storage.

Do

Before you buy the pewter chandelier that seems perfect for your living room or the flea market lamp crafted from an antique urn, check out its prospective neighbors on the home front. Where do you plan to put the lighting fixture? Is it compatible in size and scale with adjacent furnishings, such as an oversize table, a chunky sofa, or a lightweight end table? Does it fit the style of your room? Your answers can forecast whether your fixture find will be a hit or a miss. Over a dining table, the diameter of a hanging fixture should be about one-third the table's width. For a table lamp, the visual weight of the base—not the actual dimensions—should be about two-thirds of the entire lamp, with the shade making up the remaining third.

Don't

DON'T fly too high. Proportionately, the ceiling-hugging chandelier, ABOVE, is too small to complement the round table and chairs. The high-flying fixture also leaves a gaping hole above the tabletop, where gracious light belongs. Against the bold-patterned wallcovering in this room, the puny pendent fixture all but disappears.

DO come down and spread out. With graceful arms radiating over the tabletop, the chandelier, RIGHT, becomes a focal point. It hangs low, working as a unit with the table. Choose a hanging fixture that drops to 2 to 3 feet above the tabletop—high enough not to block diners' views of each other.

Do

CHAPTER 21

Accessories

What treasure delights your eye, warms your heart, or simply makes you smile, remembering that rainy day when you found "it" at the flea market? Choosing accessories is your chance to surround yourself with what's important to you and make your rooms truly personal. Shells, an old oar, and nautical art in this living room are clues to the seafaring spirit of the homeowners. What messages do you want your rooms to send? This chapter will help you tell your story with accessories.

"Past Perfect" Cottage

"Past Perfect" Cottage
SHIRLEY ZYLSTRA OF CORONADO, CALIFORNIA

PREVIOUS PAGES: Because they steal less floor space, a few larger storage pieces, such as the painted pine armoire for entertainment gear, are wise choices in this small cottage. Window shutters made from hinged boards trimmed with molding are freestanding. Originally a temporary fix for privacy, they looked so good, Shirley left them in place. Beneath a display of framed art, a console table serves as a sideboard and mini-office. An unusually small corner cupboard is the right size for a kitchen broom closet. **BELOW:** Shirley Zylstra tends her garden in the latticed outdoor "room" she created just beyond the front door of her cottage. **OPPOSITE:** In the living room, pale walls and brown and cream striped slipcovers on seating create a neutral backdrop for colorful porcelain pieces and antiques. The oversize ottoman is upholstered in an old kilim rug.

When Shirley Zylstra traded a rambling Victorian home for a Lilliputian cottage, this collector turned into an editor. The challenge? To squeeze her treasures—lots of blue and white porcelain, books, art, and vintage mementos and furniture—into a mere 700 square feet of living space. After all, she says, accessories are the storytellers that give homes their happy endings. "Isn't that what decorating is all about? When you walk into a room, you get a sense of who lives there, their favorite things, and their personal treasures. It's all those things that make you who you are, and when you find that, you're content," she says.

NEW START WITH OLD FRIENDS
Neutral colors and fabrics give Shirley's "granny flat"—as her daughter affectionately calls it—some breathing room because her collections deliver the color. Blue and white porcelain from the 1700s and 1800s has been her passion since she discovered the Oriental character for "double happiness" on a ginger jar. "That's such a wonderful thought. I was stuck," she says.

She masses much of her porcelain in 9-inch-deep built-in shelves that span a living room wall; this gives the pieces more weight and prominence. "It made the living room more interesting, and I needed a place for the blue and white, books, and pictures of the grandchildren," she says. A porcelain garden stool serves as an end table.

Merged with the kitchen, the cottage's miniscule dining room gets its personal look from wall-hung accents—plate and garden racks for colorful dishes, as well as whimsical art, such as fish prints and a distinguished bulldog in a gilt frame. "I love having art in the kitchen," Shirley says. "It makes it feel so much warmer."

Small spaces call for restraint, so her vignettes are light, with a few silver pieces, sugar shakers, and antique bottles on table tops and shelves. But she found places for her favorites, from Oriental rugs to mellow English pine. "If you've got a little bit of traditional in you, that doesn't go away," Shirley says.

OPPOSITE: Floor-to-ceiling built-ins across a living room wall pay big rewards in this small space, adding architectural interest and giving Shirley plenty of room to display her porcelain, art, books, and mementos. **1** Six feet long, this English pine base cabinet probably graced a big manor-house kitchen in the early

1800s. Today, it delivers character and extra-deep storage for pots and pans. **2** Although this wire rack is designed for the garden, it was drafted as pretty countertop storage for floral-motif dishes because there was no room for upper cabinets. **3** To give the bed a coordinated look, the bed skirt and upholstered headboard are made with sheets. **4** A new corner shower opens space for needed storage. The pine chest was too deep before Shirley shaved five inches off the back. Above the towel rack, the wall-hung cabinet that displays antique vanity bottles is the top of an old grandfather clock case.

The Personal Touch

Imagine this living room without accessories—no tabletop treasures or old volumes to explore and no art and artifacts coaxing your eye to every corner and every shelf. But collectors live here, so accessorizing with favorites was as important as comfy seating in their design scheme. Accessories always infuse a room with personality, and putting those accessories in perfect balance adds visual comfort. So play, rearrange, experiment, and rotate accessories. But take your time; as your tastes and interests change, your rooms become dynamic works-in-progress.

■ **ADD A DASH OF THE UNEXPECTED.** Symmetry is synonymous with formality and asymmetrical groupings play in casual settings. Sometimes, however, drama falls flat if everything pairs up. For variety, use identical porcelain vases to frame an asymmetrical grouping of objects on a mantel—an interesting bit of symmetry and asymmetry in one vignette.

■ **FIND YOUR FOCAL POINT.** A mantel, a built-in bookcase, or an empty wall makes an obvious starting point for personal touches. In the space shown here, collections turn bookshelves into a grand entry to the window sitting spot beyond; denser, visually weightier shelf arrangements on one side balance taller objects on the opposite side.

■ **PERFECT YOUR BALANCING ACT.** Apply the same tenets of scale and visual weight to everything from tabletop and shelf vignettes to the room as a whole. To avoid that "listing ship" feeling, even out the visual weight of your accessories, balancing one side of the room against the other.

■ **VARY THE PACE.** Don't accessorize every wall or surface. Good decorating schemes mix slow-paced, uncluttered zones with high-drama, high-energy areas.

■ **KNOW WHEN TO STOP.** Love what you display—but don't display everything you love. By rotating your treasures—even boxing some things up for a while—you not only cut the clutter but ensure that your favorite things will continue to delight and surprise you as you rediscover them again and again.

RIGHT: Varying the scale and elevation of objects makes vignettes more interesting. Aged leather-clad volumes on the shelves give a boost to tiny treasures, such as Chinese mud men figures. In front of the windows, European collectibles cluster on the drop-leaf table, which features distinctive barley-twist legs.

Gather for Impact

Like birds of a feather, collections that flock together make a stronger design statement

than objects that are sprinkled around a room. In choosing collectibles for a high-impact display, spread out your potential candidates and look for a link—for example, color, form, texture, or theme. In the living room (opposite), paintings of colonial American birds make the wall a topic of conversation. On a mantel, time-worn finishes and sculptural form could tie old frames and candlesticks together. *(To learn more about the basics of arranging related accessories, turn to pages 300–305 and 308–309 in the "Elements" chapter.)*

REPEAT AFTER ME

Some types of accessories—smaller pieces or those with more detail—often look best when grouped together for impact. Beautifully detailed botanical prints can turn a dull wall into a garden; carry the theme to seating by adding pillows in floral fabrics. For fun, mix flat and three-dimensional works into the same grouping. For example, hang pieces of architectural salvage near art in vintage frames for added texture and interest. Or tuck a framed cat print or photo behind a lineup of cat figurines on a shelf.

OPPOSITE: In this treasure-filled living room, prints of colonial birds by 18th-century British watercolor artist Mark Catesby are framed alike and grouped to turn the wall behind the camelback sofa into a focal point. A tole tray tops the coffee table, and a salesman's sample chest from the 1840s sits on the end table. RIGHT: Chinese exportware dating to the 19th century mixes easily with the rich hues of leather-covered antique books in this 1770 English secretary. The lamp carries the eye toward the top of the piece, where vases continue the color theme. FAR RIGHT: Confessing to a penchant for pitchers, this collector clusters some of her flow-blue, spongeware, and ironstone favorites on a quilt-topped bedside table. A collectible iron doorstop perches on the books, fitting into the floral theme.

Set Your Stage

If you love decorating and view it as a lifelong hobby,

you don't intend for your home to ever be truly finished. You'll add items as you find things you love, and you'll shift others to different rooms and different arrangements. Who knows what treasure will strike your fancy next? So design your rooms to welcome change.

SHOW-OFF BACKDROPS

Whatever you collect and display, make sure objects don't get lost in the backdrop or conflict with the background's pattern and color. In the rooms opposite and below, a gallery-style backdrop and streamlined furnishings show off art glass, contemporary art, miniature clocks, and a variety of funky finds, including sculptural plastic foods. A bold rainbow of collectible color pops on this all-white stage, and arrangements can be remixed anywhere with ease.

A MOVABLE FEAST

Sometimes it takes a while for accessories to find the spot where they look best. Move them around and place them in different groupings and different rooms. For flexibility, this collector's haven includes a museum-inspired half-inch-wide indentation about three-quarters of the way up the walls so artwork can be hung—and rehung—without unsightly nail holes. For art on the go, prop framed pictures on mantels, shelves, or easels while you ponder their eventual home; you may like the look and leave them propped.

OPPOSITE LEFT: Set on the the sideboard, sparkling art glass pieces show off their colors and shapes against plain painted walls. Beneath a sculptural, lighted soffit, the sleek dining room has a frosted glass-top table. **OPPOSITE RIGHT:** Sleek contemporary design meets pure fun in the open-plan living space, where glass hats perch on the coffee table. As far as the eye can see, art and accessories deliver more color and smiles. **ABOVE:** Deadlines? This collector never misses one, thanks to an extensive and delightful collection of miniature clocks on her desk. She's mastered the "surround yourself with things you love" rule, but when daylight saving time rolls around, she works overtime resetting her treasures.

Tell Your Story

What do your chosen accessories and collections reveal about you? Do they give visitors a sense of what and whom you love, where you've been, and where you're going? For example, this sari-swathed guest/meditation room speaks eloquently of the homeowners' world travels and their passion for the colors and decorative artistry of exotic cultures.

CAST YOUR CHARACTERS

Decorating books and magazines are invaluable resources for ideas on accessories and display, but only you can write your story.

■ **WEAVE A TALE.** Grouped together, certain objects can create a narrative of your life. The story may be literal—perhaps told by photographs that show you and your family over the years. Or you may prefer an anecdotal approach, displaying items that jog wonderful memories and become conversation pieces as you recount their origins to friends.

■ **FORAGE ROOM TO ROOM.** View your possessions with a fresh eye. Walk through your rooms, gathering things that speak to you—seashells you collected on a tropical vacation, a stack of bowls you bought at a flea market, or a limited-edition print from an art fair. Shop your attic and albums for family photos and have some copied, enlarged, and framed.

■ **EDIT FOR IMPACT.** Whether they're written in words or accessories, the best stories have a point. Leave out extraneous objects that clutter your intended message.

OPPOSITE: Inspired by a trip to Morocco, this guest/meditation room showcases a creative way to display a beautiful collection of silk saris and set an exotic mood. The saris form a dramatic tent over an antique Balinese "love bed" piled with pillows in more exotic fabrics. RIGHT: The same hardware that holds the saris in place works for the no-sew window treatment; lengths of bronze "drapery scarf" fabric are loosely swagged from the outside rods over the center rod. Gold cording embellishes the translucent fabric.

Pretty Hang-Ups
Whether you rack it up, tie it up, or simply let it hang, put that collection of yours on display for all to enjoy.

ABOVE: If the treasures you want to display don't line up easily on shelves or tabletops, hang them creatively on a wall. In a bygone era, elegant ladies carried the lovely purses that now dress this sitting room wall. A peg rack in an unusual star shape is the perfect hanger to show off their charming shapes, sparkly beads, and dangling trims. **ABOVE RIGHT:** Even if you're a novice collector, you may find what you need for a one-of-a-kind display by rooting through your cupboards or by giving commonplace, inexpensive items a creative twist. Adding personality to a hard-to-decorate corner, the platters and plates vary in size and shape, but they share a color theme and fancy openwork threaded with ribbon hangers.

BELOW: Color and pattern pop against the whitewashed backdrop of a timeworn shelf that holds vintage dishes. With its simple turnings and handcrafted charm, the shelf looks as if it were plucked from a farmhouse in Ireland, where the collector once lived. Make the hanger an important part of your composition by choosing antique shelves or pegged racks with character befitting what's on display.

ABOVE: Collections and blank walls are made for each other. In the living room, a vintage 1900 spool rack, all wrapped up in colorful yarn, creates a countrified focal point. It also gives this century-old farmhouse a sense of place, because the rack came from an old woolen mill nearby. Quilts, painted furniture, and Native American kachina dolls reveal the collector's wide-ranging passions. **OPPOSITE BOTTOM:** Heighten the impact of your collections by creatively arranging the furniture that displays them. A chest and wall-hung shelf pair up, hutch-style, to showcase exquisite English and Chinese teapots, transferware, and figurines from the 1700s and 1800s. Teapots "spill" onto the chest top, linking it with the shelf display above. Wall-hung plates frame it all.

PicturePerfect

When you're hanging pictures and composing gallery-style arrangements, trial and error often results in walls resembling Swiss cheese. Before you pick up hammer and hooks, get out paper and pencil. Arrange pictures on the floor on a large piece of paper, trace frame outlines, and then tape the paper to the wall as a map for nail holes. Or cut paper templates of each picture, tape them to the wall, and move them around until you like the mix.

CREATE SPECIAL EFFECTS

■ EVOKE INTIMACY by hanging pictures low to visually link them with furniture. Generally, walls that are wider than they are high call for horizontal groupings; narrow spaces welcome vertical arrangements.

■ ARRANGE YOUR ART OR PHOTOS within an imaginary framework that includes a strong horizontal anchor. To unify a grouping, keep the spaces between frames approximately equal.

■ ORGANIZE AROUND A THEME. Use a theme—family snaps, pet pictures, or landscapes, for instance—for each artwork or photograph grouping. Color itself—even a theme as simple as "blue paintings"—unifies an artwork grouping.

■ FRAME FOR IMPACT. Presenting small photos in large mats and gallery-style frames gives them presence. Minimal frames enhance modern art; traditional paintings often call for decorative frames and multilayered mats. Instead of a hodge-podge of photos and frames, select a few and reframe them with similar frames and mats for unity.

■ BE PLAYFUL. For fun, loop cording around old architectural finials, aged drawer pulls, and vintage crystal doorknobs and use them as dimensional picture hangers.

OPPOSITE: Whether you're arranging collectibles or art, link elements by making color the focus. White connects the oil painting of roses with a snowy parade of shapely ironstone pitchers and plates arranged on a late-19th-century dry sink. ABOVE: Seafaring images in vacation photos inspired the cheery dining spot's color scheme. Against a pastel backdrop, snapshots gain gallery appeal when surrounded by big mats. A chair rail mounted at one-third the wall height reinforces the strong horizontal lines of the arrangement. RIGHT: Taking its cue from the vibrant tomato red walls, this gallery of family photos dons layered mats in warm red, gold, and orange. For dimension and unity, all the photos are displayed in similar shadow-box frames.

Spark Up a Fireplace

In any room lucky enough to have one, a fireplace is an unrivaled focal point and always a cozy mood-setter. Hang the predictable picture and plop a couple of candlesticks on the mantel, and you're done decorating, right? Wrong. No matter how handsome your rugged stone or carved oak hearth is, expanding your decorating horizons and rethinking mantel accessories can make a dramatic difference in the attractiveness of the fireplace. To make the most of your fireplace, first look at the backdrop. Does a white mantel disappear into a white wall? Would painting the wall in a warmer hue bring out the rich wood tones in the mantel? Next, forget that ho-hum formula—two candlesticks and a picture—and work some mantel magic by dipping into your favorite collections.

Do

Don't

DON'T blur the focus. On the rustic fireplace, LEFT, a high-contrast combination of chalky-white limestone and dark mortar overwhelms the eye and steals attention from the focal-point hearth. A sprinkling of accents gets lost on the chunky mantel, which needs a more extensive arrangement to match its visual weight.
DO brush on star power. Priming and painting the stone and mortar in white gloss paint erased the distracting light-and-dark contrast and put the focus where it belongs, on the rugged texture of the stone, ABOVE. A new painting introduces eye-popping orange and lemon—as colors and as themes—and a collection of bowls on the mantel echoes the color scheme.

Do

Don't

DON'T chill out. With a generous mantel and classic carving, the fireplace, RIGHT, has the potential to shine. Stark contrast between the natural oak and the white walls, however, give the fireplace a surprisingly chilly look. Glass doors create another contrast problem, exposing the black firebox to surrounding white tile.

DO warm with color. Sponged-on amber-tinged paint warms the walls, ABOVE, and brings out the mantel's golden tones. In front of the firebox, a folding screen in neutral hues bridges the color gap by bringing the warm feeling of the walls to the fireplace opening. More interesting than the original single piece of artwork, the horizontal trio of prints is more in scale with the length of the mantel.

Index

Contributors

Page 4 Designer: Sandra B. Chancey, Sandra B. Chancey Interior Design, Inc.,1860 Avenue Republica de Cuba, Tampa, FL 33605; 813/247-3203. Architect: Walton H. Chancey, Walton H. Chancey & Associates, 1860 Avenue Republica de Cuba, Tampa, FL 33605; 813/248-9258. Regional Editor: Stephanie M. Davis. Photographer: William Stites

Pages 6–7 (Left) Architect/Designer: Carol Maryan, (AIA), Carol Maryan Architect, PC, 212 W. 79th St., Suite 1C, New York, NY 10024; 212/787-7800. Regional Editor: Stephanie M. Davis. Photographer: William Stites. (Center) Designer: Debbie Clifton Perez, Peridot Decorators, Inc. 4816 S. Sunset Blvd., Tampa, FL 33629; 813/831-6878. Regional Editor: Stephanie M. Davis. Photographer: William Stites

Page 8 Designer: Marc Strait, Strait Design Associates, Ltd. 200 N. Dearborn St., Suite 1307, Chicago, IL 60601; 312/251-8282. Regional Editor: Mary Anne Thomson. Photographer: Alise O'Brien.

Page 60 Designer: Gary McBournie, Gary McBournie, Inc., 33 A N. Main St., Sherborn, MA 01770; 508/655-3887.

Page 62 (Left) Designer: Alessandra Branca, Branca Inc., 1325 N. State Pkwy., Chicago, ILL 60610; 312/787-6123.

Pages 66–67 Regional Editor: Andrea Caughey. Photographer: Ed Gohlich

Pages 72–73 Designer: Marc Strait, Strait

Design Associates, Ltd. 200 N. Dearborn St., Suite 1307, Chicago, IL 60601; 312/251-8282. Regional Editor: Mary Anne Thomson. Photographer: Alise O'Brien

Pages 74–77 Designer: Jane Hardin, 2201 N. Spruce St., Little Rock, AR 72207; 501/664-3969. Architect: John Allison, (AIA), Allison Architects, 300 Spring Bldg., Suite 717, Little Rock, AR 72201, 501/376-0717. Regional Editor: Nancy E. Ingram. Photographer: Jenifer Jordan

Pages 80–83 Designer: Sandra B. Chancey, Sandra B. Chancey Interior Design, Inc., 1860 Avenue Republica de Cuba, Tampa, FL 33605; 813/247-3203. Architect: Walton H. Chancey, Walton H. Chancey & Associates, 1860 Avenue Republica de Cuba, Tampa, FL 33605; 813/248-9258. Regional Editor: Stephanie M. Davis. Photographer: William Stites

Pages 90–91 Designer: Jane Hardin, 2201 N. Spruce St., Little Rock, AR 72207; 501/664-3969. Architect: John Allison, (AIA), Allison Architects, 300 Spring Bldg., Suite 717, Little Rock, AR 72201; 501/376-0717. Regional Editor: Nancy E. Ingram. Photographer: Jenifer Jordan

Page 94 Designer: Beth Sachse, S.R. Hughes Interior Design, 1345 E. 15th, Tulsa, OK 74120; 918/582-4999. Regional Editor: Nancy E. Ingram. Photographer: Jenifer Jordan

Page 96 Designer: Gary McBournie, Gary McBournie, Inc., 33 A N. Main St., Sherborn, MA 01770; 508/655-3887

Page 98 Architect/Designer: Carol Maryan (AIA), Carol Maryan Architect, PC, 212 W. 79th St., Suite 1C, New York, NY 10024; 212/787-7800. Regional Editor: Stephanie M. Davis. Photographer: William Stites

Pages 102–103 (Left) Designer: Debbie Clifton Perez, Peridot Decorators, Inc. 4816 S. Sunset Blvd., Tampa, FL 33629; 813/831-6878. Regional Editor: Stephanie M. Davis. Photographer: William Stites. (Center) Architect/Designer: Robert Maschke, (AIA), Robert Maschke Architects, 1849 W. 24th St., Cleveland, OH 44113; 216/241-6711. Regional Editor: Diane DiPiero. Photographer: Jeff Rycus

Page 106 (Top) Regional Editor: Betsy Harris. Photographer: Jim Hedrich

U.S. UNITS TO METRIC EQUIVALENTS

To Convert From	Multiply By	To Get
Inches	25.4	Millimeters (mm)
Inches	2.54	Centimeters (cm)
Feet	30.48	Centimeters (cm)
Feet	0.3048	Meters (m)

METRIC UNITS TO U.S. EQUIVALENTS

To Convert From	Multiply By	To Get
Millimeters	0.0394	Inches
Centimeters	0.3937	Inches
Centimeters	0.0328	Feet
Meters	3.2808	Feet